Euro Horror

NEW DIRECTIONS IN NATIONAL CINEMAS

Jacqueline Reich, editor

EURO HORROR

CLASSIC EUROPEAN HORROR CINEMA IN
CONTEMPORARY AMERICAN CULTURE

Ian Olney

INDIANA UNIVERSITY PRESS

Bloomington & Indianapolis

This book is a publication of

INDIANA UNIVERSITY PRESS
601 North Morton Street
Bloomington, Indiana 47404-3797 USA

iupress.indiana.edu

Telephone orders 800-842-6796
Fax orders 812-855-7931

© 2013 by Alexander Ian Olney

All rights reserved

No part of this book may be reproduced or utilized in any form or by any means, electronic or mechanical, including photocopying and recording, or by any information storage and retrieval system, without permission in writing from the publisher. The Association of American University Presses' Resolution on Permissions constitutes the only exception to this prohibition.

⊖ The paper used in this publication meets the minimum requirements of the American National Standard for Information Sciences – Permanence of Paper for Printed Library Materials, ANSI Z39.48-1992.

*Manufactured in the
United States of America*

Library of Congress
Cataloging-in-Publication Data

Olney, Ian.
 Euro horror : classic European horror cinema in contemporary American culture / Ian Olney.
  p. cm. – (New directions in national cinemas)
 Includes bibliographical references and index.
 ISBN 978-0-253-00648-6 (cl : alk. paper) – ISBN 978-0-253-00652-3 (pb : alk. paper) – ISBN 978-0-253-00658-5 (eb) 1. Horror films – Europe – History and criticism. 2. Motion picture audiences – United States. I. Title.
 PN1995.9.H6 O46 2013
 791.43'6164 – dc23
                    2012027225

1 2 3 4 5   18 17 16 15 14 13

FOR JILL – LOVE ALWAYS

You had been set adrift in a world of European exploitation movies, unstable mixtures of poetry and gothic melodrama and outright pornography – Belgian vampires, Italian cannibals, Spanish sex murderers, hooded inquisitors from Portugal – and now there was no easy way out.

GEOFFREY O'BRIEN, *The Phantom Empire*

CONTENTS

Preface xi

Acknowledgments xv

Note on Film Titles xix

PART 1 TOWARD A PERFORMATIVE THEORY OF EURO HORROR CINEMA

1 Academic Hot Spots and Blind Spots: Horror Film Studies and Euro Horror Cinema 3

2 Fast, Cheap, and Out of Control: The Academic Case against Euro Horror Cinema 23

3 Playing Dead, Take One: Euro Horror Film Production 46

4 Playing Dead, Take Two: Euro Horror Film Reception 61

5 Return of the Repressed: Euro Horror Cinema in Contemporary American Culture 83

PART 2   CASE STUDIES IN EURO HORROR CINEMA

6   Blood and Black Lace: The *Giallo* Film   *103*

7   The Whip and the Body:
     The S&M Horror Film   *142*

8   Cannibal Apocalypse:
     Cannibal and Zombie Films   *182*

CONCLUSION   From the Grindhouse to the Arthouse:
              The Legacy of Euro Horror Cinema   *217*

Works Cited   233

Index   243

PREFACE

Euro Horror explores a surprising development in American popular culture: the substantial cult following garnered since the late 1990s by films from the golden age of twentieth-century Continental European horror cinema. Between the mid-1950s and the mid-1980s, these Euro horror movies emerged from countries like Italy, Spain, and France in astonishing numbers and were shown in the United States at rural drive-ins and at urban grindhouse theaters of the sort that once filled Times Square in New York City. Gorier, sexier, and just plain stranger than most British and American horror films of the time, they were embraced by hardcore genre fans and denounced by critics as the worst kind of cinematic trash. Eventually, the changing tastes of movie audiences, reflected in the Reagan era resurgence of Hollywood and the contemporaneous decline of film industries in Europe, led to the end of Euro horror's golden age and the disappearance of these movies from circulation. Today, however, they have reappeared on DVD and Blu-ray, on cable and satellite television, at film festivals and retrospectives, and in midnight movie programming and theatrical re-releases. Their re-emergence has inspired cinematic homages from directors like Quentin Tarantino, Robert Rodriguez, and Eli Roth, who have claimed artistic kinship with Euro horror auteurs like Dario Argento, Jess Franco, and Jean Rollin; more significantly, it has inspired the devotion of a whole new generation of American fans, who have built home video collections, joined online communities, and created fan art to celebrate their favorite Euro horror movies, directors, genres, and stars. Unfortunately, despite the crucial place of Euro horror in the history of horror cinema and the buzz surrounding it in contemporary American popular culture, little has been written about it in the field of Film Studies. This book aims to correct that oversight by exploring some of the most popular genres of Euro horror cinema – including the *giallo* film, the S&M horror film, and the cannibal and zombie films – and by developing a theory that explains their considerable appeal to audiences today.

Euro Horror is divided into two main parts. In part 1, I develop a performative theory of Euro horror cinema. I begin by noting that although there has been a surge of interest in horror cinema among scholars over the last several decades, classic European horror movies have received relatively little attention within the field of Film Studies – despite their obvious importance to the genre, their close relationship with contemporaneous European art films that enjoy a privileged status in film theory and criticism, their unprecedented availability in the United States today, and their substantial popularity among contemporary American viewers. The reason for this, I argue, has to do with certain lingering aesthetic, ideological, theoretical, and cultural prejudices that continue to define which films are considered worthy of serious study within academia. Its marginalization is unfortunate because Euro horror represents, in my view, what many scholars have been looking for in more mainstream forms of horror cinema: a nexus not just of revolting bodies, but of bodies in revolt. I suggest that the radical potential of Euro horror cinema has to do with the distinctive manner in which it affords viewers the opportunity to approach film spectatorship as a form of "play" or performance. In the first place, Euro horror movies foster spectatorship-as-performance because of how they were originally made: the uniquely postmodern qualities of Euro horror cinema prompt viewers to adopt multiple viewing positions and experiment with a range of subjectivities in a fashion generally proscribed by mainstream cinema and the dominant social order. Additionally, Euro horror movies foster spectatorship-as-performance because of how they are now watched: the digital remediation and repurposing of Euro horror cinema as home entertainment in the United States and the perceived "paracinematic" character of Euro horror cinema in the present American cultural context have allowed viewers the opportunity to refashion their identities and lay claim to individual agency as Euro horror fans, while also performing their resistance to current cinematic and cultural norms. I conclude part 1 by discussing the appeal to contemporary American audiences of the kind of performative spectatorship that Euro horror makes possible.

Part 2 of this book comprises three case studies in which I apply the performative theory of Euro horror cinema outlined in part 1 to different kinds of Euro horror movies. The first case study focuses on the *giallo* film, a violent and erotic type of murder mystery movie that originated in Italy in the 1960s. An example of "anti-detective" cinema – a cinema whose pleasures for viewers lie not in the solution of a central mystery, but rather in an embrace of the postmodern principles of disruption, transgression, undecidability, and uncertainty that it celebrates – the *giallo* film, I contend, invites spectatorship-as-performance primarily through its play with gender identity. The second case study covers the Euro horror S&M film, a genre that blends elements of horror and pornography to tell stories that interrogate the imperatives of patriarchal power and pleasure. I argue that the straight and queer S&M fantasies in Euro horror encourage spectatorship-as-performance by demonstrating to viewers that the grounds of the sexual are constantly shifting and that the power that dictates representations of sex and gender is unfixed and up for grabs. The third case study deals with the zombie film and the cannibal film, two related genres of Euro horror cinema that chronicle what happens when East *eats* West – when white interlopers pay the ultimate price for intruding upon the domain of the Other. I suggest that these films prompt spectatorship-as-performance by addressing issues of race in a recognizably postcolonial fashion, deconstructing the power dynamics at the heart of the historical relationship between the colonizer and the colonized.

Following parts 1 and 2, I offer a brief conclusion that examines the legacy of Euro horror cinema. The first decade of the twenty-first century saw a new wave of horror movies emerge from Europe, and a few Euro horror filmmakers continue to direct genre movies today. I argue, however, that the form of contemporary European cinema that most closely resembles Euro horror in its elicitation of spectatorship-as-performance is the "extreme" art film – a taboo-shattering hybrid of "highbrow" and "lowbrow" cinema developed by critically acclaimed auteurs like Michael Haneke, Claire Denis, Lars von Trier, and Pedro

Almodóvar. Exploring the relationship between Euro horror and the extreme art film provides us with a better understanding both of the origins of an important movement in contemporary European cinema and of the continuing influence of classic European horror movies. It also gives us a greater appreciation for the complex interconnectedness of and frequent border crossings between European art and popular cinema – a phenomenon that is too often minimized or ignored in the field of Film Studies.

ACKNOWLEDGMENTS

This book underwent a lengthy period of gestation prior to its publication; its completion would not have been possible without the insight, feedback, encouragement, and support of a great many people. It began its life as a research project I undertook at the University of Nebraska, Lincoln. Several mentors were instrumental in helping the book through that initial stage in its development. In particular, I would like to thank Gwendolyn Audrey Foster for her unstinting assistance and honest feedback; her background in Cultural Studies benefited me tremendously as I struggled to articulate why I believed "trashy" European horror movies were worthy of scholarly rehabilitation. I also owe an enormous debt of gratitude to Wheeler Winston Dixon, who taught me to take seriously marginalized genres like horror and who generously shared his vast knowledge of cinema as I sought to understand Euro horror's place in film history. Christin J. Mamiya brought an invaluable perspective on art history to bear on my work, helping me make connections between performance art and horror film spectatorship that informed my thinking about Euro horror cinema. Finally, I want to acknowledge the contributions made by Nicholas Spencer, who passed away unexpectedly in 2008. Nick, a good friend as well as an important mentor, shaped my views about Euro horror in countless ways; as a native of England, he was able to give me a firsthand account of the experience of watching European horror movies in the theater in the 1970s and 1980s, and, as a brilliant theoretician, he helped me to see – often over cigars and bourbon at Rogues Gallery in Lincoln – how Euro horror was connected to May '68, contemporary Continental philosophy, situationist utopianism, the animal rights movement, British punk rock, Roman Catholicism, and many other equally fascinating historical, cultural, and aesthetic phenomena. He also helped me find and trust my voice as a writer. Nick is sorely missed, both by me and by the many graduate and undergraduate students who had the privilege to study under him.

The research project I pursued at the University of Nebraska underwent substantial revisions on its way to becoming the book you hold in your hands today; indeed, it was almost entirely reconceived. A number of people helped shepherd the book through the second phase of its gestation. I first need to thank my students and colleagues at York College of Pennsylvania, where I have taught Film Studies as a faculty member in the English and Humanities Department since receiving my doctorate. A course release granted by my department chair and a summer research stipend awarded by the college's Faculty Development Committee gave me the opportunity to rethink and rework my approach to the book. I was also aided in this process by the enthusiasm and encouragement of friends and fellow faculty like Todd Reid and Colbey Emmerson Reid. Finally, I have benefited a great deal from the views of my students. I have now twice taught Euro horror cinema as part of undergraduate classes on the horror film at York, and I have been inspired by the curiosity, eagerness, and critical acumen displayed by the men and women enrolled in these courses.

I have also been fortunate to receive feedback and support from outside my home institution as I wrote this book. Portions of it are based on papers that I presented at a variety of conferences over the years: chapter 6 was inspired by a paper entitled "Weaving a Tangled Web of Death: Anti-Detective Fiction and the *Giallo* Film," which I delivered at the 2006 Literature/Film Association Conference at Towson University; chapter 7 draws from a paper entitled "The Whip and the Body: Sex, Violence, and Performative Spectatorship in Euro-Horror S&M Cinema," which I gave at the joint *Film & History* and Literature/Film Association Conference in Milwaukee in 2010; chapter 8 borrows from a paper entitled "'We Are Going to Eat You!' or, Zombies, Italian Style: Thoughts on the Thirtieth Anniversary of a Euro-Trash Horror Classic," which I read at the 2009 Southwest Texas Popular Culture and American Culture Associations Conference in Albuquerque; and the conclusion is based on a paper entitled "Making *Trouble Every Day:* From Euro-Trash to a Cinema of Abjection," which I presented at the 2007 Society for Cinema and Media Studies Conference in Chicago. The kind words and constructive criticism offered by the scholars attending these conference sessions helped maintain my interest in and refine my thinking about Euro horror cinema. The same is true of the responses I received from the peers who generously offered to read the book in manuscript – most notably, Linda Schulte-Sasse and Nicholas Schlegel.

Of course, the most important advice and encouragement has come from the staff and readers at Indiana University Press. I owe the editorial board at IUP and my sponsoring editors, Jane Behnken and Raina Polivka, a debt of gratitude for their support and valuable input. Their suggestions have resulted in a leaner, better focused, and more accessible book. Jane and Raina's indefatigable assistant, Sarah Wyatt Swanson, helped me navigate a number of challenges related to the submission and production of my manuscript. Readers for the press offered not only much-appreciated endorsements of my work, but also key suggestions for further revision. To receive such incisive and enthusiastic reports was both humbling and incredibly helpful. Merryl Sloane has my sincere appreciation for her diligent copyediting; she helped me straighten tangled prose and avoid errors large and small. I am also grateful to Jacqueline Reich for her keen interest in my book and am honored by its inclusion in the New Directions in National Cinemas series she edits at IUP.

More than anyone else, however, I would like to thank my family – especially my wife, Jill; my son, Ethan; and my daughter, Emma. Without the unconditional love and support they have given me through the years it has taken to write this book, it would not have been possible to finish it. It belongs as much to them as it does to me.

NOTE ON FILM TITLES

Most of the Euro horror films discussed in this book have at least two different titles: their original, foreign-language titles and the English ones they were given upon their American theatrical or home video premiere. Many, however, have acquired other titles as they have been released and re-released in different markets over the years. Consider the (admittedly extreme) case of Mario Bava's 1971 film, *Bay of Blood*, which has played to audiences around the world under more than a dozen titles, including *Reazione a catena, Antefatto – Ecologia del delitto, Bloodbath, The Last House on the Left: Part II*, and (my favorite) *Twitch of the Death Nerve*. To avoid confusion, I have elected to introduce the Euro horror films discussed in this book by their original, foreign-language titles, followed in parentheses by the English titles under which they are most widely known and available in the United States today; all subsequent references use the English titles. Thus the aforementioned Bava film would be introduced as *Reazione a catena* (*Bay of Blood*, 1971) and thereafter referred to as *Bay of Blood*. Readers who look up a Euro horror film in the index will find the foreign-language title there, though they will be directed to the English title for a list of the pages on which the film is discussed.

PART ONE

Toward a Performative Theory of Euro Horror Cinema

ONE

Academic Hot Spots and Blind Spots

HORROR FILM STUDIES AND EURO HORROR CINEMA

There has been an explosion of interest in horror cinema among film scholars in recent years; in the first decade of the twenty-first century especially, the genre received unprecedented attention in the field of Film Studies. Perhaps the most visible sign of the current scholarly fascination with horror cinema is the record number of books on the subject being published by academic presses in the United States and abroad. Scores of monographs and edited volumes on seemingly every aspect of the genre, from its nature and history to its cultural and ideological dimensions to its notable directors and producers to its reception and fandom, now crowd the shelves. There is even a growing number of texts on horror cinema geared toward the film student – introductory guidebooks that offer overviews of the genre, as well as critical anthologies that collect the most important and influential essays on the subject – indicating that horror film studies has truly arrived as an area of academic inquiry. While the extraordinary number of books on horror cinema available today may be the most visible sign of scholarly interest in the genre, it is not the only one. Hundreds of articles on the horror film have appeared in a wide range of highly respected academic journals. Many of these journals have devoted entire issues to horror, and at least one – *Horror Studies,* a periodical published in the United Kingdom – has dedicated itself exclusively to the exploration of the genre. One might also point to the countless papers on horror cinema delivered at conferences sponsored by professional organizations like the Society for Cinema and Media Studies and the Popular Culture and American Culture associations. And this boom in horror film scholarship seems likely to continue for the foreseeable future: according to the Dissertation Abstracts Online database, dozens of doctoral dissertations on horror cinema were submitted at universities all over the world during the first decade of the 2000s, suggesting that a new generation of scholars with a substantial investment in the genre has now entered the field.

This represents a remarkable reversal of fortune for the horror film, which was at one time regarded within Film Studies as something of a bête noir – primarily because of its status as popular cinema. In the 1960s, scholars fighting to establish Film Studies as a legitimate academic discipline tended, out of necessity, to marginalize popular forms of cinema like horror. Against the notion – widespread in academia at the time – that movies were mass culture kitsch unworthy of serious attention, they argued, adopting the tenets of the newly imported auteur theory, that a film can constitute art if it expresses the unique vision of an individual "author." By creating a pantheon of auteur directors – including John Ford, Howard Hawks, Alfred Hitchcock, Fritz Lang, Jean Renoir, and Orson Welles – and differentiating the "personal" work of these masters from the "impersonal" (that is, generic or formulaic) dross of popular cinema, film scholars were able to generate cultural capital for a certain kind of "highbrow" cinema and mobilize crucial institutional support for their emerging discipline. In the process, though, they effectively placed horror and other forms of "lowbrow" cinema beyond the bounds of academic study.

Horror's standing in the field was further diminished during the 1970s with the rise of "*Screen* theory," a potent combination of semiotics, structuralism, psychoanalysis, Marxism, and feminism forged in the pages of the British film journal *Screen*. *Screen* theory argued, in essence, that popular cinema buttresses the power relations underpinning the dominant culture by symbolically "suturing" spectators into predetermined viewing positions that reflect and reinforce the social positions they occupy in real life – all under the guise of catering to their voyeuristic and narcissistic fantasies. Horror movies were mainly seen as pernicious examples of the way in which popular cinema caters to the male gaze, taking women's sexual difference as the basis both for their fetishization and for their punishment. Progressive readings of the genre were rare. True resistance to the dominant social order, it was generally agreed at the time, could only come from outside popular film – preferably in the form of a forbidding avant-garde cinema that would, in Laura Mulvey's memorable formulation, strive for the "total negation of the ease and plenitude of the narrative fiction film" (16) and destroy "the satisfaction, pleasure, and privilege" (26) of the spectator.

It was not until the 1980s and 1990s that film scholars learned to stop worrying and love the horror movie, largely because of the growing influence of Cultural Studies in academia. Often described as being less a unified academic field than an eclectic methodology that cuts across disciplinary lines, Cultural Studies deemphasized traditional, ahistorical textual analysis in favor of an examination of the diverse cultural contexts in which texts are created and received. Crucially, it also privileged the notion that mass culture products are worthy of study because their production and consumption involve not only processes of ideological manipulation or indoctrination, but also acts of resistance and appropriation on the part of both producers and consumers. This led to a reassessment of previous attitudes toward popular cinema and the horror film, in particular, during the last two decades of the twentieth century. Academic writing on the genre displayed a new sensitivity to the ideological gaps, contradictions, and ambiguities inherent in horror cinema, as well as to the ability of viewers to resist or recast the "dominant," or intended, meaning of horror movies. The horror film was reconceptualized as a dialogical text: a network of competing and conflicting discourses not reducible to a single ideological imperative. Furthermore, the experience of watching horror movies was refigured as an active and lively dialogue between spectator and screen, an intense form of negotiation not reducible to a simple process of normalization. What had been a critically ignored or maligned genre, seen simply as the province of revolting bodies, was now viewed as the home of bodies in revolt. If, in the 1960s and 1970s, horror cinema was a bad neighborhood to be avoided by film scholars at all costs, by the turn of the twenty-first century, it had been almost completely gentrified and made safe for academia. Today, it is a vital hot spot in the field of Film Studies – perhaps the single most written-about genre in the discipline.

It is all the more surprising, then, that despite its explosive growth, horror film scholarship remains quite narrowly focused in one crucial way. The vast majority of the books, articles, and papers on horror cinema focus exclusively on Anglo American horror. Relatively little has been written in English not only about non-Western – say, Latin American, Asian, or African – horror movies, but also about Western horror movies made outside the United States and the United Kingdom in countries like Italy, Spain, and France. The scholarly neglect of non-Western horror, while absolutely lamentable given the unique genre traditions in question, is perhaps not totally unexpected. As Steven Jay Schneider and Tony Williams comment, it can be seen as the result of a certain amount of Western prejudice combined with "difficulties accessing films from other parts of the globe, as well as the relative lack of interest shown by several national cinemas in this genre until the last decade or so" (1). More mystifying is that classic European horror cinema of the 1950s, 1960s, 1970s, and 1980s – Euro horror, as many of its contemporary American fans call it – has suffered such neglect. Clearly there is no cultural prejudice at work here, since other forms of European cinema dating from the same era have received much attention in Film Studies. Nor is there any shortage of films to discuss, as horror movies emerged from Europe in staggering numbers from the 1950s – when the postwar recovery of European film industries, an international surge in the popularity of horror cinema, and the decline of the old Hollywood studio system triggered a boom in horror film production on the Continent – to the 1980s, when a combination of factors, including declining movie attendance in Europe, the rise of new Hollywood blockbuster cinema, and the diminishing American market for foreign films, conspired to end Euro horror's golden age. Nor has it been particularly difficult to see these films in the years since their original theatrical releases – especially in the twenty-first century, as I will demonstrate in a moment.

There are several readily apparent reasons that classic European horror movies deserve the consideration of film scholars. In the first place, they differ markedly from British and American horror movies of the same period. As Cathal Tohill and Pete Tombs note, Euro horror drew upon a wide range of distinctly European cultural sources, including "surrealism, romanticism, and the decadent tradition, as well as early 20th century pulp-literature, filmed serials, creaky horror-movies and sexy comic strips" (5). The result was a new type of horror cinema that dispensed with the artistic unity and narrative logic privileged by Anglo American genre films, prizing the "pictorial, the excessive and the irrational" (ibid.) instead. Euro horror movies also "blended eroticism and terror" (ibid.) in a novel fashion, exploring the boundary between sex and violence in ways that were rare in the more puritanical British and American horror movies being made at the time. Finally, Euro horror produced an array of unique directors, stars, and genres completely unknown in Anglo American horror cinema. In short, to quote Tohill and Tombs: "Compared to the U.S. and U.K. [horror] scene, the developments in Europe were wild and untamed" (6). Clearly, then, an examination of Euro horror could expand our understanding of the genre and deepen our appreciation for its richness and diversity. Similarly, it could allow us to better understand and appreciate other forms of European cinema dating from the same time that have already enjoyed a great deal of attention from film scholars.

This is especially true in the case of European art cinema, which has a special, reciprocal relationship with Euro horror. Both arose from the same cultural, economic, and political milieu and responded to the same historical traumas: World War II, the Holocaust, the Cold War, and the process of decolonization, for example. Both often made use of the same production facilities and creative personnel. Studios like Rome's Cinecittà – which hosted the production of not only Federico Fellini's *La dolce vita* (1960) and Luchino Visconti's *La caduta degli dei* (*The Damned*, 1969), but also Dario Argento's *Il gatto a nove code* (*The Cat o' Nine Tails*, 1971) and Jorge Grau's *Non si deve profanare il sonno dei morti* (*The Living Dead at Manchester Morgue*, 1974) – turned out both European art films and Euro horror films. Stars like Barbara Steele – whose credits include Riccardo Freda's *Lo spettro* (*The Ghost*, 1963) and Antonio Margheriti's *Danza macabra* (*Castle of Blood*, 1964), as well as Fellini's *8½* (1963) and Volker Schlöndorff's *Der junge Törless* (*Young Törless*, 1966) – worked both in Euro horror cinema and in European art cinema, as did a variety of producers, writers, cinematographers, art directors, and other craftspeople. Both drew inspiration from earlier forms of European avant-garde cinema like Expressionism and Surrealism, as well as from classical Hollywood cinema of the studio era. Finally, the character of European art cinema is not so different from that of Euro horror cinema. Both tend to favor loosely structured plots and intense psychological subjectivity, and both push the envelope of what was then considered acceptable with regard to the onscreen depiction of sex and violence. Moreover, both share a tendency toward bold experimentation with design, color, lighting, camerawork, editing, and sound. In fact, the line between art cinema and Euro horror can be difficult to discern. Art films were often directly influenced by Euro horror, as when Fellini's *Toby Dammit*, a segment of the omnibus film *Histoires extraordinaires* (*Spirits of the Dead*, 1968), borrowed key imagery – the figure of a pretty little blonde girl with a bouncing ball as the embodiment of evil – from Mario Bava's *Operazione paura* (*Kill, Baby ... Kill!*, 1966). In turn, Euro horror movies were often inspired by art films, as when Argento's *Profondo rosso* (*Deep Red*, 1975) again cast David Hemmings, the star of Michelangelo Antonioni's *Blow-Up* (1966), in the role of an artist who witnesses a murder and becomes obsessed with solving it. The result, as Joan Hawkins has observed, is that many European pictures of the period – she offers Georges Franju's *Les yeux sans visage* (*Eyes without a Face*, 1960) as a key example – occupied "double niches" as art films and horror movies, effectively blurring the boundary between the two categories (72–85). A serious consideration of Euro horror thus reveals, among other things, not only how horror cinema participated in art cinema's "high" culture project of exploring new means of formal and narrative expression, but also how art cinema, in its quest for the shock of the new, was partly defined by its kinship with "low" culture genres like horror.

Euro horror cinema has also had a considerable impact on other films both within and outside the horror genre. The rise of Euro horror in the mid-1950s heralded the worldwide renaissance of the genre after a fallow period in the years following World War II, a time when, as Wheeler Winston Dixon writes, the horror film in Britain and America was "truly dead": "The classic monsters ... had been recycled, teamed with other of their brethren, and finally relegated to foils for burlesque comedians, and no one seemed to have any idea of how to restore them to 'life'" (*History of Horror* 63–64). Although the gothic revival movies made by Hammer Film Productions in Britain or the horror teen-pics made by American International Pictures in the United States are often credited for resurrecting horror in the late 1950s, they were actually pre-

Barbara Steele in *Black Sunday*. The "Queen of Horror" also appeared in contemporaneous art films like *8½* (American International Pictures). *Courtesy of Jerry Ohlinger Archives*

ceded by landmark Euro horror films like Henri-Georges Clouzot's *Les diaboliques* (*Diabolique*, 1955) and Riccardo Freda's *I vampiri* (1956), both of which not only helped jump-start the genre, but also exerted a powerful influence on the subsequent direction of its development. Indeed, Euro horror has often played a key role in determining the course of the horror genre over the years. The *giallo*, or Italian murder mystery film, pioneered by Mario Bava with *La ragazza che sapeva troppo* (*The Girl Who Knew Too Much*, 1963) and *Sei donne per l'assassino* (*Blood and Black Lace*, 1964), is widely regarded as an important catalyst of the original slasher film cycle in the United States during the late 1970s and early 1980s. Euro horror has also been identified by film critic David Edelstein as a major influence on what he calls "torture porn" – a new, ultraviolent type of horror cinema that includes such hit movies as *Saw* (2004) and *Hostel* (2005) (par. 2). Another measure of Euro horror's impact on the genre is the number of Euro horror films that have inspired remakes. Bava's atmospheric sci-fi/horror movie *Terrore nello spazio* (*Planet of the Vampires*, 1965) served as the basis for *Alien* (1979), while his rural *giallo Reazione a catena* (*Bay of Blood*, 1971) inspired *Friday the 13th* (1980). At the time of this writing, it is being reported that David Gordon Green, the director of *George Washington* (2000) and *Pineapple Express* (2008), is preparing to remake Dario Argento's occult thriller *Suspiria* (1977), one of the most popular and well known of all Euro horror films. When Euro horror movies have not been remade outright, they have frequently been the subject of elaborate homages that speak to their currency within the genre. *Hostel: Part II* (2007) features two Euro horror stars, Edwige Fenech and Luc Merenda, in key roles and gives Euro horror director Ruggero Deodato a cameo. *Grindhouse* (2007), Quentin Tarantino and Robert Rodriguez's retro horror double feature, heavily references Euro horror movies like Umberto Lenzi's *Incubo sulla città contaminata* (*Nightmare City*, 1980), Lucio Fulci's *Zombi 2* (*Zombie*, 1979), and Argento's *The Cat o' Nine Tails*. The same is true of contemporary European horror movies like *Amer* (2009), *Ubaldo Terzani Horror Show* (2010), and *Masks* (2011), all of which quote liberally from classic *giallo* cinema. Euro horror's influence has not been limited to the horror genre, however. As I have already noted, it had a significant impact on the European art cinema of its time. Likewise, many recent "extreme" European arthouse films – such as Claire Denis's *Trouble Every Day* (2001), Gaspar Noé's *Irréversible* (*Irreversible*, 2002), Michael Haneke's *Funny Games* (1997 and 2007), Lars von Trier's *Antichrist* (2009), and Pedro Almodóvar's *La piel que habito* (*The Skin I Live In*, 2011) – have been strongly influenced by Euro horror, as I discuss in more detail in the conclusion of this book.

Despite all this, Euro horror's distinctive films, directors, genres, stars, and conditions of production and reception have remained largely unexplored in English-language horror film studies. While a volume by Mikel J. Koven, *La Dolce Morte: Vernacular Cinema and the Italian Giallo*

Film, surveys an important genre of Euro horror, there has been no scholarly monograph offering a holistic examination of Euro horror cinema. The closest thing to a comprehensive, book-length study of Euro horror cinema hitherto produced by an academic press is Steven Jay Schneider's *100 European Horror Films,* an entry in the British Film Institute's Screen Guide series that offers brief reviews of a hundred popular Euro horror movies – not a sustained, in-depth exploration of the subject. A few edited compilations – Ernest Mathjis and Xavier Mendik's *Alternative Europe: Eurotrash and Exploitation Cinema since 1945,* Steven Jay Schneider and Tony Williams's *Horror International,* and Robert G. Weiner and John Cline's *Cinema Inferno: Celluloid Explosions from the Cultural Margins,* among them – have attempted to begin a dialogue about previously unexplored forms of horror, but they do not focus exclusively on Euro horror cinema. In fact, only a handful of essays on Euro horror have been collected in the numerous anthologies of horror film criticism and theory published since the 1980s. The majority of articles written on Euro horror thus far have appeared in a single scholarly journal, *Kinoeye.* This online periodical, which is committed to offering new perspectives on European cinema, has devoted several of its issues to the discussion of seminal Euro horror movies like *Eyes without a Face* and celebrated Euro horror auteurs like Dario Argento and Jean Rollin. Meanwhile, even the most popular and well-known Euro horror films and directors receive only passing mention, if that, in student guidebooks and readers, which, as Peter Hutchings notes, tend to define the genre as the sum of its canonical Anglo American texts: Universal monster movies of the 1930s, Val Lewton's RKO productions of the 1940s, Cold War sci-fi/horror films of the 1950s, Hammer horror of the 1950s and 1960s, Vietnam era American horror of the 1960s and 1970s, and the slasher and "post-slasher" movies of the 1980s, 1990s, and beyond (27–28).

Instead, much of the critical attention that Euro horror cinema has gotten to date has come from "fan-scholars" – a term coined by Matt Hills to describe "the fan who uses academic theorising within their fan writing and within the construction of a scholarly fan identity" (*Fan Cultures* 2) – working beyond the borders of Film Studies in the United States and the United Kingdom. Fan-scholars have produced a substantial number of books on Euro horror cinema, from historical overviews like Cathal Tohill and Pete Tombs's *Immoral Tales: European Sex and Horror Movies, 1956–1984* to collected interviews like Luca M. Palmerini and Gaetano Mistretta's *Spaghetti Nightmares: Italian Fantasy-Horrors as Seen through the Eyes of Their Protagonists* (1996) to critical filmographies such as Lawrence McCallum's *Italian Horror Films of the 1960s* (1998) and Louis Paul's *Italian Horror Film Directors* (2004) to exhaustively researched and lavishly illustrated guides to Euro horror auteurs, like those published by Flesh and Blood Press in England: Stephen Thrower's *Beyond Terror: The Films of Lucio Fulci*, Chris Gallant's *Art of Darkness: The Cinema of Dario Argento*, and Troy Howarth's *The Haunted World of Mario Bava*, for instance. One of the most impressive books about Euro horror cinema by a fan-scholar is Tim Lucas's self-published, 1,128-page tome on the life and films of Mario Bava, *Mario Bava: All the Colors of the Dark* (2007) – the product of thirty-two years of independent research and writing. In addition to books, fan-scholars have also published academic-style journals devoted to the study of Euro horror cinema. A prime example is Andy Black's periodical, *Necronomicon*, which during its irregular run has featured dozens of articles on Euro horror. A third important site of fan-scholar work on Euro horror cinema has been film fanzines like Tim Lucas's *Video Watchdog*, Steven Puchalski's *Shock Cinema*, Allan Bryce's *Dark Side*, and Stephen Thrower's *Eyeball*. The reviews of Euro horror movies, interviews with Euro horror stars and directors, and articles on Euro horror cinema that frequently appear in the pages of these fanzines constitute what David Sanjek calls "an alternative brand of film criticism, a school with its own set of values and virtues" (316). Finally, there is a relatively new locus of Euro horror fan-scholar activity: the internet. Dark Dreams, Mondo Erotico, An Angel for Satan, and other websites devoted to the celebration of Euro horror figures like Dario Argento, Jess Franco, and Barbara Steele have flourished, as have websites that offer comprehensive reviews of Euro horror home video releases: Mondo Digital, Eccentric Cinema, and Sex Gore Mutants, for example. The focal point of Euro horror fan-scholar activity on the internet, however, has arguably been the discussion forum: the virtual interpretive community whose members routinely gather online to perform what Hills calls a "discourse of connoisseurship" (*Pleasures of Horror* 73). The most sophisticated of these communities – like the Mobius Home

Video Forum and Latarnia: Fantastique International – function as sites where fans mingle, posting messages on everything from the merits of a recent Euro horror DVD or Blu-ray release to shared recollections of first experiences with Euro horror cinema to the artistic virtues or ideological complexities of a particular Euro horror film.

Why has Euro horror not received the attention it deserves from film scholars? One might argue, echoing Schneider and Williams, that it is simply because Euro horror movies have not been available for study, particularly in the United States. Although a surprising number of Euro horror films were exhibited theatrically in the United States – thanks to American International Pictures, Trans American Films, Aquarius Releasing Inc., and several other independent companies that specialized in distributing horror and exploitation movies between the 1950s and the 1980s – they typically played only limited engagements at rural drive-ins and at urban grindhouses of the sort that once lined Forty-Second Street in New York City's Times Square. Moreover, Euro horror films shown theatrically in the United States were routinely re-edited, rescored, and dubbed into English by their distributors in order to avoid censorship problems and make them more palatable to American viewers, meaning that audiences in the United States did not see the original versions of these films as exhibited in Continental Europe. At the end of their brief theatrical lives, a few of the early Euro horror films were picked up by local television stations for late-night broadcast as part of genre packages regularly put together by distributors like AI-TV, Roberts and Barry, and Thunderbird Films during the heyday of "shock theater" programming in the 1960s (Heffernan 167–170). Some of the later Euro horror films were made available on videocassette by distributors like Paragon Video Productions, Thriller Video, and Vestron Video during the home video boom in the 1980s. In addition to usually being the same Americanized versions of the Euro horror movies that played in theaters, however, the Euro horror films that appeared commercially on television and video were almost always cropped to fit the small screen – a standard industry practice that put them at a further remove from their original theatrical versions.

During the 1990s, long after the demise of shock theater programming on television and when most commercial Euro horror videos had gone out of print, the most plentiful source of Euro horror cinema in the United States was the samizdat-like network of "gray-market" mail-order video companies such as Video Search of Miami, Something Weird Video, Sinister Cinema, and Midnight Video, which sold videocassettes of public domain films and – treading into more ambiguous legal territory – films not currently licensed for home video distribution in the United States. These gray-market tapes typically offered viewers the same cropped and Americanized versions of Euro horror films that formerly appeared on television and mainstream video; moreover, since gray-market Euro horror videos were often transfers from battered sixteen-millimeter prints that had been in circulation for decades, the quality of their picture and sound was generally inferior to that of earlier television broadcasts and mainstream video releases. The few gray-market video companies that prided themselves on presenting Euro horror films in pristine condition, uncut and in their proper aspect ratio, were usually forced to rely on source materials imported from outside the United States, meaning that their Euro horror releases, while markedly better than others, often had distracting foreign-language subtitles or were simply not available in English-language versions at all. Furthermore, because gray-market video companies operated in what Joan Hawkins calls an "unsacralized cultural space" (11) outside the "'pure' marketplace of mainstream video and film distribution companies" (ibid.), their product remained more or less invisible to the general public, not to mention most of academia. As a result, Euro horror movies, though technically available to American film scholars throughout the 1990s, were much more likely to be seen only by hardcore genre fans and collectors attuned to the vagaries of "unsacralized" cultural exchange.

This is no longer the case. Once decidedly low culture, Euro horror has now drifted into the mainstream in the United States. Since the turn of the twenty-first century, Euro horror movies have become more visible and available to American consumers – academic and otherwise – than ever before, thanks largely to the explosive growth of the DVD market. In 2005, which may prove to be the year in which the DVD format peaked, given subsequent sales figures ("Home Entertainment Enjoys" par. 1), consumers in the United States spent $22.8 billion renting and buying DVDs ("Consumer Spending Reaches" par. 1) and bought an estimated

37 million DVD players (par. 5), bringing the number of American homes with the capability to play DVDs to an estimated 89 million, or 80% of all TV households, according to the Digital Entertainment Group (par. 7). The demand for films on disc drove the production of DVDs to record levels: more than 1.6 billion DVDs were shipped to retailers (par. 4). By the end of the year, there were a total of 53,737 different DVD titles available to consumers in North America, not including imports or pornographic films (Kehr par. 1).

The highly lucrative digital home video market is dominated by corporate Hollywood, which has increasingly come to depend on rentals and sales of classic hits and current blockbusters on disc to offset dwindling box-office returns; however, it has grown to the point where it supports a thriving trade not only in mainstream cinema, but also in what Jeffrey Sconce calls "paracinema": an "elastic textual category ... includ[ing] entries from such seemingly disparate subgenres as 'badfilm,' splatterpunk, 'mondo' films, sword and sandal epics, Elvis flicks, government hygiene films, Japanese monster movies, beach-party musicals, and just about every manifestation of exploitation cinema from juvenile delinquency documentaries to soft-core pornography" (535). Indeed, paracinema has proven to be one of the most rapidly expanding segments of the market, prompting a number of small, independent production companies like Blue Underground, Synapse Films, Shriek Show, and Mondo Macabro to specialize in it. Moved by a genuine paracinephilia to preserve these films and make them available to contemporary audiences or motivated by the same gold rush mentality behind the home video boom in the 1980s – and supported in either case by a vocal and growing fan base – these indie publishers, joined by larger competitors like Anchor Bay and Image Entertainment, have turned out thousands of paracinema titles on disc.

Interestingly, Euro horror represents a substantial portion of their output. Indeed, the sheer number of Euro horror titles they have released on DVD in North America thus far is remarkable; it already far surpasses the total number of Euro horror movies released commercially on video during the 1980s and 1990s, and the catalog of Euro horror films currently on disc is surprisingly comprehensive. It includes not only the work of major directors like Mario Bava, Dario Argento, Jean Rollin, and Jess Franco, but also that of relatively minor figures like Massimo Pupillo, Andrea Bianchi, Bruno Gantillon, and Claudio Guerín. If the number and range of Euro horror films now on DVD in North America is unprecedented, however, so is their availability. Because many of the home video companies specializing in Euro horror have managed to secure widespread distribution for their products, Euro horror films have become almost as ubiquitous as Hollywood movies on disc, available from consumer electronics outlets like Best Buy, bookstore chains like Barnes and Noble, music and movie retailers like f.y.e., home video rental sources like Blockbuster and Netflix, and online merchants like Amazon. Far from being hard to see in the United States, Euro horror cinema is now difficult for American consumers to avoid.

Euro horror films are not just more visible than ever before, however. They are also – once again, thanks to the advent of DVDs – being presented for the first time (commercially) in their original, uncut versions, the way they were projected in European theaters before being altered for distribution in the United States. Indeed, a number of the home video companies specializing in Euro horror cinema on disc offer these movies in deluxe editions that rival – in terms of the care taken to assemble the films from the best available print elements, to compile the most complete versions of the films possible, and to include entertaining and informative supplemental materials – those produced by Criterion, Milestone, Kino, and other elite labels dedicated to making the acknowledged masterpieces of world cinema available to consumers on high-quality DVDs.

Many Euro horror "collector's editions" have been pressed. In 2000, Anchor Bay released a limited edition DVD of Lucio Fulci's occult zombie film L'aldilà (The Beyond, 1981). Only 20,000 numbered copies of this limited edition, packaged in a special collector's tin, were made available to the public. The disc's features include an uncut, widescreen (2.35:1) presentation of the film enhanced for 16:9 televisions, a rare on-set interview with Fulci, the international theatrical trailer, the U.S. re-release theatrical trailer, a music video inspired by the film (Necrophagia's "And You Will Live in Terror"), audio commentary featuring stars David Warbeck and Katherine MacColl, the previously lost German color pre-credit sequence and main titles, and English and Italian language options. The DVD comes with six 5×7 international poster replicas and a 5×7, full-color, forty-five-page booklet featuring rare photos, a biography of Fulci, and liner notes to the film. In 2001, Anchor Bay released a three-disc limited edition DVD of *Suspiria*. Only 60,000 numbered copies were made available to the public. The first DVD includes an uncut widescreen (2.35:1) presentation of the film enhanced for 16:9 televisions, a collection of promotional materials (including theatrical trailers, radio spots, and a television spot), a music video inspired by the film (performed by the group Daemonia), a poster and still gallery, talent bios, and English, Italian, and French language options. The second disc contains a fifty-two-minute documentary entitled "*Suspiria* 25th Anniversary," which was produced for the DVD release of the film and features interviews with director Argento, co-writer Daria Nicolodi, cinematographer Luciano Tovoli, members of the Italian progressive rock band Goblin (which composed and recorded the music for the film), and stars Jessica Harper, Stefania Casini, and Udo Kier. The third disc, a CD, has the Goblin soundtrack to the film. The three discs are accompanied by eight 5×7 lobby card replicas and a 5×7, full-color, thirty-page booklet featuring photos, liner notes to the film, and an interview with Jessica Harper. In 2005, Grindhouse Releasing made available a two-disc twenty-fifth anniversary collector's edition of *Cannibal Holocaust*. Only 11,111 numbered copies were made available to the public. It features a new, high-definition, 16:9 digital restoration of the original, uncensored director's cut of the film; a new stereo remix of the film's soundtrack, as well as the original mono mix; audio commentary by director Deodato and star Robert Kerman; selected on-camera commentary; an hour-long Italian documentary entitled "The Making of *Cannibal Holocaust*," which contains rare, behind-the-scenes footage of the film's production; exclusive on-camera interviews with Deodato, Kerman, and co-star Gabriel Yorke; original theatrical trailers; an extensive gallery of stills and poster art; the original shooting script; a music video inspired by the film (Necrophagia's "Cannibal Holocaust"); and liner notes by horror journalist Chas Balun.

Of course, these films represent the high end of Euro horror in terms of their production values and are considered masterpieces by fans, so it is perhaps not surprising that they have received such lavish releases on

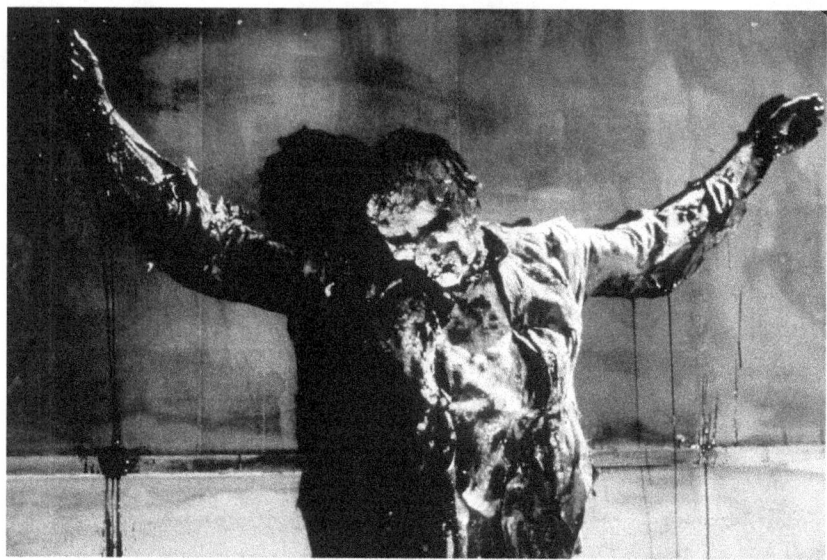

An iconic image from *The Beyond,* one of many Euro horror films to receive deluxe treatment on DVD in the United States (Aquarius Releasing). *Courtesy of Photofest*

DVD. Much the same treatment has been accorded to Euro horror films that have not been well received by contemporary American viewers, however. Take, for example, the case of three rather mediocre Euro horror zombie films made available on DVD in 2002. Anchor Bay re-released Bruno Mattei's widely reviled *Virus (Hell of the Living Dead,* 1980), a movie that most Euro horror fans regard as a shameless and inept rip-off of George Romero's *Dawn of the Dead* (1978) – a "cruddy quickie" (Naugle par. 3), as one online reviewer puts it, that "isn't worth your time unless you're a hardcore (and by hardcore I mean either incarcerated or homicidal) zombie fan" (par. 6). The disc nonetheless features an uncut widescreen (1.85:1) presentation of the film enhanced for 16:9 televisions, an all-new interview with the director entitled "Hell Rats of the Living Dead," a director biography, the original four-minute theatrical trailer for the film, and a poster and stills gallery. It is accompanied by a four-page collector's booklet and detailed liner notes. Anchor Bay also re-released Umberto Lenzi's *Nightmare City,* about which fan Mike Bracken says: "Simply put, this is one of the most inane, inept film productions I've ever seen" (par. 6). Yet the DVD features a widescreen (2.35:1) presentation of the film enhanced for 16:9 televisions, a theatrical trailer, an all-new interview with Umberto Lenzi entitled "Tales of a Contaminated City," and a director biography. Meanwhile, Media Blasters re-released Claudio Fragasso's *After Death* (*Zombie 4: After Death*, 1989), one of several charmless sequels to Fulci's *Zombie* and – once again – a film with few supporters among even the most loyal fans of Euro horror. Summing up fan reaction to the film, an online reviewer for the website Goatdog's Movies gives *Zombie 4: After Death* a rating of 0.5 out of 5 goats, calling it "a piece of garbage made to bring in a little cash with borrowed equipment and half-ass [sic] talent" (Phillips par. 6). Nevertheless, the disc features an uncut widescreen (1.85:1) presentation of the film enhanced for 16:9 televisions, lengthy interviews (totaling about a half hour) with Fragasso and stars Candice Daly and Jeff Stryker, and a collection of tie-in trailers. As with *Hell of the Living Dead*, the disc is accompanied by detailed liner notes. It is also perhaps worth noting that despite its less-than-stellar reputation among fans of Euro horror, the *Zombie 4: After Death* DVD was deemed popular enough at the time of its release to be accorded a place in the "New Releases" section at my local Blockbuster, next to such Hollywood hits as *xXx* (2002) and *White Oleander* (2002).

These DVDs were not as lavish as the limited edition, multidisc versions of *The Beyond*, *Suspiria*, and *Cannibal Holocaust* described above; however, they do rank above the bare-bones DVDs of many classic and contemporary Hollywood films, which often do not feature anamorphic widescreen presentations, liner notes, or supplements like directors' biographies, theatrical trailers, and behind-the-scenes documentaries. More to the point, they demonstrate not only that there is a wide range of Euro horror films available on disc, but also that both "good" and "bad" Euro horror films are being presented in a way that respects – and even celebrates – the original intentions of their makers. And this seems likely to continue as the home video industry transitions from the DVD to the Blu-ray format: the leading American producer of Euro horror on home video, Blue Underground, has already released high-definition versions of Lucio Fulci's *Lo squartatore di New York* (*The New York Ripper*, 1982), José Ramón Larraz's *Vampyres* (1975), Dario Argento's *Inferno* (1980), and Harry Kümel's *Les lèvres rouges* (*Daughters of Darkness*, 1971), among others.

One might note as well that the DVD and Blu-ray releases of Euro horror films do not represent the only way in which Euro horror cinema has become more visible and available to the American public. A number of Euro horror movies have also been re-released theatrically, exhibited in film retrospectives, and shown on cable and satellite television since the late 1990s. In 1998, a limited theatrical re-release of *The Beyond,* sponsored by Grindhouse Releasing, Cowboy Films, and Quentin Tarantino's Rolling Thunder Pictures, a distribution subsidiary of Miramax, drew large crowds in New York, Los Angeles, San Francisco, Chicago, Austin, Toronto, and Boston. In 2001, Grindhouse Releasing made available a newly remastered print of *Cannibal Holocaust,* which it rents to independent theaters throughout the United States and Canada for limited engagements and midnight screenings. In 2002, the American Cinematheque in Los Angeles hosted a complete retrospective of director Mario Bava's work, featuring newly struck thirty-five-millimeter prints of films like *La maschera del demonio* (*Black Sunday,* 1960), *I tre volti della paura* (*Black Sabbath,* 1963), and *Cani arrabbiati* (*Kidnapped,* 1974). After its debut, the Bava retrospective traveled the country, playing in San Francisco, Chicago, New York, and Dallas, among other cities. In addition to showing theatrically, Euro horror films have also appeared on cable and satellite television. At the same time the Bava retrospective was playing around the country, Turner Classic Movies broadcast a number of the films featured in the retrospective, including *The Girl Who Knew Too Much, Black Sunday, Black Sabbath,* and *Kill, Baby ... Kill!* In 2005, TCM showed Antonio Margheriti's *La vergine di Norimberga* (*The Virgin of Nuremberg,* 1963) and Lorenzo Sabatini's *Il castello dei morti vivi* (*Castle of the Living Dead,* 1964). Monsters HD, the first high-definition satellite television channel devoted entirely to horror cinema, broadcast a number of Euro horror movies during its time on the air between 2003 and 2009, including three films from Amando de Ossorio's popular *Blind Dead* series: *La noche del terror ciego* (*Tombs of the Blind Dead,* 1972), *El ataque de los muertos sin ojos* (*Return of the Evil Dead,* 1973), and *El buque maldito* (*The Ghost Galleon,* 1974). These theatrical screenings and television broadcasts are yet another way in which Euro horror has moved from the margins to the mainstream of American popular culture.

Given the substantial presence of Euro horror cinema on home video, in theaters, and on television in the United States, the notion that it has not received attention from scholars because it is not available for study clearly does not hold water. Rather, I would argue, Euro horror has suffered neglect in academia because of certain entrenched disciplinary prejudices that have blinded scholars to it. Some of these disciplinary prejudices stem from lingering biases against popular cinema. Despite the enthusiasm with which scholars operating under the aegis of Cultural Studies have, since the 1980s, set about "trashing the academy" – that is, "pushing the limits of the traditional cinematic canon and the constraints of conventional academic enterprise" (Sconce 539) in order to "address traditionally 'untouchable' cinematic genres such as horror and pornography" (ibid.) – the scope of their engagement with popular cinema has been limited, in my view, by an adherence to old aesthetic and ideological criteria used to determine whether a film is suitable for academic study. Popular movies that demonstrate obvious artistic merit or boast politically progressive credentials are deemed worthy of consideration; conversely, tasteless or politically incorrect forms of popular cinema – like Euro horror, which has a reputation for being not only aesthetically challenged, but also misogynistic, homophobic, and racist – remain largely beyond the pale. Another disciplinary prejudice that appears to have contributed to the marginalization of Euro horror cinema within horror film scholarship involves the nature of contemporary film theory itself. Steven Shaviro has shown that much recent film theory is "written out of the tension between a desire to reproduce and a desire to keep at a distance the voyeuristic excitations that are its object" (13). As a "phobic construct" (15), it counters the medium's invitation to "surrender to and revel in cinematic fascination" (64) with "the tools of psychoanalytic reserve and hermeneutical suspicion" (ibid.). In guarding itself against the temptations of cinematic fascination, film theory has proven to be particularly inimical to what Linda Williams calls "body genres": "low" forms of horror, pornography, and melodrama that "sensationally display bodies on the screen and register effects in the bodies of spectators" ("Film Bodies" 730). Given that Euro horror cinema combines graphic violence with frank eroticism, constituting what might be considered the body genre par excellence, it is perhaps not surprising that it has been more or less shunned by film scholars. I also suggest that Euro horror's liminal status within horror film studies has to do with the fact that, as a type of popular European cinema, it does not respond to the dominant interpretive paradigm used in the discipline to analyze European movies. In academia, "European cinema" is generally understood as "art cinema" and positioned as the polar opposite of the popular cinema of Hollywood. The result, as Richard Dyer and Ginette Vincendeau write, is that the existence and importance of popular entertainment cinema made by Europeans for Europeans – including Euro horror – have "remained stubbornly unacknowledged" (1). In the interest of documenting exactly how these disciplinary prejudices have led to Euro horror cinema's near-invisibility in academic circles – and demonstrating why this blind spot is so unfortunate – I will examine each in turn.

TWO

Fast, Cheap, and Out of Control

THE ACADEMIC CASE AGAINST EURO HORROR CINEMA

To begin, I argue that Euro horror's liminal presence in Film Studies is partly due to the fact that when making decisions about which movies to analyze, scholars continue – consciously or not – to rely upon traditional aesthetic criteria. Although ideological rather than aesthetic issues have been the primary focus of film theory and criticism since the 1970s, the old notion that a film must possess some kind of "artistic value" to be worthy of study has endured. The persistence of this notion has stalled the scholarly exploration of some forms of popular cinema despite the powerful influence of Cultural Studies in academia. In particular, as Paul Watson contends, it has led to a pervasive (if largely unspoken and perhaps unrecognized) bias against the exploitation film, that "blatantly commercial product, sold on the basis of its apparent revelatory qualities, and designed to ensure maximum possible return from the minimum investment and resources" (76):

> [F]rom its first moments Film Studies' theories and canons have been bound up with an economy of taste which influences questions not only of how to approach cinema, but questions of what cinema to approach in the first instance. Dominant notions of cinematic aesthetics have been installed and defended on the basis of the assumed excellence of taste of a relative few privileged journalists and critics, appealing to canons and principles of art in general. This is not to say that there haven't been shifts in the cinematic canon, or that those canons are uncontested, but that those shifts and contests are themselves tied to shifts in taste which have tended overwhelmingly to exclude exploitation. (68)

The "embodiment of tastelessness" (Watson 80), exploitation cinema functions as a limit of film theory because of the "dominant economy of taste" (71) upon which film theory is founded. While the study of horror obviously has not been proscribed on aesthetic grounds in Film Studies the way that the study of exploitation has, it has been delimited by the economy of taste Watson describes. Scholars tend to focus on horror movies that conform to "dominant notions of cinematic aesthetics" and ignore genre films that do not. This is especially true of horror cinema that verges on exploitation. As Ken Gelder writes:

> It has been fashionable to observe, in these postmodern times, that the once-definitive boundary between high culture and low culture has been well and truly breached. The art world now routinely borrows from low culture; and many low cultural forms have in turn been "recovered" and given some kind of social approval. This is certainly true for horror.... As one descends deeper into the cultural field, however, the obstacles to this kind of recovery can at times seem insurmountable.... Through its flaunting of "bad taste," its low-level, gross-out special effects and lurid colouration, its gratuitous and exaggerated acts of violence and dismemberment and its willing embrace of exploitation and "sexploitation" tags, modern low-budget, lowbrow horror cinema [has] made sure it remain[s] at the bottom end of the market and on the fringes of cultural analysis. (311)

This seems to be the case with Euro horror, which is vulnerable to charges of tastelessness on several counts. In the first place, it is undeniably cheap. Not only were most Euro horror movies made for very little money, they were also often made purely as opportunistic knockoffs of other films. Take the example of Italian horror of the 1960s and 1970s. Like other European countries, Italy experienced a cinematic golden age during these two decades, when a "fast-growing economy, new cultural attitudes (an emerging consumer mentality, sexual awareness) and problems encountered by Hollywood (inflexible structures of the studio system, high production costs, competition from television) created openings for European film production" (Jäckel 10). Italian cinema of the period is often equated with art films such as Michelangelo Antonioni's *L'avventura* (1960), Federico Fellini's *Giulietta degli spiriti* (*Juliet of the Spirits*, 1965), Bernardo Bertolucci's *Il conformista* (*The Conformist*, 1970), and Luchino Visconti's *Morte a Venezia* (*Death in Venice*, 1971); however, the industry was actually geared toward the production of inexpensive but lucrative genre fare: horror movies, spaghetti westerns, "peplum" (sword and sandal) epics, and "mondo" (exotic travelogue) films. Most of these movies, as Christopher Frayling notes, "were made in assembly-line circumstances which resembled those of Hollywood 'B' features, or even TV series: shooting schedules which seldom overran a five- or six-week norm; budgets averaging below $200,000; the more solid sets used over and over again; only two or three 'takes' per shot; post-synchronized sound and dialogue tracks (even in the Italian versions); and the same pieces of action footage frequently turning up in 'disguised' form" (68). The impoverished and frenetic nature of Italian genre film production meant that originality and innovation often took a backseat to imitation and repetition. It simply made economic sense to capitalize on a box-office hit by turning out more of the same, rather than spending time and money to develop something novel that might not find favor with audiences. Accordingly, the guiding principle of the industry became the concept of the *filone:* "If a given film proved successfully entertaining or titillating, a series (or, in Italian, *'filone'*) of copycat 'quickies' were hurriedly cranked out and distributed to take advantage of the short-lived trend" (Nakahara 126).

The widespread embrace of this practice resulted in the birth of what Geoffrey O'Brien calls "the Italian System" (153). The industry, he writes, "made itself the surrogate Hollywood, Hollywood's Hollywood, a low-cost recycling plant for every cast-off plot device and visual motif, not to mention every used-up actor and director: drunks, wilted starlets, aging cowboy actors, former colleagues of [D. W.] Griffith and [Thomas H.] Ince unemployable in the new Hollywood" (157). Unlike the studio system that existed during the classical Hollywood era, which – for all its restrictiveness – helped foster the creation of a new kind of popular art, "the Italian System" produced a cinema defined by "speed and violence and crudity" (152):

> In an explosion of minigenres the industry annulled any possible distinction between the beautiful and the corrupt by perfecting an ultrarefined tawdriness, a cinema of poetic cruelty whose practitioners (Mario Bava, Vittorio Cottafavi, Riccardo Freda, Antonio Margheriti, Sergio Corbucci, Dario Argento) would turn out to be the most authentic inventors of the post-postmodern movie: authentic because they invented nothing, because they stole from their own movies, because they were unable to stop obsessively tacking together a recycled dub of a dub of some archaic internalized European narrative. (O'Brien 164)

This "cinema of poetic cruelty" has essentially been ignored by scholars despite its centrality to the evolution of the Italian film industry in the postwar era. The low production values and unoriginal, profit-driven premises of the popular movies produced in Italy during the 1960s and 1970s represent an affront to the "dominant economy of taste" that governs the field. This is particularly true of the Italian horror film. As O'Brien implies – four of the six directors he cites (Bava, Freda, Margheriti, and Argento) specialized in horror – the genre has come to epitomize the cheap, exploitative nature of the Italian system. It is perhaps inevitable, then, that horror is one of the most marginalized forms of Italian popular cinema in film criticism and theory. And much the same could be said of the horror cinema that emerged under similar circumstances from other European countries between the 1950s and the 1980s: it embodies, in its "ultrarefined tawdriness," a limit of horror film scholarship.

From a present-day perspective, Euro horror is also woefully dated. Beholden to the exploitation film market, its makers aggressively exploited once-popular narrative themes and filmmaking techniques in an attempt to increase its appeal at the box office. This naked pursuit of modishness is perhaps most ostentatiously on display, once again, in Euro horror movies of the 1960s and 1970s. In terms of their settings, themes, and character types, O'Brien notes, many of these films draw upon a "common vocabulary" that had a special currency during that era, "a set of cards that could be reshuffled to generate an instant screenplay" (153):

> airport, amnesia, assassination, atom bomb, blackmail, bondage, cavern, criminal gang, desert, drug hallucination, dual personality, explosion, fashion model, fire, impalement, insanity, jewelry, jungle, laboratory, lesbianism, luxury hotel, mutilation, narcotics, nightclub, nightmare, poison, police investigator, prostitute, psychiatrist, rape, religious cult, satanism, secret society, sequestered island, speedboat, strangulation, striptease, telepathy, telephone, tomb, torture. (ibid.)

In Jess Franco's 1969 adaptation of Leopold von Sacher-Masoch's *Venus in Furs*, for example, the director interweaves narrative elements – "jazz combos, sadomasochistic orgies, stock shots of the Rio carnival and the Blue Mosque in Istanbul, Klaus Kinski wearing a djellaba, and a nude body washed up on the beach" (O'Brien 182) – that are calculated to evoke in viewers not only horror, but also a powerful impression of topicality. Likewise, in his *Necronomicon – Geträumte Sünden* (*Succubus*, 1968), Franco cobbles together voguish "S & M nightclub scenes, beautiful women who kiss and kill for lust, strange word games that end in death, mad hedonistic parties, lesbianism and mannequin terror" (Tohill and Tombs 94) to lend his tale of a mysterious and murderous dominatrix a decidedly late 1960s ambience. The period-specific atmosphere of *Succubus* is not just a product of the film's trendy narrative elements, however; it is also the result of the movie's fashionable formal qualities. Franco's use of surreal location sets (*Succubus* was filmed partly in "exotic" Lisbon), soft-focus cinematography, oblique camera angles, "crash" zoom shots, disorienting editing, portentous dialogue, and composer Jerry van Rooyen's jazzy, hypnotic musical score creates an aura of "misty abstraction, a dreamlike acid haze" (Tohill and Tombs 95). Similarly, the pronounced late 1960s vibe of *Venus in Furs* is the product not only of the far-out story, but also of "inexplicable narrative ellipses, distended zooms, soft-focus dissolves, slow-motion pursuits, red and purple filters, a score by Manfred Mann, and overheated voice-overs by James Darren" (O'Brien 182).

Perhaps no formal quality more thoroughly dates Euro horror cinema of the 1960s and 1970s, however, than its dubbing. Because Euro horror directors often worked with international casts, could rarely afford to use synchronized sound-recording technology, and mostly hailed from countries where dubbing was (and still is) a commonplace and accepted practice, they typically shot their movies silent and left it to distributors in Europe, the United States, and elsewhere to record the appropriate vocal tracks. These vocal tracks were usually hastily improvised and poorly synchronized with the image, engendering a "speech at the mercy of random lip movements, unable to deviate from an imposed syntax" (O'Brien 163). Nonetheless, the sheer number of foreign-language films imported and dubbed into English by American distributors during this period – not only horror movies from Europe, but also martial arts movies from Hong Kong, wrestling movies from Mexico, and other genre fare from around the world – suggests that audiences in the United States were more or less accustomed to this "post-synchronese" (164).

Since then, dubbing has become widely reviled in the United States, associated not just with trash cinema, but with trash cinema of a campy, bygone era. Unlike in the 1960s and 1970s, dubbing now connotes a lower standard of quality to mainstream American audiences, who equate foreign films with art cinema and expect them to be subtitled. As Antje Ascheid puts it: "Considering a film an artistically valuable 'authored original' seems to suggest the use of subtitling, whereas films categorized as short-lived, mass-produced entertainment products ease the distributor's way into employing the dubbing technique" (34). This widely held distinction is the result of several decades of campaigning on the part of American film critics, scholars, and connoisseurs who passionately believe that dubbing represents an artistic desecration of the original film. In the sixth edition of *Film Art: An Introduction,* a popular and influential introduction to the medium of cinema, David Bordwell and Kristin Thompson neatly summarize this view:

> Dubbed voices usually have a bland "studio" sound. Elimination of the original actors' voices wipes out an important component of their performance. (Partisans of dubbing ought to look at dubbed versions of English-language films to see how a performance by Katharine Hepburn, Orson Welles, or John Wayne can be hurt by a voice that does not fit the body.) With dubbing, all of the usual problems of translation are multiplied by the need to synchronize specific words with specific lip movements. Most important, with subtitling viewers still have access to the original sound track. By eliminating the original voice track, dubbing simply destroys part of the film. (326)

There is little question that the campaign against dubbing has created a pervasive bias against the practice in the United States. Alongside dubbed movies' "reputation [among Americans] for being inauthentic" (Klady AR21), however, we must consider their reputation in the United States for being laughably outdated. If subtitling indicates that a film is an "artistically valuable 'authored original,'" it also suggests that a film is technologically and culturally current. The stereotype of dubbing as "[t]ongues wagging, lips flapping . . . but rarely in sync with the words" (ibid.) is inextricably tied to the outmoded film technology and culture of the 1960s and 1970s – the heyday of "Eurotrash" and "chopsocky" movies. The failure of dubbed English-language versions of otherwise successful foreign films like Wolfgang Petersen's *Das Boot* (*The Boat,* 1981), Hervé Palud's *Un indien dans la ville* (*Little Indian, Big City,* 1994), and

Roberto Benigni's *La vita è bella* (*Life Is Beautiful*, 1997) to connect with American audiences over the years – despite the best efforts of domestic distributors to create high-quality dubs – may be attributable, then, to the widespread perception that dubbing not only cheapens foreign films, but also dates them. Like its far-out settings and trippy zoom shots, Euro horror's "post-synchronese" fosters the impression that it is simply the refuse of an earlier era, contributing to its overall aura of tastelessness.

Finally, Euro horror cinema is unquestionably sensationalistic. It privileges moments of "heightened spectacle and emotion" (Freeland 256) that "appear to be interruptions of plot – scenes that stop the action and introduce another sort of element, capitalizing on the power of the cinema to produce visual and aural spectacles of beauty or stunning power" (ibid.). Many of these moments of heightened spectacle involve what Geoffrey O'Brien calls a "science of plotless shock and dismemberment" (170). Euro horror movies are infamous for their elaborately staged scenes of gory mayhem, showcasing the "ruined-body-as-spectacle" (Pinedo 60). In these scenes, narrative development is effectively sidelined in favor of inventive and extremely graphic depictions of torture, mutilation, and murder.

Take, for example, a representative moment from a film already mentioned: Dario Argento's occult thriller *Suspiria*. Early in the movie, a female student at the Bavarian dance academy where the story is set flees the school in the middle of a late-night rainstorm, taking refuge with a friend who lives in a nearby apartment building. After rebuffing her friend's attempts to find out why she is so upset, the student locks herself in a room and begins pacing nervously, glancing out the window as if she expects someone or something to appear there. Suddenly, in a sequence choreographed to the eerie, percussive musical score created by the Italian progressive rock band Goblin, she is attacked by a demonic creature that pulls her through the glass window, stabs her repeatedly (at one point we see a close-up of the blade penetrating her exposed heart), ties a cable around her neck, and sends her plunging through the skylight above the apartment building's lobby, where she hangs in midair, blood pooling on the floor beneath her dangling corpse. (The final shot of the sequence reveals that her friend, who ran downstairs to find help after hearing her screams, has also been killed – her chest impaled and her head bisected by the glass and debris that fell from the skylight when it shattered.) This sequence, which runs for almost five minutes, does little to advance the plot of the film aside from letting viewers know that the female student has run afoul of dangerous supernatural forces – something that Argento could have accomplished in a fraction of the time the sequence takes to play out. Rather, the emphasis is on the visceral thrills produced by the spectacle of a vicious double murder.

The same could be said of the erotic scenes found in many Euro horror films. As Cathal Tohill and Pete Tombs point out, one of the most distinctive features of Euro horror cinema is the way in which it tends to mix sex with violence to tell stories that could be described as both horrific and pornographic (5). This is especially true of Euro horror movies made during the 1970s and 1980s, when film censorship was relaxed in a number of European countries, and many Euro horror directors were forced "to move sideways into the skin-flick market, where they turned out even weirder and wilder films in order to compete with the explicit attractions of porno" (ibid.). In these films, plot often takes a backseat to scenes involving explicit and prolonged sexual encounters designed purely to titillate viewers.

Walerian Borowczyk's notorious erotic horror movie *La bête* (*The Beast*, 1975) provides an instructive case in point. The film tells the story of a young British heiress who travels to France to marry the son of an aristocratic family on the decline, only to discover upon her arrival that the forest surrounding her future home is haunted by a beast with a reputation for consorting with female members of the family. Initially taken aback, the young woman eventually becomes completely obsessed with this local legend. Borowczyk ends the movie with an astonishing eighteen-minute sequence in which the woman masturbates with a rose while fantasizing about a family ancestor who, allegedly, was ravished by and in turn ravished the beast. This sequence contains virtually no dialogue (it is accompanied by a soundtrack mainly consisting of a harpsichord piece by Scarlatti) and includes most of the standard iconography associated with hardcore pornography – including a number of protracted "money shots" – despite the fact that one of the featured players is a shaggy, gorilla-like monster. Like the double-murder sequence from *Suspiria* described above, it does little, if anything, to move the plot

Aesthetically suspect: cinematic excess in the opening murder scene from *Suspiria* (International Classics). *Courtesy of Jerry Ohlinger Archives*

forward. Rather, the emphasis is once again on what Kristin Thompson calls "those aspects of the work which are not contained by its unifying forces – the 'excess'" (513): that is, it emphasizes spectacle instead of story, engaging viewers viscerally instead of involving them narratively.

There was an eminently practical reason that Euro horror directors chose to foreground cinematic excesses of a violent or sexual nature in their films: the tastes and habits of their European viewers. This audience, largely male and blue-collar or rural, went to local movie houses as much to socialize as to be entertained. In Italy, for example, while genre films of the period were frequently exported to the United States and other parts of Europe (Baschiera and Di Chiara 103), they were also geared toward a specific segment of the home market (Frayling 59). Rather than playing in the urban, middle-class *prima visione*, or first-run, theaters (Wagstaff 247), they were typically exhibited in the provincial, working-class *terza visione*, or third-run, movie houses. The audience that flocked to *terza visione* venues to see genre films was a distracted one, as Christopher Wagstaff notes:

> The audience of the *terza visione* cinema was more like the television audience than like a *prima visione* cinema audience. The viewer (generally he) went to the cinema nearest to his house (or in rural areas, the only cinema there was) after dinner, at around ten o'clock in the evening. The programme changed daily or every other day. He would not bother to find out what was showing, nor would he make any particular effort to arrive at the beginning of the film. He would talk to his friends during the showing whenever he felt like it, except during the bits of the film that grabbed his (or his friends') attention (the film would stop anyway at an arbitrary point for an intermission). People would be coming and going and changing seats throughout the performance. (253)

The behavior of the *terza visione* audience dictated to a certain extent how Italian genre filmmakers crafted their movies. Given the fact that viewers paid only scant attention to plot development, characterization, and other narrative niceties, Wagstaff writes, directors invested their energy in creating moments of spectacle that would capture viewers' attention and make them feel as if they were getting their money's worth from the films:

> The viewer was . . . offered either one or a combination of three pay-offs: laughter, thrill, titillation. They are, as it were, three physiological responses, provoked not by whole films, but by items or moments in films. Italian formula cinema simply juggled with plot items to produce the required recipe that would stimulate the appropriate number and kind of these "physiological" responses. (253)

The excessive violence and eroticism found in Italian horror cinema, then, can be seen as the product of necessity: in order to please their audiences and guarantee continued box-office receipts, horror directors strove to perfect O'Brien's "science of plotless shock and dismemberment." Much the same observation could be made about the horror cinema emerging from other European countries during this era.

If Euro horror's cinematic excess proved to be a major attraction for its original audiences (and for its later American fans), this excess has also hindered its recognition within scholarly circles. Indeed, I would argue that Euro horror's sensationalism, more than its cheapness and datedness, is the key reason for its exclusion from horror film studies on aesthetic grounds. Kristin Thompson has noted that "excess tends to elude analysis" (516) because "[a]nalysis implies finding relationships between devices. Excessive elements do not form relationships, beyond those of coexistence" (517). "The claim that a device has *no* function beyond offering itself for perceptual play," she observes, "is disturbing to many people" (516). Especially people, I would add, working in the field of Film Studies, which (like most academic disciplines devoted to the study of an art form) was founded on the basic assumption that "artistic motivation creates complete unity (or that its failure to do so somehow constitutes a fault)" (Thompson 517). It is precisely because of this assumption that contemporary Hollywood movies are generally held in such low regard by film scholars, who criticize them for jettisoning narrative (and artistic unity) in favor of spectacle (and unmotivated excess). David Bordwell has shown that this criticism of current Hollywood fare is unfounded – even in extreme cases like action movies:

> In action films, we're told, spectacle overrides narrative, and the result works against the "linearity" of the classical tradition.... [But] [e]very action scene, however "spectacular," is a narrative event, and it can advance characters' goals and alter their states of knowledge.... Just as important, if we look at the construction of action movies, most aren't significantly fragmentary. They are outfitted with all the standard equipment of goals, conflicts, foreshadowing, restricted omniscience, motifs, rising action, and closure. (104–105)

Euro horror cinema, on the other hand, because of its unique provenance, genuinely lacks much of the standard narrative equipment with which classical and contemporary Hollywood cinema is outfitted. Like the Hong Kong action films that Bordwell points to as examples of a cinema that truly favors episodic spectacle over coherent narrative, "centering on violent or comic set pieces while ignoring character change and motivic texture" (105), Euro horror movies eschew artistic unity, offering themselves up primarily for perceptual play. Given the fact that they outstrip current Hollywood blockbusters in their pursuit of cinematic excess, it is not surprising that scholars have paid so little attention to Euro horror films. Euro horror's sensationalism, coupled with its cheapness and datedness, has garnered it a reputation for tastelessness that makes its consideration within academic circles unlikely. Like other forms of exploitation cinema, Euro horror represents a limit of film theory because of the "dominant economy of taste" upon which film theory is founded.

Similarly, scholarly engagement with Euro horror has been limited partly because it fails the ideological litmus tests used – again, consciously or not – within recent film theory and criticism to determine a film's eligibility for study. While the notion that popular cinema works in a monolithic fashion to reinscribe the power relations underpinning the dominant social order has less currency in the field today, scholars continue to exhibit a preference for analyzing popular movies that are clearly politically progressive over those that could be viewed as reactionary. Horror movies, in particular, are much more likely to be the subject of attention in Film Studies if they are "ideologically pure," given the reputation for sexism, racism, and homophobia the genre has had in the past. In some instances, political progressiveness can even trump a lack of aesthetic distinction in film theory and criticism; this has been the case, for example, with some low-budget, independent American horror movies of the 1960s and 1970s, such as George Romero's *Night of the Living Dead* (1968), Tobe Hooper's *The Texas Chain Saw Massacre* (1974), and Wes Craven's *The Hills Have Eyes* (1977), which are typically lauded in academic writing on the genre for their radical gender, race, or class politics despite their formal and narrative deficiencies. Euro horror movies have not been as fortunate, since their tastelessness is matched – perhaps even outweighed – by the reactionary attitudes they often seem to adopt toward gender, sex, and race.

Leon Hunt writes that Euro horror cinema "seem[s] to confirm everyone's worst fears about the horror film as a sadistic and misogynist treatment of violence rendered into ultrachic spectacle" ("A (Sadistic) Night" 325). This is especially true, Hunt argues, of the *giallo* film, which frequently appears to revel in male-on-female violence. Consider, for example, Paolo Cavara's *La tarantola dal ventre nero* (*The Black Belly of the Tarantula*, 1971), in which a killer murders the female clients at an upscale beauty salon by first paralyzing them with a needle dipped in venom and then eviscerating them while they remain conscious of what is happening but are unable to do anything to save themselves. Or take Roberto Montero's *Rivelazioni di un maniaco sessuale al capo della squadra mobile* (*So Sweet, So Dead,* 1972), which concerns a murderer who brutally kills beautiful women who have been unfaithful to their husbands and then leaves photographs of them with their lovers at the murder scenes as proof of their adultery. In Massimo Dallamano's *Cosa avete fatto a Solange?* (*What Have You Done to Solange?*, 1972), a killer terrorizing a Catholic college for women murders his young female victims by plunging a long stiletto through their vaginas and into their wombs. Perhaps most notorious of all is Lucio Fulci's *The New York Ripper,* in which a homicidal maniac devises spectacularly nasty methods of dispatching women – especially those whom he views as being "promiscuous." In one scene he grinds a broken bottle between the legs of a live sex show performer he has trapped in a dressing room backstage, while in another he ties up a prostitute whose apartment he has invaded before using a razor blade to disfigure her face and then to bisect one of her nipples. As Hunt writes, it is "difficult to imagine a 'progressive' reading" ("A (Sadistic) Night" 326) of the stomach-churning scenes of male-on-female violence in these *giallo* films; for him, Euro horror consequently becomes "an extreme case of the genre's outlaw status" that deserves its label of "critical 'unacceptability'" (ibid.).

It has been equally difficult for film scholars to imagine progressive readings of Euro horror's representations of queer or non-white characters. Euro horror movies often appear to stigmatize gay, lesbian, bisexual, and transgender people, engaging in what Harry M. Benshoff calls "homosexual as monster" rhetoric (2). For example, lesbian vampire films like Roger Vadim's *Et mourir de plaisir* (*Blood and Roses,* 1960) and José Ramón Larraz's *Vampyres* could be criticized for the way in which their scenes of female vampires preying on other women appear to construct "a vampire that serves only as a proscription – is perceived only as a transgression" (Case 205). Similar criticism could be directed against women-in-prison films like Jess Franco's *Sadomania – Hölle der Lust* (*Sadomania,* 1981) and "nunsploitation" films like Domenico Paolella's *Le monache di Sant'Arcangelo* (*The Nuns of St. Archangel,* 1973), which in their depiction of the sexual torture suffered by captive women at the hands of sadistic lesbian wardens or Mothers Superior seem not only to connect "criminality and lesbianism" (Mayne, *Framed* 128), but also to "play on the helplessness and victimization of women" (115). Euro horror cinema is also open to charges of racism for the way in which it appears to demonize non-white characters. Most infamous in this regard are Euro horror cannibal and zombie movies. Films like Umberto Lenzi's *Cannibal ferox* (*Cannibal Ferox*, 1981) and Ruggero Deodato's *Ultimo mondo cannibale* (*Jungle Holocaust*, 1977), which obsessively chronicle what happens when white interlopers pay the ultimate price for intruding upon the exotic domains of indigenous cannibalistic tribes, resurrect the specter of Western imperialism not only by deploying the centuries-old trope of the non-white colonized subject as cannibal, but also by inviting what Fatimah Tobing Rony calls "fascinating cannibalism": in this case, the cannibalism practiced by "the consumers of the images of the bodies – as well as actual bodies on display – of native peoples offered up by popular media and science" (10). Much the same argument could be made about films such as Lucio Fulci's *Zombie* and Umberto Lenzi's *Demoni 3* (*Black Demons*, 1991), which dwell on the spectacle of black zombies attacking and devouring white adventurers in South America or the Caribbean. The apparent racism and homophobia of these films, like the seeming misogyny of the Euro horror movies described above, effectively put them beyond the pale of film theory and criticism, making their scholarly rehabilitation unlikely – even under the auspices of Cultural Studies.

Euro horror cinema is not persona non grata in academic circles simply because it is tasteless and offensive, though; its liminality is also partly due to the fact that it makes practically impossible the critical detachment demanded of scholars by modern film theory. As we have already seen, Euro horror heavily emphasizes moments of cinematic excess that violate traditional notions of artistic unity still valued in Film Studies. Excess has more than just aesthetic implications, however. The harrowing violence showcased in Euro horror movies – "blood spilling out of wounds, brains emerging from open skulls, dismembered torsos, broken joints, eviscerations, and the discharge from tissue fluids" (Brottman 13) – engages the viewer in a visceral fashion, triggering ba-

Ideologically unsound: blood-sucking lesbians in *Vampyres* (Cambist Films). *Courtesy of Jerry Ohlinger Archives*

sic somatic reactions that are both immediate and ungovernable. This makes Euro horror one of the purest examples of what Mikita Brottman calls *cinéma vomitif*: a "disreputable substream of the horror/exploitation genre" that aims to arouse "strong sensations in the lower body – nausea, repulsion, weakness, faintness, and a loosening of bowel or bladder control – normally by way of graphic scenes featuring the by-products of bodily detritus: vomit, excrement, viscera, brain tissue, and so on" (11). What makes Euro horror different – and possibly "worse" – than other types of *cinéma vomitif* is that it often confronts audiences not only with gore, but also with sexually explicit material. In Euro horror movies like Mario Gariazzo's *L'ossessa* (*The Sexorcist*, 1974), Charles Matton's *Spermula* (1976), Joe D'Amato's *Le notti erotiche dei morti viventi* (*Erotic*

Nights of the Living Dead, 1980), and Walerian Borowczyk's *Docteur Jekyll et les femmes* (*Dr. Jekyll and His Women*, 1981), priests are seduced by those whose souls they are charged with saving, female vampires are just as likely to fellate as they are to exsanguinate their male victims, reanimated zombies inspire as much lust as they do terror, and mad scientists invent potions to relieve themselves of their sexual frustrations. Euro horror's distinctive blend of graphic sex and violence arguably intensifies the effect that *cinéma vomitif* typically has on audiences. By combining the horrific with the erotic and by dwelling, as Steven Shaviro puts it, on "the physical reactions of bodies on the screen, the better to assault and agitate the bodies of the audience" (100), Euro horror exposes viewers – possibly more completely than any other kind of horror cinema – to "the infectious, visceral contact of images" (52), effectively shattering the "ideological barriers that separate the presentation from the partaking" (Brottman 3).

The radical "challenge to traditional culture's binarism of representation and participation" (Brottman 3) posed by the graphic sex and violence found in Euro horror cinema has been a basis for its marginalization by society at large. More frequently than any other form of *cinéma vomitif*, Euro horror movies have been "banned, censored, rejected, repressed, dismissed, and reviled" (1) by the governments of various countries around the world. The rationale underlying the state suppression of Euro horror cinema has typically been that its power to collapse the distance between spectator and spectacle – by viscerally involving the viewer's body in the horrific or pornographic scenes depicted onscreen – threatens not only the well-being of its audience, but also the general public health. In this "discourse of contamination," Euro horror films are likened to viral or narcotic agents, their popularity described in terms of "an addictive, infectious fan relationship sustained by cinematic zombies too attached to their media pleasures to be discerning consumers" (ibid.); the state's intervention is justified by the fact that, once addicted or infected, these contagious "cinematic zombies" might contaminate others, presumably resulting in the kind of apocalyptic scenario favored by so many of the films in question. No doubt the most infamous example of Euro horror cinema being targeted by this kind of state-sponsored "discourse of contamination" is the British Video

Recordings Act of 1984. Passed by Parliament in response to a public outcry over the "morally objectionable" nature of many of the movies that appeared on videocassette in the United Kingdom in the early 1980s, the bill required all films released commercially on video to be certified by the British Board of Film Classification. The BBFC refused to grant certificates to movies that contained depictions of sex or violence that it felt might harm young or impressionable viewers, leading to the creation of a list of banned "video nasties." Significantly, while the list of video nasties included British horror films, fully half of the seventy-four genre titles originated from Continental Europe. I would argue that the high number of Euro horror movies on the list speaks not only to the role that xenophobia played in the moral panic over the burgeoning video trade, but also to the perceived difference between the capacity demonstrated by British horror cinema to dissolve the boundary between representation and participation, and that demonstrated by Euro horror cinema.

Interestingly, a discourse of contamination similar to the one that resulted in legislation against Euro horror cinema in the United Kingdom and elsewhere has also led to its marginalization in the field of Film Studies. There, the underlying rationale is not that Euro horror's conflation of representation and participation might endanger the well-being of its audience or the public health, however, but rather that it might produce passive, uncritical viewers. As Steven Shaviro has argued:

> [Film] theory still tends to equate passion, fascination, and enjoyment with mystification; it opposes to these a knowledge that is disengaged from affect, and irreducible to images. Beneath its claims to methodological rigor and political correctness, it manifests a barely contained panic at the prospect (or is it the memory?) of being affected and moved by visual forms. It is as if there were something degrading and dangerous about giving way to images, and so easily falling under their power. Theory thus seeks to ward off the cinema's dangerous allure, to refuse the suspect pleasures that it offers, to dissipate its effects by articulating its hidden but intelligible structure. (13–14)

This is particularly true, Shaviro writes, of film theory's relationship with horror, a genre that "destroys customary meanings and appearances, ruptures the surfaces of the flesh, and violates the organic integrity of the body" (101), that "puts the spectator in direct contact with intensive, unrepresentable fluxes of corporeal sensation" (ibid.). Although Shaviro links the fear of such spectatorship primarily to semiotic and psychoanalytical theories, which counter horror's invitation to "surrender to and revel in cinematic fascination" with "the tools of psychoanalytic reserve and hermeneutical suspicion" (64), much the same connection could be made to the theoretical approaches associated with Cultural Studies. Despite the valorization of horror cinema that has taken place in film theory under the aegis of Cultural Studies since the 1980s, the assumption that the scholar should maintain a critical distance from the object of study remains entrenched. Indeed, one might argue that since film critics and theorists are now writing about previously forbidden texts, they feel more pressure than ever to cultivate the appearance of scholarly detachment, lest they be seen as simply and uncritically celebrating popular cinema. Because Euro horror retains the capacity to "move" viewers, often against their will – to involve their bodies in ways that cannot always be contained or redressed by the distancing strategies, theoretical or otherwise, that they habitually employ as spectators – it resists film theory's "endeavors to subdue and regulate the visual, to destroy the power of images, or at least to restrain them within the bounds of linguistic discursivity and patriarchal Law" (ibid. 15). Consequently, it has been marginalized within horror film scholarship at a time when other types of horror cinema are being rediscovered and rehabilitated.

Finally, Euro horror cinema owes its near-invisibility in Film Studies to the fact that, as a type of popular European cinema, it does not respond to the dominant interpretive paradigm used by scholars to analyze European movies. As Richard Dyer and Ginette Vincendeau have observed, "European cinema" is almost universally understood in academia as "art cinema" and positioned as the polar opposite of the popular cinema of Hollywood. The result, they write, is an incomplete picture of the practices of European filmmakers and the tastes of European filmgoers:

> Part of the existing map of cinema is coloured in quite clearly: there is America, which is Hollywood, which is popular entertainment, and there is Europe, which is art. Critics and historians of film have started to put new shades into the picture: the USA has, since the First World War, been massively part of European cinema, above all for audiences; aesthetic developments in European film have time and again found their way into Hollywood production (e.g., expressionism, the horror movie and film noir, the new waves and "New Hollywood Cinema"). Yet one aspect of the equation has remained stubbornly unacknowledged: popular entertainment cinema made by Europeans for Europeans. (1)

The stubborn refusal to acknowledge the importance – or even the existence – of popular European cinema is not unique to academia. It can also be found in the writings of European filmmakers from Sergei Eisenstein to Lars von Trier and European film theorists from Ricciotto Canudo to Gilles Deleuze; these filmmakers and theorists, too, have consistently sought to maintain a clear distinction between American popular cinema and European art cinema. Indeed, the development of art cinema in Europe was contingent upon this distinction: "Art cinema fed into the resistance to two filmic 'bad others': US cultural influence, including television (though Hollywood, particularly the classical era, has occupied an ambiguous place in this constellation), and the despised indigenous low traditions" (Dyer and Vincendeau 8). A willful blindness toward popular European cinema is woven into the fabric of film criticism and theory, which are dominated by "an agreed upon notion of European cinema: as *experimental* (thus with practice informing theory, theories constantly changing, and an emphasis on formal experimentation), *serious* (none of the writer/practitioners . . . wants to 'satisfy' his audience, instead each wants to challenge them) and *an art form* (this follows from the first two notions)" (Fowler 4). Clearly, this definition of European cinema "excludes 'low culture,' genre cinema and those films produced to be popular at the box office" (ibid.). In particular, it marginalizes what Ernest Mathjis and Xavier Mendik refer to as "Eurotrash" cinema – European exploitation cinema that is "prevented [from] becoming part of the cinema establishment because the films are continuously dismissed as cheap or irrelevant rubbish" ("Introduction" 4).

That a clear-cut dichotomy really exists between European art cinema and Euro horror cinema is questionable. On the surface, perhaps, such a notion seems reasonable; after all, art cinema produced groundbreaking, soul-searching examinations of the Holocaust in such films as Alain Resnais's *Nuit et brouillard* (*Night and Fog*, 1955), Marcel Ophüls's *La chagrin et la pitié* (*The Sorrow and the Pity*, 1969), and Claude Lanzmann's *Shoah* (1985), while Euro horror gave the world Nazi sexploitation movies like Sergio Garrone's *Lager SSadis Kastrat Kommandantur* (*SS Experiment Love Camp*, 1976), Cesare Canevari's *L'ultima orgia del III Reich* (*The Gestapo's Last Orgy*, 1976), and Bruno Mattei's *Casa privata per le SS* (*SS Girls*, 1977). On a deeper level, however, this apparent dichotomy breaks down. As we have already seen, Euro horror cinema has quite a bit in common with European art cinema. Many classic Euro horror movies and art films shared the same production facilities, casts and crews, and sources of financing; moreover, they frequently demonstrated related thematic interests and utilized similar formal approaches. Indeed, Paul Wells argues that Euro horror has a "style that [is] clearly inflected by the whole tradition of European art cinema" (69), and he elaborates: "It is the combination of abstract design principles – blocks of colour, impactive effects (mist and fog predominant), unusual framing – and bravura narrative elements, largely mixing the sordid with gothic 'shock' tactics, that properly distinguishes these films, and ... calls attention to the re-positioning and re-definition of art cinema motifs" (70). Thus, a film like Riccardo Freda's *I vampiri* "recalls and popularises Felliniesque touches and Viscontian composition" (69), while the work of Jess Franco is "utterly pre-occupied with the possibilities of the medium rather than the demands of the material or a particular story" (71) and "brings together horror, humour, pornography, and art cinema in a form seemingly beyond categorisation as each approach seamlessly blurs into the other" (ibid.). Likewise, a close analysis of art cinema reveals something that, as Joan Hawkins writes, "is generally overlooked or repressed in cultural analysis; namely, the degree to which high culture trades on the same images, tropes, and themes that characterize low culture" (21).

Film scholars by and large have been unwilling to concede such a point. Along with the aesthetic, ideological, and theoretical biases outlined above, the disciplinary prejudice against popular forms of European cinema has effectively stymied the recovery of Euro horror in film criticism and theory. Ironically, given the long struggle to validate the analysis of horror cinema in academia, it seems that horror film studies has developed its own hierarchy of topics worthy of serious discussion, limiting the scholarly exploration of devalued genre phenomena like Euro horror. The greater irony, though, is that Euro horror cinema is exactly what critics and theorists operating from the standpoint of Cultural Studies have been looking for in the genre: a nexus not just of revolting bodies, but of bodies in revolt. The central argument of this book is that Euro horror affords viewers the opportunity to "play dead" – to approach film spectatorship as a form of performance in which they are free to adopt multiple viewing positions and to experiment with different subjectivities in a fashion generally proscribed by mainstream cinema and the dominant social order. It is ultimately this unique characteristic of Euro horror cinema, in my view, that definitively sets it apart from British and American horror, and makes it so worthy of scholarly attention.

Euro horror movies foster performative spectatorship in two ways. On the one hand, they prompt it because of how they were originally made. As we have already seen, practical necessity forced Euro horror directors to pursue an unprecedented blend of cheapness and sensationalism in their work, marking themselves as quintessentially postmodern filmmakers. Their movies are not postmodern merely because they "invented nothing" (O'Brien 164) and practiced a "science of plotless shock and dismemberment" (170), however, but because, in churning out deliriously violent and erotic facsimiles of popular British and American horror movies, they created "surprisingly sophisticated mixes of imitation, pastiche, parody, deconstruction, reinterpretation and operatic inflation" (Newman, *Nightmare Movies* 188). Far from being "simply worthless carbon copies with a few baroque trimmings" (ibid.), these films operate on postmodern "principles of disruption, transgression, undecidability and uncertainty" (Pinedo 17). Subverting traditional formal and narrative modes – reveling in the violent disruption of the everyday world, transgressing and violating boundaries, throwing into question the validity of rationality, and repudiating narrative closure, among other things – Euro horror cinema cultivates spectatorship-as-performance by encouraging viewers to "identify with and desire against everyday modes of behavior and to play with the masks that Western culture asks us to treat as core identities" (Berenstein 262).

On the other hand, Euro horror movies foster performative spectatorship because of the way in which they are now watched. The remediation of Euro horror cinema – its translation from celluloid to video, and from video to digital format – and its repurposing as home entertainment has had an enormous impact on how contemporary American viewers engage with Euro horror films. Although Euro horror spectatorship has always been marked by a uniquely interactive relationship between text and audience, the performative dimension of this relationship has been intensified by these recent technological and cultural developments. At the same time, the performative dimension of Euro horror spectatorship has been amplified by virtue of the perspective from which these movies are now viewed by fans. During its heyday, when it was routinely (if not widely) exhibited in the United States in theaters and on television, Euro horror cinema was generally regarded by spectators as a more or less straightforward – albeit somewhat exotic and impoverished – complement to the dominant tradition of American horror. Today, though, Euro horror movies are seen much differently. Their campy qualities – their formulaic plots, excessive sex and violence, political incorrectness, awful acting, poor dubbing, and dated music and design – ensure that the response they most consistently elicit is one of ironic detachment. Interestingly, it is precisely the promise of such detachment that appeals to many contemporary American fans of Euro horror. Treating Euro horror's "flaws" as virtues, they adopt a viewing position that "renders the bad into the sublime, the deviant into the defamiliarized, and in so doing, calls attention to the aesthetic aberrance and stylistic variety evident but routinely dismissed in the many sub-genres of trash cinema" (Sconce 547). In short, they have, to an unprecedented degree, politicized the act of watching Euro horror movies. The result, once again, has been an intensification of the performativity historically associated with Euro horror spectatorship, as contemporary American fans actively cultivate "a counter-cinema from the dregs of exploitation films" in order to "explicitly situate themselves in opposition to Hollywood cinema and the mainstream US culture it represents" (542).

That such performative spectatorship has occurred in the ghetto of popular cinema suggests another possible meaning of "playing dead": if Euro horror film directors and fans seem, by dint of their strong investment in a debased form of genre cinema, to have capitulated to the cultural logic of late capitalism, they are only *playing* dead. In reality, many of them carry on quietly transgressive work by being "nonadversarial in the modernist sense" (Modleski 293), by returning "to our pop cultural past partly in order to explore the site where pleasure was last observed" (ibid.). It is in this regard that Euro horror demonstrates more clearly than other, more familiar forms of horror cinema the potentially radical politics of producing as well as consuming horror.

The second part of this book will examine how different kinds of Euro horror movies invite different modes of performative spectatorship. Before moving on to these case studies, however, I will describe in more detail the shared characteristics that make classic European horror cinema an ideal catalyst for spectatorship-as-performance in contemporary American culture.

THREE

Playing Dead, Take One

EURO HORROR FILM PRODUCTION

Euro horror movies encourage performative spectatorship because of the way in which they are made. I want to be mindful of the danger of overgeneralizing about the common identity of these films, despite – or rather because of – the fact that they are regularly lumped together by their contemporary American fans. After all, Europe comprises over fifty countries, two dozen languages, and a wide array of cultural, social, economic, political, religious, and artistic traditions. The challenge that such diversity poses to anyone wanting to make grand statements about "the" nature of European cinema is obvious. As Ernest Mathjis and Xavier Mendik write:

> There is hardly a more difficult object of media study than European cinema. Although seemingly evident by its geographical boundaries, from the Atlantic to the Urals, from the Arctic Circle to the Mediterranean, its cultural, aesthetic, economical, political and ideological demarcations are far from clear. European cinema cannot be pinned down to a small number of production strategies, or reduced to a limited series of intentions or ideological perspectives; it does not even fit barriers of language or nations. It cannot be defined through audience and reception practices, nor through its range of textual meanings. There are no straightforward genres to hold on to, no uncontested canon, not even an undisputed series of countries (Flemish cinema? Yiddish cinema? Turkish cinema? Yugoslavian cinema?), people (Alfred Hitchcock, Luc Besson, Paul Verhoeven?) or texts (*Stranger than Paradise, Buena Vista Social Club*?). ("Introduction" 1–2)

The same could surely be said of Euro horror cinema. Despite the fact that the films discussed in this book were made in the same genre at the same time on the same continent, they are the products of different national traditions, individual practices, historical circumstances, and so on. Significant distinctions, therefore, can and should be made between the character of horror cinema produced by one European country and that of another during Euro horror's golden age. Marsha Kinder has convincingly argued, for instance, that the rise of eroticized violence and horror in Spanish cinema beginning in the 1950s was connected with a larger leftist critique of the brutal Franco regime: "During the Francoist era, the depiction of violence was repressed, as was the depiction of sex, sacrilege, and politics; this repression helps explain why eroticized violence could be used so effectively by the anti-Francoist opposition to speak a political discourse, that is, to expose the legacy of brutality and torture that lay hidden beneath the surface beauty of the Fascist and neo-Catholic aesthetics" (138). Following up on Kinder's argument, Andrew Willis outlines the way in which a number of politically committed Spanish filmmakers of the 1960s and 1970s – including Eloy de la Iglesia, Vicente Aranda, and Claudio Guerín – sought "a space to work that existed outside the 'art' cinema assimilated by the regime" (75) in the horror genre, so that they "could continue to explore contemporary social and political issues in their films" (ibid.) without interference from Spain's Fascist government. Clearly, this distinguishes Spanish horror cinema of the postwar period from that of any other European country and we should be careful not to dismiss or downplay such differences when speaking about "Euro horror." Any accurate account must reckon with the complexities that problematize our understanding of it as a coherent and cohesive body of films; it would be wrong to suggest that these complexities do not exist or matter.

And yet it would be equally wrong to suggest that there are no common threads tying together the horror movies made across Continental Europe during the golden age of Euro horror cinema. We have already seen that modes of horror film production and exhibition were similar from one country to the next. We have seen that there are certain shared formal and narrative characteristics that set classic European horror movies apart from contemporaneous British and American horror movies. Most important of all is that, like other forms of "alternative" postwar European cinema, Euro horror can be seen as "set[ting] itself not just against a mainstream culture, but also against a range of [conventional] ways of thinking, politically and ideologically" (Mathjis and Mendik, "Introduction" 4). Mathjis and Mendik argue that postwar "Eurotrash" and exploitation movies generally celebrate "resistance, rebellion and liberation" (ibid.) in a manner that

> seems to point, consciously or involuntarily, to their ability to function as sites of reconfiguration of the self, as attempts to explore possibilities of reconstructing cultural frameworks. Of course, with the massive traumas of World War Two, the rise and collapse of communism, and decolonisation only a few decades behind them, both the audiences and makers of alternative European cinema could hardly ignore it. Nor can they be blind [to] the scandals and upheavals in their own local contexts, be they coup attempts, serial murders or terrorism. But it seems telling that these traumas are both acknowledged through interiorisation, and expressed through excesses, offering both soft- and shock-therapy. (ibid.)

Mathjis and Mendik do not use the term, but it strikes me that the alternative European cinema they describe could be characterized as postmodern. Although it is a highly contested concept, one that is notoriously amorphous and difficult to define, theorists typically see postmodernism as a response to the failure of the post-Enlightenment ideals of reason, knowledge, and progress implied by the cataclysmic twentieth-century events Mathjis and Mendik cite. Postmodernism involves a rejection of these ideals (and the ultimately repressive and destructive social, political, and cultural systems to which they gave rise) in favor of a new set of values: contingency over truth, relativism over universalism, indeterminacy over absolutism, hybridity over purity, pluralism over uniformity, fragmentation over centralization, and anarchy over authority. Not surprisingly, postmodern art is also hostile to earlier aesthetic regimes – especially modernist art. Rather than displaying a seriousness of purpose, it is playful and ironic; rather than striving for originality of expression, it prizes simulation and intertextuality; rather than working to preserve the distinction between high art and mass culture, it freely mixes high and low cultural forms; and rather than functioning in support of an official culture, it revels in transgression and subversion. This sounds very close to the alternative European cinema Mathjis and Mendik discuss, which "represents a unique fusion of the aesthetic sensibilities associated with the avant-garde and the visceral/erotic thrills associated with the world of exploitation" ("Introduction" 11) and demonstrates both a radical capacity to *"reconstruct cultural frameworks, and . . . [a] resistance to canons of film aesthetics"* (2, emphasis in original). It does not seem too great a leap to suggest that the characteristic that binds postwar Eurotrash and exploitation movies together, despite their surface differences, is a shared postmodern aesthetic.

Certainly I would argue that this is the case with Euro horror movies, which can be described as postmodern on a number of levels – not simply because of their cheap imitativeness and sensationalistic excess. Isabel Cristina Pinedo has defined postmodern horror cinema in the following way:

> First, fictional horror constitutes a violent disruption of the everyday world. In postmodern horror, violence is a constituent element of everyday life and the threat of violence is unremitting. Second, it is the nature of fictional horror to transgress and violate all boundaries. Postmodern horror blurs the putative boundary between good and evil, normal and abnormal, and the outcome of the struggle is at best ambiguous. Third, horror throws into question the validity of rationality. Postmodern horror constructs a nihilistic universe in which causal logic collapses and one cannot rely on the efficacy of science or authority figures. Fourth, postmodern horror repudiates narrative closure. Narratives are apt to end apocalyptically with the defeat of the protagonists, or with incipient signs of a new unleashing. Finally, what makes these anxiety-inducing elements of fictional horror not only tolerable but pleasurable is the genre's construction of recreational terror, a simulation of danger that produces a bounded experience of fear not unlike a roller-coaster ride. Much as the horror film is an exercise in terror, it is simultaneously an exercise in mastery, in which controlled loss substitutes for loss of control. The proliferation of apocalyptic, graphically violent horror films which dot the post-sixties landscape attests to the need to express rage and terror in the midst of postmodern social upheaval. (5)

As we will see, regardless of their varied national origins, individual directors, and unique circumstances of production, Euro horror movies generally adhere to the first four postmodern "principles of disruption, transgression, undecidability and uncertainty" (Pinedo 17). They stage violent disruptions of the everyday world, transgress and violate boundaries, throw into question the validity of rationality, and repudiate narrative closure. But Euro horror movies also differ from the Anglo American postmodern horror movies Pinedo describes in one crucial way. While the postmodern horror cinema she discusses seeks to provide viewers with a safe, purely recreational experience of terror, Euro horror – like other forms of alternative postwar European cinema – devotes itself first and foremost to "championing, almost anarchically, a call for liberty" (Mathjis and Mendik, "Introduction" 5). Indeed, it is my view that the single most important postmodern trait Euro horror movies share is the capacity to serve as "sites of reconfiguration" (4); through their deconstruction of social and cinematic norms, they afford viewers the opportunity to approach spectatorship as a performative experience that, far from being merely recreational, actually prompts them to rethink – and even to refashion – their own identities. In the final analysis, Euro horror functions not as a release valve for the reactionary terror and rage inspired by the postmodern condition, but rather as a catalyst for the radical restructuring of self and culture that postmodernism makes possible.

I examine the postmodern nature of Euro horror cinema more closely and discuss how it encourages performative spectatorship at greater length in the case studies that make up the second part of this book. In the interest of providing some initial support for the claims I have just made, however, I will here consider one representative example of postmodern Euro horror: Lucio Fulci's *Quella villa accanto al cimitero* (*The House by the Cemetery*, 1981). The convoluted plot of Fulci's film revolves around a self-absorbed professor of American history, Dr. Norman Boyle (Paolo Malco), who moves from New York City to rural New England with his high-strung wife, Lucy (Katherine MacColl), and their young, clairvoyant son, Bob (Giovanni Frezza), in order to complete a research project left unfinished by a colleague, who murdered his mistress and then took his own life. Occupying the same isolated country manor where these deaths occurred, Norman becomes obsessed with the legacy of the original owner of the estate, a renegade nineteenth-century surgeon named, of all things, Dr. Freudstein. Eventually, it is revealed that Freudstein (Giovanni De Nava) is still alive and hiding in the basement of the house, where he stockpiles the blood and body parts of unwary trespassers to prolong his own life. In the end, Norman and Lucy are murdered by Freudstein in his underground lair while Bob narrowly escapes into a strange netherworld – a parallel universe with nineteenth-century trappings, which is inhabited by a mysterious woman and a young girl, who, it turns out, are the ghostly apparitions of Freudstein's long-dead wife and daughter.

An analysis of *The House by the Cemetery* reveals many of the elements that Pinedo cites as being characteristic of postmodern horror cinema. In the first place, Fulci's film stages a violent disruption of the everyday world. Pinedo writes that although the classical horror film typically begins with a breakdown of the status quo, this violent disruption is "often located in or originates from a remote, exotic location" (18). Postmodern horror cinema, by contrast, "treats violence as a constituent element of everyday life" (ibid.) capable of threatening the integrity of even the most private of spaces, the human body: "In the postmodern genre, violence can burst upon us at any time, even when we least expect it, even when the sun is shining, even in the safety of our own beds, ravaging the life we take for granted, staging the spectacle of the ruined body. The postmodern genre is intent on imaging the fragility of the body by transgressing its boundaries and revealing it inside out" (19). Indeed, gore – the "explicit depiction of dismemberment, evisceration, putrefaction, and myriad other forms of boundary violations with copious amounts of blood" (18) – becomes a central metaphor in postmodern horror movies. Such carnage "violates our assumption that we live in a predictable, routinized world by demonstrating that we live in a minefield, by demanding a reason to trust in the taken-for-granted realm of 'ordered normality'" (ibid.). The destruction of the bodies displayed in these films evokes the collapse of the body politic itself. Significantly, however, postmodern horror cinema typically presents scenes of graphic violence "in an emotionally detached manner so that what fascinates is not primarily the suffering of the victim but her or his bodily ruination" (19), suggesting that the notion of social disintegration – like the spectacular rendering of bodily destruction – is to be contemplated not with dread, but with pleasure.

This is undoubtedly true of *The House by the Cemetery*. Fulci's film trades heavily in the "ruined-body-as-spectacle" (Pinedo 60). One of the first images of the movie, underscored by pulsing synthesizers and grossly exaggerated sound effects, is that of a young woman who is stabbed in the back of the head with a butcher knife with such force that the point emerges from the shocked O of her open mouth. Other, similarly gory moments punctuate the film: one character is slowly, painfully decapitated with a carving knife, another is skewered repeatedly with a fireplace poker, and another has his throat torn out by the villain, who uses his bare hands. While the gruesomeness of these scenes is definitely unsettling, they are so artfully staged and so extreme that they generally prompt fascination (or disbelieving laughter) rather than repulsion. We find ourselves responding less to the plight of the victim than to the fetishization of his or her "wet death" (Pinedo 51). We also find ourselves cheering on the breakdown of ordered normality itself. Because the gore serves as a metaphor for the violent disruption of the everyday world – occurring, as it does, entirely in the domestic sphere – its artfulness and excess encourage us to regard such disruption with delight. Like other forms of postmodern horror cinema, then, *The House by the Cemetery* recognizes the connection between the destruction of the body and the collapse of the body politic and, moreover, implicitly endorses the latter through its gleeful pursuit of the former.

In addition, Fulci's film transgresses and violates boundaries. While the classical horror film, in Pinedo's formulation, "draws relatively clear boundaries between the contending camps of good and evil, normal and abnormal" (22), the postmodern horror film blurs these boundaries, operating "on the principle of undecidability" (23). This principle is first and foremost embodied in the postmodern horror narrative by the figure of the monster, which threatens society not only because of the violence it perpetrates, but also because – through "the disruptive qualities of its own body" (21) – it "dissolv[es] the basis of [society's] signifying system, its network of differences: me/not me, animate/inanimate, human/nonhuman, life/death" (ibid.). Undecidability is woven into the fabric of the postmodern horror film at the "cinematographic level" (23) as well, so that its very form expresses this principle – as when, for example, a movie like *A Nightmare on Elm Street* (1984) "repeatedly blurs the boundary between subjective and objective representation by violating the conventional cinematic (lighting, focus, color, music) codes that distinguish them" (ibid.).

The House by the Cemetery clearly exhibits the tendency toward undecidability that Pinedo notes in postmodern horror cinema. Narratively speaking, Fulci's film is a baffling pastiche of other horror films. It begins, intelligibly enough, as a routine slasher flick: before the opening credits roll, two promiscuous teenagers have sex in an abandoned house and then are stalked and graphically slain by an unseen assailant. Just as we adjust our expectations accordingly, however, the film disorients us by mutating into a knockoff of Stanley Kubrick's *The Shining* (1980) – which also features a clairvoyant boy with unbalanced parents who encounter ghosts in an isolated gothic manor – and then, bewilderingly, into a mad scientist movie featuring a villain who is an outlandish amalgamation of Sigmund Freud and the Frankenstein monster. Whereas most horror movies restrict themselves to delivering a few variations on an otherwise familiar narrative theme, *The House by the Cemetery* mates several seemingly incompatible scenarios, planting an overabundance of genre signposts that confound our efforts to situate the story.

This kind of undecidability affects our relationship with the movie's characters as well, especially in the case of its nominal antagonist, Dr. Freudstein. Like monsters in other postmodern horror movies, Freudstein "blurs boundaries and mixes categories that are usually regarded as discrete" (Pinedo 21). A tall, gaunt, weirdly insectoid zombie who, dressed in a surgeon's smock, murders unsuspecting victims in order to obtain their life-sustaining body parts, he challenges a number of the binary oppositions – animate/inanimate, human/nonhuman, life/death – upon which our understanding of the natural order is based. Moreover, he defies the clear-cut distinctions made in classical horror movies between good and evil, normal and abnormal. While Freudstein perpetrates a series of heinous crimes in Fulci's film, these crimes can be interpreted not just as purely selfish deeds meant to ensure his continued survival, but also as bizarrely protective acts aimed at preserving the new family that has moved into his home, as well as the traditional notion of family in general. Indeed, Freudstein can be seen as grotesquely maintaining the legacy of one of his namesakes by keeping the Boyle clan under constant surveillance and fanatically eliminating any threat to its model tripartite (father-mother-son) structure. Although he eventually kills Norman and Lucy – after much hesitation and arguably in self-defense – when they invade his basement laboratory-cum-abattoir at the end of the film, Freudstein's murderous impulses are otherwise almost invariably directed at those characters whose desires run counter to the Oedipal norm represented by Norman and his family: Norman's former colleague and his mistress, the two teenagers who engage in clandestine, premarital sex in the film's prologue, a mysterious babysitter who apparently has adulterous designs on Norman. Given that Freudstein engages in "evil" or "abnormal" behavior partly to uphold what is widely considered "good" or "normal," it is difficult for us to know whether we are supposed to abhor or applaud him as a character.

Like other postmodern horror movies, *The House by the Cemetery* also transgresses and violates boundaries at a formal level. Cultivating a truly schizophrenic style – alternately artful and amateurish, classically influenced and postclassically inclined, firmly rooted in the narrative and completely divorced from it – Fulci intensifies the aura of undecidability about the film, further confounding our attempts to come to terms with it. The traditional gothic atmosphere evoked by the camerawork, design, and lighting is frequently destroyed by frenetic Steadicam ramblings, disorienting zoom shots, and perplexing focus pulls – many of which are neither motivated by preceding events nor explained by events that follow. Likewise, the flow of the film is often disrupted by inexplicable jump cuts and other violations of the rules of continuity editing, while the suspense is compromised by a wistfully romantic musical score that seems to belong to a different film. Are such instances of stylistic excess the result of deliberate choices on the part of the director or evidence of his inability to achieve artistic unity in his work? Whatever the answer, they clearly transgress and violate well-established aesthetic boundaries, keeping the viewer continuously off-balance and providing yet another link between postmodern horror and Fulci's film.

There is an equally strong connection to be made between the way that both postmodern horror and *The House by the Cemetery* throw into question the validity of rationality. If the horror genre generally "exposes the limits of rationality and compels us to confront the irrational," writes Pinedo, the "trajectory of the classical narrative is to deploy science and force (often together as when science is put into the service of the military) to restore the rational, normative order" (23). Conversely, postmodern horror cinema "defies the Cartesian construction of reason that reduces it to instrumental rationality and pits it against emotion and intuition" (25), creating a "nihilistic universe" in which characters "cannot rely on the efficacy of science or authority figures" (26). Indeed, such figures often appear as the villains in postmodern horror films, and such is the case with *The House by the Cemetery*, which features a monster who is symbolically aligned with one of the most famous scientific authorities of the twentieth century: Sigmund Freud. With very little effort, Fulci's film can be read as an allegorical critique of the way in which psychoanalytical theory obsessively tries – and inevitably fails – to define or represent desire according to the procrustean logic of the Oedipal drama. Freudstein's fanatical attempts throughout the movie to preserve the idea of the nuclear family work to expose the disciplinary nature of the psychoanalytical gaze. Fulci renders this gaze visible at the conclusion of the film in a climactic high-angle shot of Lucy and Bob desperately struggling to escape the basement through an eye-shaped aperture in Freudstein's tombstone, which, fittingly, is embedded in the floor of the family's living room. *The House by the Cemetery* contests the scientific authority of psychoanalysis not only by literalizing its repressiveness here, but also by hinting at an alternative to its phallocentric rule. While Norman and Lucy are too large – too conditioned by years of submission to this rule – to slip through the symbolic aperture in Freudstein's tombstone, the younger, smaller, and more "unformed" Bob succeeds in doing so. He is pulled into a parallel universe inhabited by Freudstein's deceased wife and daughter, who adopt him into their nontraditional, matriarchal family and spirit him away from the house by the cemetery. If, according to the "Cartesian construction of reason, rationality is masculine, associated with mastery, and requires the domestication of irrationality, which is feminine and associated with the body and disorder" (Pinedo 25), the implication of this mystical ending is that irrationality – (dis)embodied by the ghosts of Freudstein's wife and daughter – can never fully be contained by the forces of reason. Moreover, Fulci takes pains to demonstrate, by dwelling on the grotesque nature of Freudstein's existence, the high cost of succumbing to the illusion that such mastery is possible. Like other postmodern horror movies, *The House by the Cemetery* "confronts us with the necessity for an epistemology of uncertainty" (Pinedo 29).

A final characteristic shared by postmodern horror cinema and Fulci's film is that both repudiate narrative closure. As Pinedo observes, classical horror cinema has a vested interest in providing such closure: "In the classical horror film, the monster is an irrational Other who precipitates violence and transgresses the law. It is evil because it threatens the social order; the suppression of the unleashed menace is a priority for the agents of order. The violence of the law restores repression, and the social order is reestablished. This is the ending that best conforms to the status quo and regards departures from it as chaotic and evil" (30). But while the classical horror film "constructs a secure universe characterized by narrative closure, one in which (hu)man agency (human agency understood as male agency) prevails and the normative order is restored by film's end," "violating narrative closure has become *de rigueur* for the postmodern genre" (29). Postmodern horror cinema refuses not only to make "the monster unambiguously evil, [or] the social order unambiguously good" (31), but also to give audiences the comfort of a happy ending or even narrative closure. While the postmodern horror film may come to an end, it is typically an "open ending" (29) in which "the monster triumphs or the outcome is uncertain" (31).

Both of these things could be said of the conclusion of *The House by the Cemetery*. By most measures, the monster triumphs at the end of Fulci's film. Instead of killing Freudstein and restoring the social and natural order, Norman and Lucy are themselves killed. Their deaths are symbolic of the disintegration of the social order, devastating not only to Bob, but also to the very notion of the status quo upheld by classical horror cinema. The film leaves quite open the possibility that Freudstein will continue his ghastly existence in the titular house, forever prolonging his life at the expense of others; indeed, the circularity of the film – it opens with news of the deaths of Norman's colleague and his mistress and closes with the deaths of Norman and Lucy – suggests as much. The fact that Bob escapes from Freudstein does little to provide the film with a sense of narrative closure and actually injects yet more uncertainty into the ending, leaving us with more questions than answers. How is Bob able to cross over into the otherworldly realm inhabited by Freudstein's deceased wife and daughter? Where are they going in the final shot of the film, which shows the trio disappearing into the distance as they walk down a country lane leading into a wintry, twilit forest? Fulci does not tell us. Instead, he pans left to show us the Freudstein manor, its windows lit and chimney smoking, and superimposes an epigraph attributed to Henry James – "No one will ever know whether children are monsters or monsters are children" – before fading to black. It is difficult to know what to make of this conclusion. The image of the occupied house can be interpreted as a final reminder that the monster has triumphed, that

Freudstein's reign of terror will continue; it can even be read as an indication that fresh victims have already arrived to take the place of the Boyle family. The surprising quotation from James poses more of a quandary. Does it suggest that Bob's ability to commune with spirits makes him somehow monstrous or that Freudstein's psychotic devotion to the traditional family can be seen as a form of infantile regression, further eroding any distinction that might be made between good and evil in the film? Perhaps the only thing we can say with any certainty about *The House by the Cemetery* is that, like other postmodern horror films, it fully embraces uncertainty, creating "a universe out of control where extreme violence is endemic and virtually unstoppable" (Pinedo 65).

Crucially, there is one respect in which *The House by the Cemetery* does not fit Pinedo's definition of postmodern horror cinema. In her formulation, postmodern horror produces a bounded experience of fear, "an exercise in recreational terror, a simulation of danger . . . not unlike a roller-coaster ride" (38). For its audience, it functions as a means of "coping with the terrors of everyday life" (39), a way of "express[ing] and thus, to some extent, master[ing] feelings too threatening to articulate consciously" (40). In particular, Pinedo argues, the postmodern horror film answers the contemporary viewer's "need to express rage and terror in the midst of postmodern social upheaval" (48), providing an experience that is finally "as much an exercise in mastery as it is an exercise in terror" (50). This suggests that postmodern horror cinema paradoxically offers the promise of a respite from the ambiguities and uncertainties of the postmodern condition. If postmodern horror movies stage a violent disruption of the everyday world, transgress and violate boundaries, throw into question the validity of rationality, and repudiate narrative closure, they do so, it would seem, not in order to celebrate postmodernity, but rather in order to allow viewers the chance to exorcise (if only temporarily) its specter from their lives. Seen in this light, the postmodern horror film looks politically conservative, even reactionary.

Although it is not clear that Pinedo means her commentary as a critique of postmodern horror cinema, it strongly echoes the negative assessments that other critics and theorists have made about the political valence of postmodernism over the years. Fredric Jameson, in his landmark writing on the postmodern condition, famously suggested that while "the older modernism functioned against its society in ways that are variously described as critical, negative, contestatory, subversive, oppositional, and the like" (202), postmodernism "replicates or reproduces – reinforces – the logic of consumer capitalism" (ibid.). Mas'ud Zavarzadeh and others have expressed the same reservation, arguing that postmodernism's proclamations about the "disappearance of the real" and the "death of the subject," as well as its proscriptions of "totalizing theories" and "grand narratives," preclude meaningful opposition to – indeed, amount to an apologia for – the repressive and alienating system of late capitalism: "The world that emerges from the ludic theory of dispersed power is one in which ... there are no ruling or ruled classes because, in a world articulated by the playfulness of signifiers producing representations of reality, 'class' – like all 'concepts' – is an undecidable category and as such is in no sense a determining factor of subjectivity, representation, or the political calculus of power and exploitation" (Zavarzadeh 34–35).

This argument has been made about the postmodern horror film specifically. Christopher Sharrett, for example, contends that rather than articulating what opportunities and options for political resistance and intervention remain to us in a world in which spectacle threatens to become – or perhaps has already succeeded in becoming – reality, contemporary horror movies are "filled with conventions that throw the [genre] ideologically in reverse while keeping up the postmodern montage and allusionism that seems to make them hip, self-aware, self-reflexive" (269). In other words, there is a significant disconnect between what postmodern horror cinema promises and what it delivers. While this may be true of some horror movies routinely described as "postmodern," I argue that it is not true of postmodern horror cinema as a whole. Indeed, one might suggest that horror films that work to contain the terrors of contemporary everyday life they call forth are not "postmodern" at all – that it is the unabashed celebration of the postmodern principles of disruption, transgression, undecidability, and uncertainty that defines postmodern horror films and distinguishes them from classical horror films, which *do* characteristically offer the bounded experience of fear that Pinedo describes. At the very least, one should make a distinction, as Hal Foster does, between the kind of neoconservative "postmodernism of reaction" that Sharrett decries – postmodernism "conceived in therapeutic, not to say cosmetic, terms... as a return to the verities of tradition (in art, family, religion...)" (Foster xii) – and the oppositional "postmodernism of resistance" that is "concerned with a critical deconstruction of tradition, not an instrumental pastiche of pop- or pseudo-historical forms, with a critique of origins, not a return to them" (xii). Horror movies that fall into the latter category revel in the postmodern condition and encourage us to do the same. They offer the viewer not an exercise in mastery, but rather a lesson in letting go – in giving oneself over to the postmodern reconfiguration they make possible. I hope to show that this is the case with Euro horror cinema. By embracing the postmodern, Euro horror affords spectators the possibility of a genuinely transformative viewing experience.

This viewing experience is akin to what Rhona J. Berenstein calls "spectatorship-as-drag." Berenstein argues that certain horror movies open "a space for an attraction to figures that revel in sex and gender fragmentation" (261), inviting viewers to adopt "fluid subject-positions" and "engage in roles similar to those appropriated by actors in the performance of drag" (232). Such role-playing "provides a framework for addressing gender behaviors as modes of performance" (232–233) and encourages viewers to "identify with and desire against everyday modes of behavior and to play with the masks that Western culture asks us to treat as core identities" (262). Ultimately, by positing "something more than the conventional sex-role and gender options available to men and women in American patriarchy" (261), the horror cinema about which Berenstein writes "throws into question the notion of an authentic spectating self" (233).

The House by the Cemetery prompts viewers to approach spectatorship as a form of performance that involves play not only with gender, but also with the concept of identity itself. Fulci undercuts any desire we might have to identify with the "masculine" forces of reason that traditionally triumph over the "feminine" forces of irrationality in horror cinema by making the monster, Freudstein, the representative of rationality in his film. By inviting viewers to identify against Freudstein and with the female spirits who adopt Bob at the end of the movie, Fulci can be seen as celebrating "malleable spectatorial positions, the dissolution of conventional sex and gender categories, the fragility of the heterosexual couple and the family, and the precariousness of Western patriarchal institutions and values" (Berenstein 262). Such a move not only taps into what Steven Shaviro refers to as "film's radical potential to subvert social hierarchies and decompose relations of power" (64) on a textual level, but also enables what Gilles Deleuze and Félix Guattari describe as a process of "becoming-other" at the level of spectatorship. By reconstructing cultural frameworks in a postmodern fashion, Fulci's film serves as a site of reconfiguration, promoting a performative cinematic experience in which the "subject is born of each state in the series, is continually reborn of the following state that determines him at a given moment, consuming-consummating all these states that cause him to be born and reborn" (Deleuze and Guattari, *Anti-Oedipus* 20).

In the second half of this book, I focus on how Euro horror cinema in general follows *The House by the Cemetery* in fostering spectatorship-as-performance not only through its deconstruction of gender, but also through its dismantling of sexuality and race as traditional markers of identity and sources of viewer identification. Given that Euro horror movies have often been condemned as misogynistic, homophobic, and racist, I take a certain amount of satisfaction in noting that they actually work against such reactionary ideological positions in many cases. My aim, however, is not to argue that the postmodern textuality of Euro horror films renders them uniformly transgressive; such an argument strikes me as being dubious at best, considering that, like all horror movies, Euro horror films are networks of competing and conflicting discourses. Instead, I hope to demonstrate that because of its postmodern textuality, Euro horror lends itself uncommonly well to a kind of performative spectatorship that is transgressive insofar as it insists on treating identity as an ongoing process of transformation and reconfiguration rather than as a fixed, continuous state of being. In view of this, I suggest, Euro horror cinema demands "new protocols for reading the positivity of horror and abjection, not as representational (as pedagogical object-lessons: don't try this at home) but as functional dysfunctions that make other things happen" (Halberstam and Livingston 14).

FOUR

Playing Dead, Take Two

EURO HORROR FILM RECEPTION

Postmodern filmmaking practices provide part of the explanation for the performative spectatorship fostered by Euro horror cinema, but not a full account. For that, we need to consider the uniquely performative ways in which Euro horror movies are now being watched in the United States. To a certain extent, film viewing always involves an element of performativity. In her phenomenological account of the cinematic experience, Vivian Sobchack appropriates Maurice Merleau-Ponty's description of the "intertwining" or "chiasmus" of subject and object that takes place at the moment of perception in order to argue that watching a movie should be thought of not as an act, but rather as a dialogue that involves the audience and the film as equal participants. Writing that a movie "is as much a *viewing subject* as it is . . . a *visible* and *viewed object*" (51), Sobchack demonstrates that spectatorship is necessarily "a dialogical and dialectical engagement of *two* viewing subjects who also exist as visible objects" (52). Despite the fact that there are "always two embodied acts of vision at work in the theater, two embodied views constituting the intelligibility and significance of the film experience" (53), though, we often fail to recognize this, missing entirely the "dynamic activity of viewing that is engaged in by both the film and the spectator, each as *viewing subjects*" (45). Rather than treating the movies we watch as partners in dialogue, we tend to see them as events to which we must play passive witnesses. As a rule, the "returned gaze" (Dixon, *It Looks at You* 2) of cinema goes unmet.

There is at least one important exception to this rule, however. The "*intersubjective* basis of objective cinematic communication" (Sobchack

38) is vigorously cultivated by many horror movies – a fact not lost on film theorists and critics, who have identified performative spectatorship as one of the central characteristics of the genre. Philip Brophy, for example, defines contemporary horror cinema as a "mode of fiction, a type of writing that in the fullest sense 'plays' with its reader" (279), engaging the viewer in a "game that is impervious to any knowledge of its workings" (279). He adds, somewhat ominously: "The contemporary Horror film *knows* that you've seen it before; it *knows* that you know what is about to happen; and it knows that you know it knows you know" (ibid.). Carol J. Clover echoes Brophy's playful characterization of the performative nature of horror film spectatorship in her description of the unique exchange that takes place between contemporary horror movies and their audiences:

> No one who has attended a matinee or midnight showing of a horror film with a youth audience can doubt the essentially adversarial nature of the enterprise. The performance has the quality of a cat-and-mouse game: a "good" moment (or film) is one that "beats" the audience, and a "bad" moment (or film) is one in which, in effect, the audience "wins." Judged by the plot alone, the patterns of cheering and booing seem indiscriminate or unmotivated or both. It is when they are judged by the success or failure of the film to catch the audience by surprise (or gross it out) that the patterns of cheering and booing fall into place. At such moments, the diegesis is all but short-circuited and the horror filmmaker and the competent horror viewer come remarkably close to addressing one another directly – the viewer by shouting out his approval or disapproval not to the on-screen characters but to the people who put them there, and the people who put them there, in their turn, by marking the moment with either a tongue-in-cheek gesture ... or an actual pause to accommodate the reaction – both amounting to a silent form of second-person address. (202)

As Clover's vivid sketch plainly illustrates, horror is one of the few forms of cinema that actively embraces the inherently performative nature of film spectatorship. Within the genre, however, there are varying degrees of performativity to be found. In the pages that follow, I argue that Euro horror cinema offers unusually rich opportunities for spectatorship-as-performance – especially given the unique ways in which viewers are interacting with Euro horror movies in the United States today.

As we have already seen, the relationship between Euro horror cinema and its original European audience was deeply marked by performativity. In Italy, the mode of viewing favored by the *terza visione* audience – for which horror movies were primarily made – was, as Leon Hunt writes, "closer to the 'distracted' gaze associated with theories of television spectatorship than the more intensive immersion associated with cinema" ("Boiling Oil" 177). The rural, working-class viewers "went to the pictures several times a week, talked through the boring bits, enjoyed plenty of action and noise, ... were accustomed to an arbitrary intermission while the projectionist changed reels, and unless captivated by a surprise ending liked to walk out before the end" (Frayling xi). In order to capture their attention, Italian horror directors made sensationalistic movies that spoke directly to the viewers' interests, engaging them in an intersubjective dialogue. Much the same could be said of the relationship that formed between Euro horror cinema and its original American audience. In their fond memoir, *Sleazoid Express: A Mind-Twisting Tour through the Grindhouse Cinema of Times Square,* Bill Landis and Michelle Clifford recall that one of the most fascinating aspects of the experience of watching Euro horror movies at Deuce theaters like the Liberty and the Cinerama was that "the audiences would talk back to the characters on screen in an ongoing call-and-response rhythm" (xii). The viewers, Landis and Clifford write, "demanded that the exploitation movies the theaters screened lived up to the promises made by their graphic, outrageous ad campaigns and shocking trailers" (3). If the movies let them down, they would react by "shouting, tossing food containers, and physically damaging the theaters" (ibid.); if the movies "were as much fun as their lurid ads and trailers promised" (196), then the "shuffling in the aisles would be punctuated by spontaneous jokes and loud laughter from the audience" (ibid.). The more extreme films even left viewers "shaking, cowering, and occasionally hollering out in sympathetic pain" (205).

Clearly, the relationship between Euro horror cinema and its audiences has historically been "a very lively and often self-conscious one" (Tohill and Tombs 22). But what of that relationship today? Does it still retain its performative dimension? After all, with the exception of the occasional limited re-release, festival screening, or special retrospective, Euro horror movies are no longer shown in theaters; the context in which this unique relationship was originally formed no longer exists. Nonetheless, I suggest that the performativity that has historically marked the interaction between Euro horror cinema and its viewers is in fact more intense today in the United States than it ever has been before. This has partly to do with how Euro horror movies have been remediated – translated from celluloid into video, and from video into digital texts – and repurposed as home entertainment products in the United States. As I have already discussed, the reincarnation of Euro horror cinema on DVD made it much more broadly available to viewers than it had been in the past. In addition, the DVD format has made Euro horror movies obtainable in special editions that restore them as closely as possible to their original versions and repackage them as collector's items, transforming them from lowbrow "gore-objects" into highbrow "art-objects" (Guins 29). The result has been a dramatic increase in the size and widening in the demographic of Euro horror's audience in the United States.

The remediation of Euro horror cinema has also had an enormous impact on the way in which contemporary American fans engage with these movies. Landis and Clifford touch on this when they reflect on the curious afterlife of grindhouse era cinema:

> The old Times Square was killed, but the films – the life force of those grindhouses and the blood that ran through their veins – remain alive. These films are like tiny pieces of the Deuce, spreading to millions across the globe through video and DVD. With 42nd Street gone, wildly successful home-entertainment companies have sprung up to fill the void, selling the films that once haunted the Deuce. Walk into any mainstream video store and you'll see exploitation genres sublimated into euphemisms like *independent, horror, supernatural, documentary, action/adventure,* or *mature adult*. No more hard seats, sticky floors, and menacing audience members. Exploitation movie lovers now enjoy their entertainment in the safety of their bedrooms, watching their favorite films over and over, gleefully programming their own double and triple features, recreating the art of the arrangement of a Deuce triple bill. (6)

As Landis and Clifford suggest, the migration of Euro horror from the theatrical arena to the domestic sphere has allowed spectators greater opportunity to shape their viewing experiences. With immediate and unfettered access to the Euro horror films in their DVD collections and the benefit of home theater technology, which enables them to view these films in private at any time and in any way, contemporary American fans exercise an unprecedented degree of power over where, when, and how they watch Euro horror cinema. To quote Anne Friedberg, the home video viewer – who "commands fast forward, fast reverse, and many speeds of slow motion; who can easily switch between channels and tape; who is always able to repeat, replay, and return" (75–76) – is a "spectator *lost in* but also *in control of* time" (76). As viewers in the United States master Euro horror at home, not only in terms of their ability to manage the way they watch it (starting and stopping the DVD at will, playing back favorite moments), but also in terms of their familiarity with it (developed through repeated encounters with the films themselves and with extra-filmic texts such as directors' commentaries and "making of" documentaries), they interact with it more performatively than was possible during its initial, theatrical life.

The new power of viewers in the United States to act as programmers, as well as spectators, of Euro horror movies is only one way in which the remediation of Euro horror has enhanced the performative nature of its relationship with its audience. The reappearance of Euro horror movies on commercial home video has also encouraged contemporary American fans to develop passionate attachments to them – to weave them deeply into the fabric of their lives – thereby strengthening the intersubjective connection Euro horror has always enjoyed with its viewers. Barbara Klinger observes that when films are introduced into the home, they often become highly personalized, attaining a "quasi-familial status that affects their meaning and influences individuals' perceptions of themselves and the world" (139). As fan testimonials posted widely across the internet attest, the pleasures of Euro horror cinema for many viewers in the United States today are "discursively constructed through micro-narratives of biography as well as through notions of belonging to a fan culture and through notions of horror-as-art" (Hills, *Pleasures of Horror* 73). The intense personalization of Euro horror cinema made possible by its remediation and repurposing also manifests in a range of spectatorial activities – "rearranging narrative priorities, altering the rhythms of anticipation to deemphasize tension and heighten pleasure through foreknowledge, and using cinema for comfort" (Klinger 156), for instance – in which contemporary American fans engage when watching Euro horror movies. This kind of spectatorship involves not only a performative transformation of the films themselves, in a kind of cognitive play born of textual mastery, but also a performative transformation of the viewer's self, as Euro horror cinema is incorporated into the process of identity formation. Fans return to their favorite Euro horror DVDs again and again to "amplify or change moods, to insulate themselves from the world, [or] to address or compensate for problems" (Klinger 164). Ultimately, these movies come to embody "a road map through their lives, autobiographical landmarks that represent points of orientation to the past as well as to the present" (174–175). They also provide a means for fans to "secure and maintain individual and community identities within this group of viewers" (184). While such spectatorship-as-performance doubtlessly occurred during Euro horror's past lives on film, television, and videotape, its digital reincarnation in the United States has not only provided viewers with far more opportunities to engage with it performatively, but also amplified the performativity of these encounters.

It is important to note, though, that the recent remediation and repurposing of Euro horror cinema only partly explains why the performative dimension of Euro horror spectatorship is more pronounced in American culture now than ever before. The rest of the explanation has to do with the perspective from which Euro horror movies are typically watched by viewers today. During its heyday from the 1950s to the 1980s, when it was routinely (if not widely) exhibited in the United States in theaters and on television, Euro horror cinema was generally regarded by spectators as a more or less straightforward – if somewhat exotic and impoverished – complement to the dominant tradition of American horror. Today, however, Euro horror movies are seen much differently. Their paracinematic qualities – their formulaic plots, excessive sex and violence, political incorrectness, awful acting, poor dubbing, and dated music and design – ensure that the response they most consistently elicits is one of ironic detachment. Interestingly, it is precisely the promise of such detachment that seems to attract many contemporary American fans, who take pleasure in a "renegade, neo-camp" (Sconce 535) appreciation of classic European horror movies. Exhibiting a kind of performativity rare in earlier audience interactions with Euro horror, they celebrate its "flaws" as a means of promoting "an alternative vision of cinematic 'art,' aggressively attacking the established canon of 'quality' cinema and questioning the legitimacy of reigning aesthetic discourse on movie art" (536). The result has been an unprecedented politicization of Euro horror spectatorship, involving fans' promotion of "their tastes and textual proclivities in opposition to a loosely defined group of cultural and economic elites, those purveyors of the status quo who not only rule the world, but who are also responsible for making the contemporary cinema ... so completely boring" (536–537).

In this respect, American Euro horror fans resemble the devotees of other forms of paracinema who consciously politicize their taste in movies, performatively "cultivating a counter-cinema from the dregs of exploitation films" (Sconce 542) in order to "explicitly situate themselves in opposition to Hollywood cinema and the mainstream US culture it represents" (ibid.). Indeed, it is largely this shared viewing position that defines "paracinema," which, Jeffrey Sconce observes, is "less a distinct group of films than a particular reading protocol, a counter-aesthetic turned subcultural sensibility" (535) that "renders the bad into the sublime, the deviant into the defamiliarized, and in so doing, calls attention to the aesthetic aberrance and stylistic variety evident but routinely dismissed in the many sub-genres of trash cinema" (547). To a certain extent, the paracinematic approach to reading films resembles the "camp" sensibility famously described by Susan Sontag; however, as Sconce notes, whereas camp "was primarily a reading strategy that allowed gay men to rework the Hollywood cinema through a new and more expressive subcultural code" (536), paracinematic culture seeks "to valorize all forms of cinematic 'trash,' whether such films have been either explicitly rejected or simply ignored by legitimate film culture" (535).

Sconce thus champions the agency of fans, casting them, rather than a specific set of transgressive filmmaking practices, as the primary source of paracinema's "politics of excess" (551). While I give due weight in this book to the postmodern textuality of Euro horror cinema as a catalyst of transgressive spectatorship-as-performance, I follow Sconce in also locating such performativity in fan responses to Euro horror films. In my view, it is perhaps most accurate to say that Euro horror texts and audiences "activate" one another, giving Euro horror cinema the capacity "to answer Brecht's famous call for an anti-illusionist aesthetic by presenting a cinema so histrionic, anachronistic and excessive that it compels even the most casual viewer to engage it ironically, producing a relatively detached textual space in which to consider, if only superficially, the cultural, historical and aesthetic politics that shape cinematic representation" (Sconce 553). In this way, Euro horror spectatorship substantiates Barbara Klinger's claim that when viewers engage with older films, "cinematic variables – stars, narratives, *mise-en-scènes,* cinematography, and/or sound – provide the materials for a wrestling match between the past and the present in which the older artifact becomes a vehicle for expressing the concerns of contemporary society" (248). If Euro horror's postmodern textuality fosters a radical form of spectatorial performativity, this performativity is complemented – and enhanced – by the way in which Euro horror movies are now watched by contemporary American fans, whose politicization of these films is rooted firmly in an active resistance to current cinematic and cultural norms.

This is not to say, of course, that the political valence of Euro horror spectatorship is uniformly progressive. One of the pitfalls of writing about spectatorship from a Cultural Studies perspective is to assume that it is *necessarily* resistant in nature, always producing "oppositional" readings that challenge the "dominant" or "preferred" readings of texts that "have the institutional/political/ideological order imprinted in them and have themselves become institutionalized" (Hall 98). Many scholars have voiced concerns about the dangerous naiveté of this assumption, which, as Robert Stam points out, stresses "spectatorial agency and freedom, ironically, just as media production and ownership have become ever more centralized" (234). Judith Mayne expresses doubt that "all unauthorized uses of film, and therefore spectatorial positions that depart from the presumed ideal of capitalist ideology, are virtually or potentially radical" (*Cinema and Spectatorship* 99). Similarly, Patricia White cautions: "The idea of the 'appropriation' of mass media by spectators for their own purpose endows viewers with a problematic degree of self-consciousness and intentionality and ignores the temporal dimensions and *experience* of spectatorship" (196). Even paracinematic spectatorship, with its explicit politicization of filmic excess, does not guarantee a progressive audience. Despite the fact that "the paracinematic audience cultivates an overall aesthetic of calculated disaffection, marking a deviant taste public disengaged from the cultural hierarchies of their overarching taste culture" (538), Sconce concedes that "the paracinematic community, like the academy and the popular press, embodies primarily a male, white, middle-class, and 'educated' perspective on the cinema" (537–538). These demographic facts are not insignificant, given that, as Joanne Hollows writes, the "'radicalism' of cult [cinema] is only sustained by processes of 'othering'" (49). Pointing out that "fan practices in cult [cinema] are constructed as masculine" and "work structurally to exclude women" (36) while at the same time setting themselves "in opposition to an imagined feminized 'mainstream'" (41), Hollows demonstrates that "although it is usually associated with a challenge to cultural hierarchies and with resistance, transgression and radicalism, [cult cinema] serves also to reproduce cultural distinctions and cultural hierarchies along the lines of gender" (49). We should be careful, then, to avoid generalizations about Euro horror spectatorship that paint it as wholly "radical."

On the other hand, we need to be equally careful about repeating the mistake of past film scholars who have assumed that fans of cult cinema – and horror movies in particular – are passive dupes of the dominant social order. It would be a critical error to imagine that horror, as Kelly Hurley wryly puts it, "endlessly and monotonously enact[s] narratives of repression and displacement to an unsophisticated audience compulsively returning to the theater for yet another healing (or normativizing) catharsis" (209). There have been a number of empirical studies that confirm that horror film fandom engenders an active and lively dialogue between spectator and screen, an intense form of negotiation not reducible to a simple process of normalization. In her study of viewer responses to violent films, for instance, Annette Hill finds that, contrary to "media fantasies of 'depraved devotees' of violent movies" (3), there is "no evidence to suggest a) viewers are passive, b) they are exclusively male, and c) that watching violent movies acts as a cathartic release" (4). Instead, Hill's research leads her to the conclusion that "the viewer is active, male and female, and is able to differentiate between fictional violence and real violence in a way that indicates real violence is perceived as disturbing and abhorrent" (ibid.). Moreover, it shows that viewers respond to fictional violence in ways that can be considered positive and constructive on an individual level. By testing personal boundaries, for instance – "identifying a threshold of violence and choosing whether to self-censor or not" (Hill 66) – viewers "interpret fictional violence on their own terms" (52) and can thus experience through it "a sense of achievement and/or liberation" (ibid.). In his study of the pleasures of horror film fandom, Matt Hills also focuses on how typical fan behavior – like using horror texts to "perform and display types of agency, whether this is a knowledge of narrative worlds, of specific aesthetics, or of production and genre histories" (*Pleasures of Horror* 91) – signals that these viewers are in fact engaged in an "ongoing and reflexive, subcultural project of the self" (ibid.).

Research has not simply demonstrated that fans utilize horror movies to test and transform themselves, however; it has revealed also that these viewers employ horror cinema as a means of collective resistance to the social and cinematic status quo. Fans of paracinema use "trashy" movies to attack established film canons and promote an alternative vision of cinematic art. Horror fans have also used their favorite films to challenge dominant social ideologies. For example, in her study of female horror fandom, Brigid Cherry shows that despite the "seeming invisibility of female horror fans" (43), women do watch horror movies in significant numbers and, moreover, practice forms of spectatorship – many linked to "female masquerade" (52) and other extreme expressions of femininity – that can be seen as "rituals of resistance against social norms" (54) involving gender. Empirical studies like these imply that while we should not take it for granted that Euro horror spectatorship is progressive, we should also not overlook the possibility that contemporary American fans actively exploit Euro horror as a platform not only to fashion and refashion their own identities, but also to defy mainstream cinema and culture.

I discuss the potentially radical nature of Euro horror spectatorship in the United States today at greater length in the case studies. In the interest of providing some initial support for my claims about the ways in which Euro horror movies are now being watched by American viewers, however, I will consider one example of contemporary Euro horror fandom here: the cult popularity of Claudio Fragasso's *Troll 2* (1990). *Troll 2* tells the story of a young boy, Joshua Waits (Michael Stephenson), who is able to communicate with the spirit of his recently deceased grandfather. Grandpa Seth (Robert Ormsby) tells Joshua stories about goblins – evil, forest-dwelling monsters that use a magical green potion to transform humans into plants and consume them – and warns him that they are real, not just fairy-tale creatures. Worried about Joshua's claims that he is in contact with his dead grandfather, the boy's parents,

Michael (George Hardy) and Diana (Margo Prey), decide to take him and his teenage sister, Holly (Connie McFarland), on a month-long trip that will involve swapping houses with a family living in the rural town of Nilbog. As Joshua realizes shortly after their arrival, however – "Nilbog! It's 'goblin' spelled backwards!," he exclaims – their vacation destination is actually the kingdom of the goblins. Led by their queen, Creedence Leonore Gielgud (Deborah Reed), and disguised as normal townspeople, the goblins plan to trick Joshua and his family – along with Holly's boyfriend, Elliott (Jason Wright), who has secretly followed the Waitses to Nilbog with his buddies Arnold (Darren Ewing), Drew (Jason Steadman), and Brent (David McConnell) – into eating food laced with the magical green potion. Only Joshua, with the help of Grandpa Seth, who has acquired supernatural powers in the afterlife, can destroy the goblins and save his family from becoming their dinner.

As this brief synopsis suggests, *Troll 2* is in many ways a fantastically bad film. Bankrolled by Filmirage, an Italian production company headed by Joe D'Amato (the preferred pseudonym of Euro horror producer-director Aristide Massaccesi), it was shot over just a few weeks in the summer of 1989 on a budget of less than half a million dollars. Endeavoring to appeal to American audiences, whose interest in Euro horror had been almost completely eroded by Hollywood blockbuster cinema at this point, D'Amato had Fragasso make the movie in English and on location in rural Utah, employing a cast of locals. Following current trends in horror, Fragasso and his wife, Rossella Drudi, developed a script – originally entitled *Goblins* – that aped then-popular genre pictures like *Gremlins* (1984), *Ghoulies* (1985), and *Troll* (1986). Unfortunately, despite Fragasso's best efforts to tailor his movie to the American market, distributors were simply not interested. After managing a brief theatrical run for the film in Europe, D'Amato was only able to broker home video and cable television deals in the United States, selling it as *Troll 2* in a desperate attempt to capitalize on whatever limited cachet the original *Troll* might still have. Several years after it was shot, *Troll 2* finally appeared on the shelves at video rental stores and in the late-night programming schedules of HBO and Showtime.

In retrospect, it seems incredible that D'Amato and Fragasso could have thought that *Troll 2* would meet with commercial success in the United States. Judged by the standards of mainstream cinema, it is a failure on almost every level. The script does not measure up to even the modest benchmark set by the B-grade horror movies it imitates. Full of stereotyped characters, stilted dialogue, and wacky situations, it is at once completely unconvincing and totally outlandish. In one early scene, the Waits family arrives in Nilbog to find that their hosts have left them a supper of suspiciously green-colored food. Grandpa Seth appears to Joshua and warns him not to let them eat, lest they fall victim to the goblins' evil plans. Urging Joshua to think of something fast, Grandpa Seth magically stops time for thirty seconds. With sober determination, Joshua climbs up on his chair, unzips his pants, and urinates all over the meal. When Grandpa Seth releases the family from his spell and they discover what Joshua has done, Joshua's incensed father drags the boy to his room, shouting, "You can't piss on hospitality! I won't allow it!" In an even stranger scene later on, the grotesque queen of the goblins transforms herself into a sexy temptress and attempts to seduce one of Elliott's friends, Brent, with a corncob. "Do you like it? Shall we eat it together?," she asks suggestively. "Actually, I like popcorn," he stammers. "No problem," she responds. "All we have to do is heat it up." Putting the corncob in her mouth, she falls upon him lustily and they devour it together, face-to-face; sure enough, popcorn begins to fly through the air, filling the screen and eventually burying the witless Brent. Finally, in the film's wonky climax, the instrument of salvation for Joshua and his family turns out to be a "double-decker bologna sandwich" – a secret weapon provided by Grandpa Seth for Joshua to use as a last resort against the vegetarian goblins, who plead with him not to eat it. "Don't do it!," they shriek. "Think about the fats in your blood! Think about the cholesterol! Think about the toxins!" Undeterred, he bites into the sandwich with gusto and the monsters disappear in a puff of smoke. The inanity of the writing here and in the rest of the script goes a long way toward explaining why the film was deemed unreleasable in the United States upon its completion. Hopelessly clichéd, embarrassingly inept, and downright bizarre, it is simply impossible to take seriously.

The dreadfulness of the film's screenplay is more than matched by its abysmal acting, production design, and special effects. The cast, which was composed almost entirely of amateurs who were unable to understand the Italian-speaking director and his crew, turns in performances that run the gamut from hopelessly wooden to spectacularly over the top. In one particularly excruciating scene, Darren Ewing, who plays Elliott's friend Arnold, has visible difficulty registering terror as he watches a young woman, Cindy (Christina Reynolds), being turned into plant matter and devoured by the goblins in their lair. "They're eating her!," he exclaims tonelessly. "And then they're going to eat me! Oh my Gaaaaaaahhhhd!" The moment is made all the more painful by the fact that, as he recites his lines, he is also attempting to ignore a fly that has unexpectedly landed on his forehead. While Ewing has trouble getting into his character in this scene, Deborah Reed, who portrays the queen of the goblins, has the opposite problem. Eyes bulging and head rolling, she mugs shamelessly, essaying a terrible imitation of Bela Lugosi. "She is *pur*-ifying herself," Reed gloats as the unfortunate Cindy dissolves into a puddle of green goo before her. "*Now* she is *one* with the *veg*-etable world! *Now* she is *food* for my *chil*-dren!" Although the performances are especially atrocious here, each scene brings fresh evidence of the actors' incompetence: they stumble around awkwardly, glance occasionally at the camera, and struggle to convincingly deliver lines like "Stop, I say!" and "Oh dear God, what can we do?" (Their job was not made easier by the fact that Fragasso apparently only gave them a few pages of the script at a time and insisted that they deliver its hopelessly unidiomatic English dialogue verbatim.)

The production design, meanwhile, is on par with that of the average high school play. Props are constructed out of papier-mâché and chicken wire, while atmosphere is provided by fog machines, strobe lights, and patently artificial cobwebs. The costumes are equally unimpressive. The goblins, in particular, look exactly like what they are: little people dressed uncomfortably in burlap sacks, wearing hand-me-down fright masks and gloves and carrying spears fashioned from tree branches. Even the special effects, usually a point of pride in Euro horror, leave much to be desired. They consist mostly of green food coloring poured over actors whose characters are supposed to be turning into plants. Given all of this, it hardly seems surprising that *Troll 2* failed to impress American distributors; indeed, it is astonishing that D'Amato was able to sell the home video and cable television rights in the United States. More astonishing, however, is that, rather than fading into obscurity after gathering dust in the discount bins at video rental stores and quietly dropping out of regular rotation on cable television, it has become a bona fide cult sensation.

Troll 2's American fan base initially built slowly, since its expansion was dependent largely on happenstance – a blind video rental or an unplanned encounter on late-night cable television – and word of mouth. The film became popular first among viewers in their teens and twenties, who stumbled upon it accidentally, were astounded by its awfulness, and felt compelled to share it with friends, wearing out their VHS tapes at impromptu screenings held in their apartments or college dormitories. Over the course of the 1990s, these scattered private screenings developed into something of an underground phenomenon, spawning *Troll 2* parties at which guests ritualistically donned goblin masks, ate green-colored food, and played drinking games inspired by the film. Then, in the first decade of the twenty-first century the movie's American following gained real mass and momentum, cohering into a fan movement visible to the public at large. The release of the film on DVD in 2003 – which brought it a bigger audience and a modicum of mainstream respectability – was partly responsible for the explosive growth in its cult popularity. More important catalysts, though, have been its unlikely celebrity in cyberspace and its even unlikelier emergence as a midnight movie favorite in theaters across the country.

Troll 2's exalted cult status in the United States today owes much to the internet, where fans of the film have created *Troll 2*–themed websites, message boards, discussion forums, blogs, and social network pages to celebrate what they fervently believe is the "best worst movie" of all time. This virtual community has experienced tremendous growth as its members, not content with merely preaching to the choir, have set out to spread the gospel of *Troll 2* throughout cyberspace. The original nexus of fan activity online was the Official *Troll 2* Fan Website, launched in September 2006 by Michael Stephenson, the former child actor who plays Joshua in the film. (This website has since been folded into another one, BestWorstMovie.) In interviews, Stephenson has discussed his amazement at discovering earlier that year that the film, about which he had long been embarrassed, was the subject of such fan adoration. He was especially struck by the uniquely viral nature of its cult popularity, realizing: "*Troll 2* is not just another bad film. It's unbelievably, hilariously bad. . . . It's an infectious disease providing a new form of contagious, absurd entertainment" ("Nightmare Theatre Presents" par. 6). He created the Official *Troll 2* Fan Website to commemorate the activities of "dedicated fans who feel compelled to share *Troll 2* awfulness with the rest of the world" ("Nightmare Theatre Presents" par. 5). Visitors to the website were invited to become members – or "goblins in disguise" – by creating profiles for themselves that included their goblin names, the names of their hometowns (spelled backward, of course), and a goblin avatar. Once they were members, they had full access to the website's many features, which included a message board called the "Nil-Blog"; announcements about upcoming *Troll 2* parties and screenings; behind-the-scenes photographs from the production of *Troll 2* and pages from the original shooting script; downloadable *Troll 2* goblin mask cut-outs, desktop wallpaper, webpage banner codes, and media files; and links to *Troll 2* fan art. Judging from the traffic at the website – it claimed over 42,000 visitors and 700 members in the year after it went live and boasted almost 200,000 visitors and 1,500 members by the end of the decade – Stephenson succeeded in making it a central location for *Troll 2* fandom in cyberspace. It has by no means been the only gathering place on the internet for fans of the film, however; many more have sprung up, including *Troll 2* pages on Facebook, *Troll 2* profiles on Myspace, and *Troll 2* entries on Wikipedia, Uncyclopedia, and other wiki sites.

As impressive as the fan participation on these various websites is, the most fascinating indication of *Troll 2*'s cult fame in cyberspace may be the remarkable fan art the film has inspired. Much of this fan art has taken the shape of amateur videos uploaded to file-sharing sites like YouTube. While some of these videos are simply fans' favorite scenes or compilations of clips from the film, others represent more creative reinterpretations of *Troll 2*. For example, K80, cofounder of the internet-based Beta-Unit Productions, has posted a mash-up trailer on YouTube that cleverly reinvents the movie as a dysfunctional family comedy along the lines of the indie hit *Little Miss Sunshine* (2006), complete with a feel-good pop score and critical raves superimposed over the images.

Another YouTube mash-up, created by Abnws, reimagines *Troll 2* as an Oscar-winning film, presenting a montage of images from Fragasso's movie with a syrupy musical score, slow fades, and portentous intertitles ("Sometimes we forget . . . about love . . . and the unbreakable bonds of blood . . . and it takes a child to remind us") of the sort found in trailers for the heavy-handed Hollywood melodramas favored at the Academy Awards. Fans have also posted music videos inspired by *Troll 2* on YouTube: Jaron edited clips from the infamous corncob sex scene and set them to the tune of Justin Timberlake's pop single "SexyBack," while Xenogigas sampled moments from the movie and mixed them to a dance beat. Other *Troll 2* fan art online includes everything from tribute songs by garage bands – such as Operation Popcorn's rock 'n' roll ode to a staple of the goblins' diet in the film, "Don't Drink the Nilbog Milk" – to T-shirts bearing the movie's more memorable lines: "Goblins Still Exist!" or "You Can't Piss on Hospitality!" Some fans, like Adam Ross, have recorded downloadable, feature-length, *Mystery Science Theater*-style commentaries for viewers to listen to as they watch the film; others, like James M. Tate, who has posted a 129-page, 19-episode serial screenplay for a sequel to *Troll 2* entitled *Monstrous Beings,* have set out to expand the movie's fictional universe. These instances of *Troll 2* fan art offer a testament not just to the size of the following Fragasso's film has attracted via the internet, but also to its unusual fervor. They suggest a depth of devotion rare outside long-established fandoms like those surrounding the *Star Wars* or *Harry Potter* movies. Together with the other fan activities that have led to the film's internet celebrity, fan art has played an instrumental role in making *Troll 2* the cult phenomenon it is in the United States today.

Another catalyst of *Troll 2*'s cult popularity among contemporary American viewers has been its ironic emergence as a midnight movie favorite in theaters across the country – many years after it failed to attract a domestic distributor. The film's rise to fame as a midnight movie began in April 2006, when it received a special screening as part of a cast reunion held at the Starry Night Theater in Provo, Utah. The event's organizers were surprised when more than a hundred fans showed up to watch the movie and ask questions of the actors who were present. Later that year, in September, a heavily promoted late-night screening of *Troll*

2 took place at the Upright Citizens Brigade Theatre in New York City. Once again, a number of the original cast members were invited to attend and participate in a post-screening Q&A. This time, hundreds of fans, many of them dressed up as their favorite characters, waited for hours in the rain for the opportunity to see the film and mingle with the actors. Once inside the theater, they spontaneously performed vignettes from the film, chanted dialogue in unison with the movie, and threw popcorn and bologna at the screen during the corncob sex and double-decker bologna sandwich scenes. When news of the show circulated on the internet, fans from all over the country immediately posted pleas for similar events to be held in their hometowns; in response, the sponsors of the *Troll 2* midnight movie experience took it on tour. Subsequent sold-out screenings – the most recent benefiting from the discovery of a pristine thirty-five-millimeter print of the film – have taken place at venues in major American cities, including Austin, San Francisco, Houston, Seattle, Boston, and Los Angeles. The enthusiasm with which *Troll 2* has been received at each stop, both among long-time fans and among "virgins," recalls the passion inspired by the original midnight movie screenings of *The Rocky Horror Picture Show* (1975); indeed, George Hardy, who plays Joshua's father in the film, has dubbed Fragasso's film the "*Rocky Horror* of the Myspace generation" (qtd. in Roberts par. 2). While it may be too early to tell whether *Troll 2* will achieve the same lasting cultural impact as that landmark film, there is no denying that its success as a nationwide midnight movie sensation is one that few cult pictures ever experience. Like its celebrity in cyberspace, its triumphant – if belated – arrival in theaters has helped fuel the explosive growth of its cult popularity.

On the face of it, *Troll 2*'s journey from decidedly humble origins to exalted cult status in the United States may seem inexplicable. Even those involved in the film's production appear not to fully understand its current appeal to American viewers; original cast members Michael Stephenson and George Hardy have made a feature-length documentary, *Best Worst Movie* (2009), dedicated to investigating the *Troll 2* phenomenon. As baffling as its dramatic reversal of fortune might seem at first blush, however, there is, in my view, a relatively simple reason that this spectacularly bad Italian horror movie made more than twenty years ago has been so eagerly embraced by American audiences. I would argue that the film's current cult popularity stems from the opportunities for performative spectatorship it affords to viewers.

That fans engage with *Troll 2* performatively is apparent, in the first place, from the way in which they have used the film to help define themselves on both a personal and a social level. Barbara Klinger shows that when viewers form a passionate attachment to a text, they open it to "a potentially intense refashioning" (156) that "affects [its] meaning and influences individuals' perceptions of themselves and the world" (139). Ultimately, such texts come to embody "a road map through their lives, autobiographical landmarks that represent points of orientation to the past as well as to the present" (174–175), and a means for viewers to "secure and maintain individual and community identities" (184). Reading comments posted by fans online, it quickly becomes clear that, for many of them, *Troll 2* serves as an important means of establishing individual identity. Blogger Austin Wolf-Sothern, in a post entitled "Why I Love *Troll 2:* For All the Right Reasons," rejects the widely accepted idea that the film is "so bad, it's good," claiming passionately: "*Troll 2* is a movie that is so good, it's fucking amazing. Every second of it makes me feel fucking awesome, and I love it to death, with full sincerity" (par. 7). The same sentiments have been voiced across cyberspace. For example, a number of Myspace users have devoted their profiles to communicating how much the film means to them personally. swansong writes: "I want to put the time and effort into creating my own expression of what this movie has done for me. My life has been changed forever, and I'm glad that if you are reading this, that yours has as well" (par. 3). Fans have also commented on how their love of *Troll 2* helps them define themselves on a social level by making them feel like part of a larger community. In a lengthy thread devoted to the movie at the Mobius Home Video Forum, Adam Tyner writes: "A friend of mine back in 1991, I guess it was, sold me on *Troll 2* when it was in rotation on one of the movie channels (HBO?), and ever since then, I've always felt a special kinship to anyone else who's seen it. Everytime I've brought up *Troll 2* and someone in earshot has suffered through it, they always get wide-eyed and start quoting/referencing every other scene in the movie. *Troll 2* brings people together!" (par. 2). On his blog, thegreatob gives a remarkable account of being transformed by his experience of seeing the film in a theater with an audience:

> The atmosphere was utterly unbelievable, I had never, ever, experienced anything quite like it. People wooped and cheered, they cried with laughter, shouted the lines out before they were even uttered. It was like watching a film with all of your friends (beer in hand to add to the experience) realising that you are all unified and joined together in a church of film.
>
> I still can not get over it now, the buzz and energy was what I have been waiting to experience within a film screening for so long. Finally it had happened, the audience reacting as one whole, viewing body. (pars. 6–7)

When the screening ended, thegreatob recalls: "I was left with so many emotions flooding through my very being. I came to the realisation that this is how all film screenings should be. And if it has taught me one thing, it is to encourage more people to watch *Troll 2*, as it was passed to me I shall pass it unto others" (par. 10). The "average multiplex-Joe" might not recognize the value of a movie like *Troll 2*, the blogger concludes, "but for a select few (myself included) we realise these are the films made for sharing" (ibid.). Such testimonials indicate that fans have performatively woven *Troll 2* into the fabric of their lives, making it integral to their senses of self and community. The film facilitates both their conceptualization of themselves "*as agents who display expertise and authority*" (Hills, *Pleasures of Horror* xi, emphasis in original) and their efforts "to pleasurably imagine and demarcate the boundaries of [their] fan culture" (73). The fact that *Troll 2* offers viewers the opportunity to engage in such self- and community-defining acts of performative spectatorship is part of the reason that it has earned such a rabid cult following in the United States.

The rest of the explanation, I think, has to do with the way in which *Troll 2* affords viewers the chance to perform their resistance to current cinematic and cultural norms. By taking pleasure in a "renegade, neo-camp" (Sconce 535) appreciation of *Troll 2*, fans of the movie follow devotees of other forms of paracinema in "cultivating a counter-cinema from the dregs of exploitation films" in order to "explicitly situate themselves in opposition to Hollywood cinema and the mainstream US culture it represents" (542). In a review of *Troll 2* on the website Fatally Yours, The Film Fiend distinguishes between fans of the movie and other, more middle-of-the-road viewers:

> Though you may watch hundreds of thousands of motion pictures over the course [of] your pathetic little existence, there are just some films you simply

cannot forget no matter how hard you try. For many, that may be a timeless classic such as *Casablanca,* or perhaps a life-affirming epic like *Schindler's List.* Others may be quick to champion the likes of *Star Wars,* or even *Raiders of the Lost Ark* and its handful of sequels. . . .

However, if you're an ever-blogging loser not unlike myself who prefers the company of *Sorority Babes in the Slimeball Bowl-O-Rama* to anything by Steven Spielberg or Akira Kurosawa, that unforgettable celluloid experience just may be . . . *Troll 2.* (pars. 1–2)

For some fans, it is *Troll 2*'s originality that makes it more memorable than the more widely seen and culturally respectable movies cited by The Film Fiend. Blogger Austin Wolf-Sothern argues that *Troll 2* "may not be brilliant in the sense that it's actually a satire, or that the whole people turning into plants thing is some kind of metaphor for the general state of human loneliness and sense of isolation. But there is a kind of brilliance to how strange it often gets. There's nothing else like this movie. It's an original, it's fucking innovative. There are things in *Troll 2* that you could never see in any other movie" (par. 5). For other fans, it is *Troll 2*'s entertainment value that sets it apart. In a review of the film on the Internet Movie Database, superhero has this to say: "Everytime I walk out of a movie theater, no matter what movie I had just seen, I always think to myself, 'this was no *Troll 2* . . .' No movie since has been made that has left such an impact on me as a serious film critic. Why is this movie so great? Unlike 99% of movies out today, *Troll 2* accomplishes something most movies don't even come close to and usually fail at, it's entertaining" (par. 1). Whether it is because of *Troll 2*'s originality or entertainment value, though, fans agree that the film is not just different, but better than the movies that are routinely glorified in American culture. On his blog, Rich Knight goes so far as to claim that it is superior to the film that many critics have called the best American movie ever made: *Citizen Kane* (1941). In his view, "a good movie is any film that makes you feel all warm and fuzzy inside, and one that you can watch over and over and over again, ad nauseum without getting tired of it" (par. 3):

[T]hen let's see, would I rather watch *Citizen Kane,* Orson Welles' masterpiece that basically drew the ire of the entire entertainment industry for his criticism on William Randolph Hearst, or *Troll 2,* which features a whole group of actors who just learned their lines the day prior to shooting the movie? Let's weigh it on the hand scale, shall we? *Citizen Kane,* well, I've seen it three times already, but don't think I can ever watch it again. And *Troll 2*, which I've also seen three times already but want to see it a few hundred times more for good measure.

So, weighing it like THAT, I guess I'm going to have to go with *Troll 2* then and say that it's the better film. Yep, I'm saying it loud and proud, *Troll 2* is BETTER than *Citizen Kane*. (pars. 4–5)

Rather than simply enjoying *Troll 2* as the holy grail of bad movies, fans like Rich Knight perversely insist upon treating its formal and narrative defects as virtues that set it apart from – and above – other films, mundane and acclaimed alike. For them, its awfulness is precisely what makes it special and worth celebrating. Fan commentary about the uniqueness of the film, then, can be seen as a political critique of dominant notions about cinema and culture – one that playfully reverses the hierarchical relationship between the mainstream and the marginal, arguing for the superiority of the latter over the former.

This sort of critique also manifests in many of the instances of *Troll 2* fan art – especially the mash-ups. These ersatz movie trailers clearly derive much of their humor from the ridiculous suggestion that Fragasso's film commands the same cultural capital as an acclaimed independent film or an award-winning Hollywood movie. As Barbara Klinger notes, however, mash-ups are "hybrid parodies" that by definition satirize more than one text: "This is 'strange bedfellows' humor, created out of a choreography of affinities and dissimilarities between texts that seeks to mine the comic possibilities of dissonance" (222). More than merely poking fun at how far from the top of the cinematic hierarchy *Troll 2* lies, fan mash-ups can be seen as "aggressively attacking the established canon of 'quality' cinema and questioning the legitimacy of reigning aesthetic discourse on movie art" (Sconce 536). As Robert Ryang, the creator of a famous faux trailer that reimagines *The Shining* as a romantic comedy, has said, the mash-up strikes a chord with viewers because it "mock[s] how formulaic Hollywood movies are" (qtd. in Kornblum par. 4). In doing so, it works to "expose official seriousness as sham" (Klinger 225) and can thus be considered a "critical [response] to the empire of corporate capitalism and the media mythos that supports it" (ibid.). Like the fan commentary discussed above, these instances of fan art allow viewers the opportunity to perform their resistance to cinematic and social norms. This provides the rest of the explanation for *Troll 2*'s cult popularity in the United States today. Fans have responded so passionately to the film because it offers them not only a means of challenging entrenched cultural values, but also a way of imagining alternatives to them. It fulfills, in the words of blogger thegreatob, the promise of a "Cult film-Revolution!" (par. 11).

While *Troll 2*'s paracinematic qualities are more pronounced than those of most other Euro horror movies, and while it has (perhaps as a consequence) attracted a larger cult following in the United States, it is my contention that Euro horror cinema in general fosters the same kind of spectatorship-as-performance as Fragasso's film does because of how it is now being watched. Euro horror's recent remediation and repurposing have enabled viewers to use it both to define themselves as individuals and members of a community, and to express their opposition to conventional film culture and the dominant social order it represents. Clearly, its new cult status and its fundamentally postmodern character – a result of the way in which it was originally made – have made Euro horror a powerful conductor of performative spectatorship in the United States today. But important questions still remain. Why is this kind of spectatorship such a draw? What allure does "playing dead" hold for contemporary American viewers? To answer these questions, it is necessary to understand the larger cultural context within which Euro horror and its fans are currently interacting in the United States.

FIVE

Return of the Repressed

EURO HORROR CINEMA IN CONTEMPORARY
AMERICAN CULTURE

As we scan the landscape of mainstream cinema in the United States today, it becomes easier to understand why Euro horror movies like *The House by the Cemetery* and *Troll 2* currently hold such allure. For all its commitment to crowd-pleasing spectacle, contemporary Hollywood cinema simply does not offer audiences the same opportunities for performative spectatorship that Euro horror does. Bland, safe, and boring – despite their emphasis on nonstop action, celebrity actors, and flashy special effects – Hollywood films lack the postmodern qualities that afford Euro horror fans the chance to try out different points of view and play with a range of often transgressive subject positions. Moreover, rather than presenting itself as a partner in dialogue and prompting the viewer's active participation in a conversation, the dominant cinema is largely invested in masking its gaze and colonizing ours. It denies the intersubjectivity that defines the cinematic experience by presenting itself simply as a vehicle for our entertainment and encouraging us to just go along for the ride. In short, it is a form of disposable entertainment intended to be consumed and quickly forgotten, a roller-coaster ride designed to thrill audiences without asking them to think too much or feel too deeply.

The state of mainstream American cinema today has much to do with the corporatization of Hollywood, which has accelerated dramatically since the 1980s. As Hollywood studios like Warner Brothers, Paramount, and 20th Century Fox have become subsidiaries of gigantic, multinational media conglomerates like TimeWarner, Viacom, and News Corporation, they have mainly focused on producing the blockbuster film: "a high-cost, high-speed, high-concept entertainment machine propelled by a nationwide 'saturation' release campaign" (Schatz 19). The goal is to create an "event movie" – "one that gains prominence in the wider culture, beyond the cinema screen; one that everyone seems to be talking about, that is almost impossible to avoid" (King 52) – that will attract a mass audience and generate immense profits at the box office. The event movie, however, functions not only as a theatrical attraction, but also as a merchandising tentpole, the center of a corporate franchise that might eventually comprise future sequels and home video releases, as well as ancillary products like books, soundtracks, toys, and games, all of which the parent company can sell through the media outlets it owns or through licensing agreements with other companies.

Because an event movie is extremely expensive to make and market – the average cost of a Hollywood film reached a record $106.6 million in 2007 (Kilday par. 7), the last year that the Motion Picture Association of America (MPAA) publicly disclosed this information – media conglomerates have devised an array of strategies to minimize the financial risk inherent in such a venture while maximizing its potential profits. In addition to favoring movies that fit neatly into established genres, boast spectacular special effects, and feature major stars, they routinely attempt to "presell" films by basing them upon properties already familiar to the moviegoing public. As Geoff King writes: "The potential benefits of pre-sold properties are considerable. Money can be invested with some confidence that an audience already exists. Pre-sold properties have credentials and a track record; they appear less risky" (54). Many Hollywood blockbusters have been based on popular novels, Broadway shows, comic books, video games, and even theme park rides – as is the case with Disney's *Pirates of the Caribbean* film franchise. More than any other type of presold property, however, media conglomerates have come to rely on remakes, reboots, and sequels. In just the five years prior to the publication of this book, a staggering number of these were released, including *Pirates of the Caribbean: At World's End* (2007), *Spider-Man 3* (2007), *Shrek the Third* (2007), *Harry Potter and the Order of the Phoenix* (2007), *Hairspray* (2007), *Harold & Kumar Escape from Guantanamo Bay* (2008), *Indiana Jones and the Kingdom of the Crystal Skull* (2008), *The Dark Knight* (2008), *Get Smart* (2008), *The Mummy: Tomb*

Film the ride, ride the film: the logic of corporate Hollywood as embodied by *Pirates of the Caribbean: The Curse of the Black Pearl* (Buena Vista Pictures). *Courtesy of Jerry Ohlinger Archives*

of the Dragon Emperor (2008), *The Pink Panther 2* (2009), *Transformers: Revenge of the Fallen* (2009), *Terminator Salvation* (2009), *Land of the Lost* (2009), *Star Trek* (2009), *Clash of the Titans* (2010), *Iron Man 2* (2010), *The Twilight Saga: Eclipse* (2010), *The Karate Kid* (2010), *TRON: Legacy* (2010), *The Hangover Part II* (2011), *Footloose* (2011), *Rise of the Planet of the Apes* (2011), *Arthur* (2011), *Mission: Impossible – Ghost Protocol* (2011), *21 Jump Street* (2012), *The Three Stooges* (2012), *Men in Black III* (2012), *The Bourne Legacy* (2012), *Total Recall* (2012), and many, many more.

Ironically, the moviemaking practices of corporate Hollywood owe much to those pioneered by exploitation filmmakers in earlier eras; indeed, one could argue that exploitation cinema provided the business model that saved the American film industry in the 1960s and 1970s, after the old studio system finally imploded. As David A. Cook has noted:

> [T]he 1948 consent decrees and two decades of enormously costly films reconfigured the system, culminating in the "Recession of 1969" and attendant corporate buy-outs. This convulsion, combined with demographic shifts in audience composition and the replacement of the Production Code by the MPPA

[sic] ratings system, led the majors to embrace exploitation as a mainstream practice, elevating such previous B genres as science fiction and horror to A-film status, retrofitting "race cinema" as "blaxploitation," and competing with the pornography industry for the "sexploitation" market share. Grindhouse-style gore was injected into seemingly conventional Westerns and gangster films, and four-letter words became obligatory in all but family-rated genres (G and GP categories). By 1974, sequels and series, the very fodder of B-film production during the studio era, loomed as a major strategy for risk reduction among the majors, who have since devoted approximately 10 percent of their rosters to these categories.... Finally... the majors borrowed the distribution tactic known as saturation booking – opening a film in many theaters simultaneously, accompanied by intensive advertising – from the exploitation field, where its main purpose was to generate quick profits before bad reviews and word of mouth killed business, and customized it as the standard mode for launching blockbusters, or "event" films. (3–4)

While corporate Hollywood may have come to rely upon some of the production and distribution strategies once associated with exploitation cinema, however, the movies it manufactures differ substantially from those churned out in the past by exploitation filmmakers working in the United States and abroad. In order to generate the hundreds of millions of dollars in revenue necessary to offset costs (much less make a profit), Hollywood blockbusters must appeal to the widest possible audience. Accordingly, they are calculated to be as safely mainstream and blandly inoffensive as possible in both form and content. Absent entirely are the taboo-breaking tastelessness and lack of technical polish characteristic of true exploitation fare. Absent too – partly as a consequence – is the type of interactivity fostered by paracinema, which offers viewers "the freedom of speculating on the story, and polishing or radicalizing the style on the film's behalf" (Mathjis and Mendik, "Editorial Introduction" 3). Smoothly impersonal and completely self-contained, contemporary Hollywood cinema resists our involvement in the construction of its meaning. No wonder, then, that more and more viewers are turning away from Hollywood movies in a search for more interactive forms of entertainment.

The signs of this defection have become increasingly evident. In 2005, the American film industry experienced a much-publicized downturn in business, which industry observer Edward Jay Epstein dubbed "Hollywood's death spiral" (par. 8). That year, according to figures published by the MPAA, total box-office receipts in the United States fell

5.7% from the previous year, from $9.54 billion to $8.99 billion (Motion Picture Association of America, "U.S. Theatrical Market" 23), while the total number of theater admissions fell 8.7% from the previous year, from 1.54 billion to 1.4 billion (24). These numbers bespoke a serious decline for an industry that had, up to 2005, experienced three decades of almost unchecked annual growth in theatrical revenue. Even worse, DVD sales, which by 2004 had come to represent 47.9% of the total income earned by Hollywood movies (compared to the 23.1% they earned in theaters), simultaneously began to plateau after increasing steadily for the better part of a decade (Adams Media Research), suggesting that home video could no longer be counted on to offset losses or augment gains at the box office.

A number of different theories were offered to explain the setbacks that corporate Hollywood suffered in 2005. Many commentators suggested that a drop in the quality of mainstream films, rising ticket prices, and the inconveniences associated with watching movies in a theatrical venue were to blame. Surveys of moviegoers indicated that almost a fifth felt that their last moviegoing experience was not worth their time and money (Snyder par. 18). Viewers complained about the "sameness of everything" (Waxman par. 10) coming out of Hollywood – that "a steady diet of formulaic plots, too-familiar special-effects vehicles and remakes of television shows [had], over time, left the average moviegoer hungry for better entertainment" (par. 6). This frustration with the standard Hollywood fare provided a convincing explanation for the underwhelming box-office performances of even the most highly anticipated blockbusters, which tended to open strongly and then sink like stones, their earnings dropping by as much as 50 or 60% in the second week of release as bad word of mouth and the buzz surrounding the premiere of the next big event movie helped to kill their prospects for long theatrical runs. In addition, other commentators pointed to the emergence of state-of-the-art home theater systems, the impact of video piracy on the film industry, and the fragmentation of the mass audience that Hollywood once courted so successfully, arguing that these factors were to blame for the empty seats at multiplexes across the country in 2005 as well.

Also persuasive was the case made by some industry observers that the popularity of mainstream movies had declined because of the rise of newer, more interactive entertainment technologies. Chief among these was the internet, which had, by 2005, evolved into a medium that privileged user-generated content in the form of blogs, wiki entries, personal profiles on social networking websites, and uploads to file-sharing websites. According to a study published by the *New York Times,* the average number of hours on the internet spent each year by Americans rose 76.6% between 2000 and 2004 (Holson par. 14). Also, video games had become progressively more popular, particularly among a demographic long crucial to the financial health of corporate Hollywood: young men in their teens and twenties. Rather than watching movies in the theater or at home, men in this age group increasingly preferred playing ever-more-sophisticated, interactive video games – often over the internet, where massively multiplayer online games like *EverQuest* and *World of Warcraft* allowed for the collaboration of millions of concurrent gamers worldwide. It is interesting to note, moreover, that with the advent of more nontraditional interactive video games – simulation games like *The Sims* or virtual world games like *Second Life,* for instance – the medium's fandom had expanded well beyond the young, male demographic to include groups historically averse to gaming, including young women. The *New York Times* study found that there was an overall 20.3% increase in the average number of hours Americans spent each year playing video games between 2000 and 2004 (Holson par. 14). For Neal Gabler, these developments spoke to the growing dissatisfaction of viewers in the United States with the passivity demanded by the dominant cinema and a concomitant desire for media technologies that allow them to take a more active role in their entertainment:

> It is certainly no secret that so much of modern media is dedicated to empowering audiences that no longer want to be passive. Already video games generate more income than movies by centralizing the user and turning him into the protagonist. Popular websites such as Facebook, Myspace and YouTube, in which the user is effectively made into a star and in which content is democratized, get far more hits than movies get audiences. Myspace has more than 100 million users worldwide, and Fortune magazine reported that 54 million of them spend, on average, 124 minutes on the site for each visit, while 11.6 million users spend 72 minutes a visit on Facebook. YouTube's most popular videos attract more than 40 million hits, which is substantially larger than the audience for all but a very, very few movies. (par. 15)

Although Gabler does not mention it, the skyrocketing use of digital home video technologies at this time also suggested a movement toward more interactive media entertainment. The growth in the average number of hours Americans spent watching movies at home between 2000 and 2004 – 53% – was second only to the growth in internet use (Holson par. 10). To be sure, many of the films watched on DVD in the United States during this period were Hollywood blockbusters that offered viewers little more in the way of interactivity than they did in theaters; as we have already seen, however, a significant number were examples of paracinema – like Euro horror – that secured a sizable audience by providing opportunities for performative spectatorship. They, too, should be classified as a new type of interactive entertainment medium and seen as part of the reason that the public's appetite for mainstream movies shrank so dramatically in 2005.

The explosive growth in the popularity of cutting-edge interactive entertainment technologies in the first few years of the twenty-first century did not, of course, spell the end of the dominant cinema. Desperate to reverse the losses it suffered in 2005, corporate Hollywood redoubled its commitment to producing presold event movies designed to clean up at the box office and serve as the basis for future corporate franchises, while at the same time exploring new exhibition technologies – digital 3-D and IMAX projection systems, for example – with the potential to lure audiences back to the multiplex. To a certain extent, its efforts paid off. In 2006, buoyed by the success of blockbusters like *Pirates of the Caribbean: Dead Man's Chest, Night at the Museum,* and *Cars,* all of which were released that year, the total domestic box office reached $9.4 billion, a 5% increase over 2005 (Halbfinger par. 14); this upward trend continued in 2007, as event movies such as *Spider-Man 3, Shrek the Third,* and *Transformers* boosted box-office gains to $9.7 billion, an increase of 4% over 2006 (Barnes, "Film Year Full of Escapism" par. 2). And in 2009, a year when Americans sought solace from the worst economic downturn since the Great Depression in Hollywood fantasies like *Transformers: Revenge of the Fallen, Harry Potter and the Half-Blood Prince,* and *Avatar,* domestic box-office returns topped $10 billion for the first time ever (Barnes, "Distressed Year, Hollywood Smiles" par. 3).

The gains made in 2006 and 2007 are less impressive, however, when one considers that, adjusted for inflation, box-office receipts from those years were considerably lower than they were in 2002, corporate Hollywood's most profitable year to date (Media by Numbers). Not even the remarkable sales from 2009 matched 2002's inflation-adjusted record of just over $11 billion (Barnes, "Distressed Year, Hollywood Smiles" par. 8). In addition, as a number of commentators have noted, bigger box-office returns do not necessarily mean that more people are going to the movies, especially given ever-escalating ticket prices. In fact, movie attendance in 2007 remained flat, after a slight increase in 2006 and three previous years of sharp declines (Barnes, "Film Year Full of Escapism" par. 2). At the end of 2009, admissions were still down about 12% from 2002, the attendance peak of the decade (Barnes, "Distressed Year, Hollywood Smiles" par. 6). In 2011, box-office receipts in the United States dropped 4% after remaining flat in 2010 (Motion Picture Association of America, "Theatrical Market Statistics" 9), while attendance dropped 4% (ibid. 9) after a decline of 6% in 2010 (Barnes, "A Year of Disappointment" par. 5). And surveys have found that 60% of American moviegoers intend to spend less time and income on moviegoing in the future (Gabler pars. 3–4), indicating that this downward trend can be expected to continue. Finally, according to the Digital Entertainment Group, DVD sales fell for the first time ever in 2007 ("Home Entertainment Enjoys" par. 1) – and have fallen steadily since then, faster than the Blu-ray and video-on-demand sales, which were supposed to offset this lost revenue, have risen (Snider par. 1) – confirming that the film industry can no longer count on home video to make up for dwindling box-office sales. Meanwhile, the popularity of newer, more interactive entertainment media has continued to explode.

The position that corporate Hollywood finds itself in today resembles the one occupied by old Hollywood during the 1950s, in the final days of the studio system, when it was forced to confront its growing irrelevancy as emerging entertainment technologies like television became increasingly popular and younger audiences displayed a distinct lack of interest in the kind of escapist fantasies the industry had been mass producing for decades. Interestingly, corporate Hollywood has adopted the same kind of tactics used by the studio system in the 1950s to maintain its cultural relevancy, devoting the greater part of its cinematic output to spectacular, epic movies and exploiting exhibition gimmicks like 3-D and larger screens in an effort to recapture the public imagination. It has even, perhaps in some unconscious attempt at a homeopathic cure, been remaking Hollywood movies and television shows from that era at a frantic rate, giving us *Far from Heaven* (2002), *The Quiet American* (2002), *The Alamo* (2004), *Around the World in 80 Days* (2004), *War of the Worlds* (2005), *The Honeymooners* (2005), *House of Wax* (2005), *3:10 to Yuma* (2007), *The Invasion* (2007), *Journey to the Center of the Earth* (2008), *The Day the Earth Stood Still* (2008), and *Alice in Wonderland* (2010) – with many more announced as being in development or production, including *Father Knows Best, East of Eden, Strangers on a Train, Forbidden Planet, The Blob, Harvey, 20,000 Leagues Under the Sea, Creature from the Black Lagoon, When Worlds Collide, A Star Is Born,* and *The Incredible Shrinking Man.* Ultimately, of course, it *was* the formula for the blockbuster movie – perfected with *Jaws* (1975) and *Star Wars* (1977) – that proved to be Hollywood's salvation from the financial difficulties it began to experience in the 1950s. As we have already seen, however, it is unlikely that this formula will save the American film industry in the twenty-first century. Quite simply, audiences seem to be fed up with the thrill-ride mentality and boring uniformity of mainstream films and have little interest in returning to the multiplex for more of the same.

The same is true, it is important to add, of viewers' attitudes toward contemporary American horror movies – although it might seem at first glance that the genre has never been more popular in the United States than it is today. Horror cinema actually underwent something of a renaissance in the middle of the first decade of the twenty-first century, earning a record $1 billion in box-office revenues in 2005 alone – a 15% increase over 2004 and a 78% increase over 2003 (Lieberman par. 2). This rebirth was largely triggered by the moviegoing public's embrace of *Saw, Hostel, The Devil's Rejects* (2005), and other films that eschewed the hip self-reflexivity and tongue-in-cheek humor of 1990s horror in favor of the gritty realism and absence of irony associated with 1970s horror. It was also partly driven by a broadening of the genre's traditional audience – especially in terms of gender, as young women began for the first time to flock to horror movies in numbers equal to or greater than those of young men (A. Williams, "Up to Her Eyes" pars. 5–6). A third key factor seems to have been an increased interest on the part of bankable stars – particularly "top-tier actresses" like Halle Berry, Sarah Michelle Gellar, and Hilary Swank (Moerk par. 8) – in appearing in horror movies.

In the wake of these developments, Hollywood studios moved quickly to establish horror divisions or to affiliate themselves with production companies devoted to making horror movies. These studio units, including Dark Castle (Warner Brothers), Rogue (Universal), and Fox Atomic (20th Century Fox), were joined in their search for profits by independent mini-majors like Lionsgate and the Weinstein Company, as well as smaller outfits, some of which – like Sam Raimi's Ghost House and Eli Roth's Raw Nerve – were run by newly empowered horror auteurs. The result was a boom in horror film production that effectively resuscitated the genre, recalling the American horror revivals spearheaded by New Line Cinema in the 1980s and Dimension Films in the 1990s. Significantly, as with those earlier revivals, the new boom was not confined to theatrical horror films; it also involved a surge in the production of direct-to-video horror movies. Following in the footsteps of pioneering direct-to-video companies like Lloyd Kaufman's Troma Entertainment and Charles Band's Empire Pictures, newcomers like Image Entertainment, Anchor Bay, and Lionsgate all began making genre films aimed specifically at the home video market – many of them, such as those released by Lionsgate as part of its *After Dark Horrorfest: 8 Films to Die For* DVD series, boasting name actors and fairly substantial budgets. Although these movies did not have the benefit of wide theatrical releases or intensive marketing campaigns, they were, crucially, stocked by major brick-and-mortar and online video rental stores, where they did a brisk business.

One might point out as well that this horror film revival is not the only indication of the massive popularity horror now enjoys in the United States. There has also been an explosion of genre programming on satellite, cable, and network television. In addition to Monsters HD, the first high-definition satellite television channel devoted entirely to horror cinema, NBC Universal and DirecTV partnered in 2007 to create Chiller, a digital cable channel completely dedicated to the broadcasting of horror movies. Other cable television channels with more diverse programming have developed popular horror series. From 2005 to 2007, Showtime aired *Masters of Horror*, an anthology series featuring episodes directed by veteran genre filmmakers like John Carpenter, Tobe Hooper, and Joe Dante. Currently, one of Showtime's most popular programs is

Dexter (2006–), a show about a forensics expert working for the Miami police department, who leads a double life as a serial killer. Meanwhile, HBO has struck ratings gold with *True Blood* (2008–), which charts the uneasy coexistence of humans and vampires in rural Louisiana, and AMC has a hit with *The Walking Dead* (2010–), which details the struggles of a small-town southern sheriff and his family to survive a zombie apocalypse. Horror programming is not confined to the rarified realms of satellite and cable television, though. A plethora of horror series have appeared on network TV – CBS's *Medium* (2005–2011), ABC's *Ghost Whisperer* (2005–2010), and WB's *Supernatural* (2005–), to name just a few – perhaps more than at any time since the late 1960s and early 1970s, when shows like ABC's *Dark Shadows* (1966–1971), NBC's *Night Gallery* (1969–1973), and ABC's *Kolchak: The Night Stalker* (1974–1975) were on the air. Moreover, the tradition of late-night shock theater programming has been revived: popular new horror hosts like Penny Dreadful, Dr. Gangrene, and Count Gore De Vol preside over the broadcast of classic horror movies on regional network and cable-access television in an homage to the original horror shows of the 1950s and 1960s: *The Vampira Show* on KABC in Los Angeles, *Zacherley's Shock Theater* on WABC in New York City, and *Sivad's Fantastic Features* on WHBQ in my own hometown of Memphis, among them.

Along with its increased presence in the more traditional arena of television, horror has established a significant foothold in newer media like video games and the internet. Genre-themed video game franchises such as *Doom, Resident Evil, Silent Hill, BloodRayne,* and *Alone in the Dark* (all of which, notably, have been turned into films) have skyrocketed in popularity across a number of different gaming platforms. Horror fans have also colonized the internet, creating an astonishing variety of websites devoted to the genre, including horror movie news sites like Bloody-Disgusting, discussion forums like the Classic Horror Film Board, niche fan sites like Pretty/Scary (devoted to women in horror) and BlackHorrorMovies (devoted to African American horror), and horror podcasts like Deadpit and Rue Morgue Radio. In all of these ways and others, horror has clearly emerged as an important part of American popular culture. There have even been signs that the genre has acquired a certain amount of prestige in the eyes of the arbiters of "high" culture: witness, for example, the mammoth, five-week horror retrospective – entitled "It's Only a Movie: Horror Films from the 1970s and Today" – that New York City's Museum of the Moving Image mounted in 2007, featuring over thirty genre movies, past and present, as well as panel discussions of their aesthetic, cultural, and political implications.

Upon closer inspection, however, the phenomenal popularity that horror enjoys in the United States today is not as straightforward as it might seem. It is complicated by the fact that audience interest in contemporary American horror cinema has waned significantly in recent years. Indeed, it now appears that the enthusiasm with which viewers greeted new horror movies in the first decade of the twenty-first century has all but evaporated. The turning point in the moviegoing public's love affair with contemporary American horror cinema seems to have been 2007, which saw not only the conspicuous box-office failures of high-profile horror films like *Hostel: Part II*, *Grindhouse*, *The Reaping*, *Vacancy*, *Captivity*, and *The Mist*, but also a $79 million drop in the combined box-office receipts of the top ten highest-grossing horror films compared to the total from the year before (Kiernan par. 2). These developments led many industry observers to declare the horror boom officially over (obituaries appeared in national newspapers like the *New York Times* and the *Los Angeles Times*) and corporate Hollywood to dramatically scale back its plans for future horror film production. Of course, horror movies continue to be made in the United States – a few, like those in the *Paranormal Activity* and *Twilight Saga* series, have even enjoyed considerable commercial success – and no doubt American horror cinema, in typical cyclical fashion, will at some point rebound. For the moment, however, it has clearly fallen out of favor with viewers in the United States.

The decline in the fortunes of American horror cinema seems, like the more general "Hollywood death spiral" discussed earlier, to be due in part to audiences' weariness with the formulaic nature of the movies currently being produced by the film industry. Echoing comments made by mainstream moviegoers, horror fans have complained, in discussion forums and blogs across the internet, about the "sameness of everything" being released today in their favorite genre. One factor contributing to the sad state of contemporary American horror cinema, fans agree, is the astonishing number of remakes, reboots, and sequels that clog theaters.

In the five years prior to the publication of this book, we have had *Halloween* (2007), *The Hills Have Eyes II* (2007), *Resident Evil: Extinction* (2007), *The Hitcher* (2007), *Diary of the Dead* (2007), *Saw V* (2008), *It's Alive* (2008), *April Fool's Day* (2008), *Day of the Dead* (2008), *Prom Night* (2008), *My Bloody Valentine* (2009), *Friday the 13th* (2009), *The Last House on the Left* (2009), *Sorority Row* (2009), *The Stepfather* (2009), *The Wolfman* (2010), *The Crazies* (2010), *A Nightmare on Elm Street* (2010), *I Spit on Your Grave* (2010), *Don't Be Afraid of the Dark* (2010), *The Thing* (2011), *Fright Night* (2011), *Scream 4* (2011), *Final Destination 5* (2011), *Paranormal Activity 3* (2011), *Silent House* (2011), *Underworld: Awakening* (2012), *Prometheus* (2012), *Piranha 3DD* (2012), and *Dark Shadows* (2012), among others, with new versions of *The Evil Dead, Near Dark, The Birds, Hellraiser, Child's Play, Poltergeist, Carrie, Pet Sematary, The Brood, Godzilla,* and *An American Werewolf in London* announced as forthcoming. Even the "original" horror movies being released by Hollywood, however, are seen by viewers as little more than glib imitations of genre classics. On the "Sci-Fi, Horror & Fantastic Cinema" board at the Mobius Home Video Forum, John W. McKelvey summed up the feelings of many fans in his response to a discussion thread tellingly entitled "What Do You Miss Most in Today's Horror Films?, What's Missing?" He responded: "original stories. Non-remakes. Yes, I know there are still a bunch of non-remakes being made, but even then, they're not really original. Most of the non-remakes just aren't remakes because they didn't pay for the name of the older film they're copying, or because they're copying two or three films at the same time" (par. 1). Ironically, this criticism has been leveled perhaps most often at the flood of retro, 1970s-style "realist" horror movies released by the studios on the heels of *Saw* and *Hostel*. If these films were initially welcomed as a refreshing departure from the usual genre fare, fans quickly grew tired of their slick standardization, which seemed to be a stark contrast to the grittiness and authenticity of the movies they self-consciously modeled themselves after.

For many fans, however, the banality of contemporary American horror cinema is just part of the problem; also at issue is the way in which it fails to maintain the traditionally intersubjective relationship between the horror film and its viewers. An editorial posted on one fan website argues that many modern horror directors are unable to "speak" to the

The mutants claim another victim in *The Hills Have Eyes,* one of dozens of horror film remakes to dismay genre fans in recent years (Fox Searchlight Pictures). *Courtesy of Jerry Ohlinger Archives*

audience because they are insufficiently familiar with the genre, seeing it in purely careerist terms as a "cheap and easy way to break into the business": "How many filmmakers toss out these useless celluloid disasters without ever having seen the horror of Chaney's reveal in *The Phantom of the Opera*? ... Masterpieces that are willing to take the time to produce true fear are cast aside in favor of the latest borefest involving the newest crop of teens to seek hiatus from their weekly drama series. Time after time I find myself sitting through unimaginative drivel created by people who don't even care about the genre" (MovieMaven par. 4). According to this editorialist, a major symptom of the lack of knowledge about and feeling for the genre displayed by many modern horror directors is an overreliance on gore to frighten the audience: "Whatever happened to the craft of making a horror film? Where is the atmosphere? Where is the suspense? Is showering us with viscera the only way these people know how to elicit a response? ... Anyone can poke out an eye to make us gag but only a true master can give us the willies" (pars. 2–3). The problem with recent American horror movies is not the abundance of gore in and of itself – "Don't get me wrong," MovieMaven assures her readers, "I am a gore hound. I love to see the limbs and entrails fly when it fits the story" (par. 2) – but rather the breakdown in intersubjective communication that the abundance of gore implies. If horror has historically been a "mode of fiction, a type of writing that in the fullest sense 'plays' with its reader" (Brophy 279), fans like MovieMaven feel that it has lately lost its way in the United States, that American horror movies no longer foster the kind of intense interaction between viewer and film that once defined the genre. It is for this reason, as well as because of their unhappiness with the derivative nature of these films, that viewers have increasingly refused to support them at the box office, contributing to the decline in the fortunes of Hollywood horror.

If the unprecedented popularity of horror in the United States today has little to do with contemporary American horror cinema, what then is its basis? Interestingly, it seems to be rooted in a sense of nostalgia for the past. Most of the signs cited above suggesting horror's cultural ascendancy – the appearance of horror-themed channels on satellite and cable television, the reemergence of shock theater programming on regional network and cable-access television, the explosive growth in the number of websites devoted to classic horror on the internet, the horror film exhibition hosted by the Museum of the Moving Image – are indicative of a "retrospective orientation" (Hantke 197) toward the genre. Even the brief renaissance that American horror cinema underwent in the first decade of the 2000s was predicated on a return to the style and substance of 1970s horror, the last truly celebrated period in the history of the genre. Given the current state of American horror cinema, it should come as no surprise that fans in the United States are stuck in the past. They are looking for horror movies that still provide them with the opportunity to engage in performative spectatorship. That, in my view, is what explains the cult status Euro horror cinema presently enjoys in the United States. The rediscovery of Euro horror by contemporary American audiences represents, to borrow Robin Wood's famous phrase, a true "return of the repressed" (182). Banned by governments, dismissed by critics, and largely ignored by scholars, it has been embraced by fans because it promises a radically different cinematic experience than the one offered by corporate Hollywood movies – a cinematic experience not characterized by sameness and banality, but rather by postmodern subversion and intense intersubjectivity.

Once upon a time in Film Studies, an embrace of the pop cultural past as a means of resisting contemporary cinematic and social norms would have been seen as self-defeating, a capitulation to the logic of late capitalism and an endorsement of the oppressive structures of mainstream cinema critiqued within the field. Only by working in an oppositional fashion outside the bounds of the dominant cinema, scholars would have argued, can we hope to free ourselves of that logic and dismantle those structures. Now, however, film critics and theorists widely recognize the ability of viewers to create a counter-cinema from the graveyard of pop culture via a process that Patricia White calls "retrospectatorship" – a form of spectatorship that involves the "irreducible play of past and present, the joining of audiences and artifacts" (xxiv). Indeed, one of the key tenets of recent reception theory is that when viewers engage with older movies, "cinematic variables – stars, narratives, *mise-en-scènes,* cinematography, and/or sound – provide the materials for a wrestling match between the past and the present in which the older artifact becomes a vehicle for expressing the concerns of contemporary society" (Klinger 248). As we have seen, not all older movies and their present-day fans have received serious scholarly attention; exploitation fare like Euro horror cinema continues to represent something of a blind spot in academia, even while horror itself has become a hot spot. The striking popularity of Euro horror movies in the United States today, though, "invites us to re-encounter something we've seen before but didn't yet know what the encounter could mean to us" (White 215).

My argument in the first part of this book has been that Euro horror cinema is worthy of consideration in Film Studies because it affords viewers the opportunity to approach film spectatorship as a form of "play" or performance. Interacting with Euro horror performatively, fans are able not only to adopt a variety of viewing positions and to experiment with different subjectivities in a potentially transgressive way, but also to define themselves on a personal and social level while challenging cinematic and social norms – all spectatorial activities that contemporary Hollywood movies do not generally facilitate. Many contemporary American fans have evidently already come to this conclusion and have been quietly carrying on subversive work by being "nonadversarial in the modernist sense" (Modleski 293), by returning "to our pop cultural past partly in order to explore the site where pleasure was last observed" (ibid.). Let's follow them there.

PART TWO

Case Studies in Euro Horror Cinema

SIX

Blood and Black Lace

THE *GIALLO* FILM

Mario Bava's *Blood and Black Lace* chronicles in gruesome detail the crimes of a silent, black-clad, white-masked killer, who, armed with an iron claw, stalks and brutally slays half a dozen beautiful female models employed at a fashion salon in Rome. The chain of murders begins in the opening scene, when the first victim, Isabella (Francesca Ungaro), returns to the salon after a night on the town only to be ambushed on the grounds by the anonymous killer, who savagely slashes her face, throws her against a nearby tree, and finally strangles her to death before dragging her body into the bushes. When her mutilated corpse is discovered the following day, the police are contacted and proceed to question her former employers, the suave Massimo Morlachi (Cameron Mitchell) and the attractive, recently widowed Countess Cristiana Como (Eva Bartok), and her former co-workers, few of whom seem genuinely distressed by her horrific death. Although the motive behind Isabella's murder is at first obscure – the investigating detective, Inspector Silvestri (Thomas Reiner), initially speculates that the person responsible might be a "homicidal sex maniac" driven to kill by "the female beauty" – it soon becomes apparent that she was murdered because of her intimate knowledge of the sordid private lives of her colleagues. When her incriminating diary is discovered and circulated among the models at the salon, the killer begins to eliminate them one by one. As the bodies pile up, the mystery surrounding the identity of the masked murderer grows, frustrating the police and terrifying potential victims.

Blood and Black Lace occupies a special place in the history of Euro horror cinema as the first true *giallo* film, a violent and erotic type of murder mystery that flourished in Italy during the 1960s and 1970s. The plot of the *giallo* film typically revolves around the efforts of an amateur or professional detective to solve a chain of grisly, sexually charged murders committed in an urban setting by a faceless, black-gloved killer whose methods are elaborate, whose motives are ambiguous, and whose identity is always in question. As in other types of Euro horror cinema, however, story often takes a backseat to style; the plot can frequently seem like little more than an excuse to present a series of extravagantly staged sequences showcasing the gory deaths of the killer's victims, who are often beautiful young women. During their heyday, *giallo* films enjoyed substantial popularity not only in Europe, but also in the United States, where, dubbed and recut, they played regularly at drive-ins and grindhouses. As they have subsequently undergone remediation in the United States – migrating from film to video to DVD and Blu-ray – *giallo* films have garnered a loyal cult following. Indeed, this is perhaps the single most popular kind of Euro horror cinema among American fans today.

Not surprisingly, given its overt sensationalism and apparent misogyny – as well as its low production values, dated mise-en-scène, and poor dubbing – the *giallo* film has not received the attention that it deserves in academic circles. But there have been signs that scholars are beginning to take it more seriously. Several works on the *giallo* film have been published in the twenty-first century, and many of the introductory texts on horror cinema mentioned in the first part of this book now recognize the genre's historical importance – especially in terms of the role it played in helping to push horror toward the kind of psychological terror and graphic violence pioneered by Alfred Hitchcock's *Psycho* (1960), and the role it played in inspiring the first wave of American slasher movies in the late 1970s and early 1980s. Some of these texts have also identified the *giallo* film as a crucial bridge between the Hollywood tradition of horror cinema and the European tradition of art cinema, pointing to its emergence as the moment at which the horror film "became self-conscious both in regard to the previous traditions of the genre drawn from the American context, but also in the ways that art cinema had drawn upon a whole range of other art forms to enhance its credentials and create a counter cinema to the classical Hollywood style" (Wells 69).

Despite these stirrings of scholarly interest in the *giallo* film, however, there is as yet little consensus concerning its exact nature. There has not even been agreement in all quarters that it can properly be called an example of horror cinema. As Peter Hutchings notes:

> Some horror critics have argued that this type of film does not belong to the horror genre in any meaningful way, while others have seen it as comprising an important development within horror, one which in its focusing on extreme psychological states and scenes of sexual violence anticipates later American horror films. But its precise place within a cyclical model of horror history is not clear. Simply viewing it as an early version of the American slasher films of the late 1970s and early 1980s arguably misrepresents it, for in many important respects the Italian *giallo* is different from that type of film. Nor can it simply be seen as an attempt to cash in on the box-office success of Hitchcock's *Psycho* (1960). While there might be a shared emphasis on representing madness within contemporary settings, the *giallo* favours a far more baroque and artificial approach than that adopted by Hitchcock. (29)

Another debate over the *giallo* film among scholars – one even more fundamental than the dispute over whether it can be called an example of horror cinema – has to do with the question of whether it represents a coherent genre in the first place. In his essay on the *giallo*, Gary Needham concedes that it exhibits identifiable thematic and stylistic tropes, but argues that it is "not so much a genre ... but a body of films that resists generic definition" ("Playing with Genre" 136). Consequently, he suggests, we should attempt to define it not in generic and historical terms, but rather in "a more 'discursive' fashion, as something constructed out of the various associations, networks, tensions and articulations of Italian cinema's textual and industrial specificity in the post-war period" (138).

Although Needham's thesis is provocative, it is not, finally, very helpful: seen as "a conceptual category with highly moveable and permeable boundaries that shift around from year to year" (Needham, "Playing with Genre" 135), the *giallo* film becomes at once all things and nothing, a play of signs with no meaning in itself – only in its relation to other textual, industrial, and cultural phenomena. In this case study, I argue that if we want to understand the significance of the *giallo* film, we need to recognize the importance of its generic and historical dimensions. While I do not dispute Needham's contention that *giallo* is "quite difficult to pin down as a body of films" ("Playing with Genre" 144), and while I want to be careful of allying myself too closely with what he calls the "Anglo-American taxonomic imaginary that 'fixes' genre both in film criticism and the film industry in order to designate something specific" (136), I do believe that the *giallo* film possesses a strong generic identity and that an understanding of this identity affords us a clearer picture of its relationship with horror cinema in general, as well as an explanation for its cult popularity among contemporary American viewers.

In my view, the way to locate the *giallo* film's center of gravity as a genre is to trace its roots in popular fiction. The term *giallo* (which means "yellow" in Italian) originally referred to a series of classic British and American detective novels printed with yellow covers by the Mondadori publishing company in Italy starting in 1929. The years of censorship and deprivation ushered in by Fascist rule and World War II initially curtailed sales of *giallo* novels, but in the postwar era, their popularity exploded (Tani 27–29). The public's embrace of the genre prompted Italian authors like Giorgio Scerbanenco and Leonardo Sciascia to begin writing detective stories as well. While the prewar Anglo American *giallo* novels by Agatha Christie, Cornell Woolrich, Edgar Wallace, and others fell squarely into the rational-deduction tradition of detective fiction inaugurated by Edgar Allan Poe and Arthur Conan Doyle, the postwar Italian *giallo* novels, influenced by the nascent postmodern movement in European and American literature, were closer to what Stefano Tani calls "anti-detective" fiction. The anti-detective story, as Tani describes it, is a text that "frustrates the expectations of the reader, transforms a mass-media genre into a sophisticated expression of avant-garde sensibility, and substitutes for the detective as central and ordering character the decentering and chaotic admission of mystery, of nonsolution" (40). This final point is especially salient, Tani emphasizes, for while in the detective story, the solution to the crime "is the final and fulfilling link in the . . . [narrative] sequence, the one that gives sense to the genre and justifies its existence" (41), what seems like "suspense that promises fulfillment" (42) in the anti-detective story "actually proves [to be] unfulfilled suspense . . . [when] the delay of the solution becomes nonsolution" (ibid.).

It is no coincidence that the *giallo* film was born during the 1960s, just as the anti-detective novel reached the height of its popularity in

Italy. Indeed, I suggest that *giallo* filmmakers consciously modeled their movies after the contemporaneous fiction of Scerbanenco, Sciascia, and others, as well as certain Italian art films of the period – Bernardo Bertolucci's *La commare secca* (1962) and Michelangelo Antonioni's *Blow-Up*, for example – that were themselves partly inspired by the anti-detective novel. Like their work, which, as Tani writes, initiates a "teasing, puzzle-like relationship between the text and the reader" (45) in order to unmask "a tendency toward disorder and irrationality that has always been implicit within detective fiction" (46), the *giallo* film amplifies, in a postmodern manner, the bias toward disruption, transgression, undecidability, and uncertainty inherent in horror cinema, prompting a uniquely performative kind of spectatorship.

The *giallo* film's debt to anti-detective fiction is already apparent in *Blood and Black Lace*, the earliest true example of the form. Consider the narrative of the film. Although it is often described as a supreme example of what Geoffrey O'Brien calls Bava's "science of plotless shock and dismemberment" (170) – the literal English translation of its original Italian title, *Sei donne per l'assassino*, is "six women for the murderer" – *Blood and Black Lace* does have a plot. It is, however, an extremely convoluted and unconventional one that perfectly fits Tani's definition of an anti-detective story. While the film begins, as most traditional detective stories do, with a murder mystery, it very quickly mutates into something else entirely. Ultimately, Bava transforms it into a text that, to borrow from Steven Shaviro, is "multiple and anarchic, nonintentional and asubjective" (30) – one that is "no longer subordinated to the requirements of representation and idealization, recognition and designation" (30–31), but rather "pushes toward the condition of freeplay" (38), in which "all fixed points of reference and self-reference, all lines of perspective, and all possibilities of stabilizing identification and objectification are banished" (53). Bava achieves this effect, in the first place, by constructing a plot that toys mercilessly with viewers, inviting them to make certain assumptions or take certain positions vis-à-vis the unfolding story and its characters, only to pull the rug out from under them again and again. To some extent, the traditional detective film operates in this way also. As David Bordwell, Janet Staiger, and Kristin Thompson observe, it "encourages the spectator to erect erroneous first impressions, confounds the viewer's most probable hypotheses, and stresses curiosity as much as suspense" (40); however, they also emphasize that it remains "finally bound by classical precepts. First, the narration still depends chiefly upon suspense and forward momentum: the story is primarily that of an investigation, even if the goal happens to be the elucidation of a past event. Secondly, the mystery film relies completely upon cause and effect, since the mystery always revolves around missing links in the causal chain. Third, those links are always found, so even the gaps of the mystery film are temporary, not permanent" (40).

Bava's film, in contrast, does not offer viewers a traditional detective story that they can follow carefully as it unfolds, gathering clues and keeping an eye on likely suspects until they feel as though they have enough evidence to indict one of the characters. Instead, it keeps viewers perpetually off-balance with an astonishing number of unexpected twists, turns, and reversals – some "fair" (those that follow conventional narrative logic), others not. At the drop of a hat, heroes and villains change places; victims become killers and killers become victims. Because of this, we can trust no one, and as the narrative plays out we shift our sympathies and suspicions from one character to another and back again. Our efforts to identify (or identify with) a protagonist or an antagonist are continually stymied; consequently, we entertain and discard any number of different hypotheses about the characters' motives and invest in and abandon any number of different characters' perspectives. We eventually find ourselves adopting a free-floating mode of spectatorship that operates in between set viewing positions.

One might add that rather than providing a plausible and satisfying solution to its central mystery, *Blood and Black Lace* in the end offers an explanation that is so improbable and unsatisfying that we are denied any real sense of closure. In the third act of the film, we learn that the owners of the fashion salon, Morlachi and Cristiana, have been murdering the models together, donning the same anonymous disguise and claiming victims on an alternating basis in order to confound investigators. Initially, they sought only to rid themselves of Isabella, who had been blackmailing them because she found out that they were responsible for the "accidental" death of the Countess's late husband; after Isabella's diary came to light, however, they acted jointly to silence anyone who might have discovered their crime from its pages. As they kill more and more of their employees, Morlachi convinces Cristiana that in order to clear themselves of suspicion, they must frame someone else for the murders. Accordingly, the Countess drowns one final model as the unfortunate woman bathes at home, slitting her wrists afterward to make it look like she committed suicide in a fit of guilty remorse. Just as Cristiana is putting the finishing touches on this incriminating tableau, though, she is startled by a loud knock at the front door. Believing that the police are outside, she climbs out the bathroom window in a desperate attempt to escape via the roof; she does not realize that the person at the door is Morlachi, who has decided to betray her in an effort to save himself. His plan seems to succeed: as Cristiana traverses a ledge, she loses her footing and plummets to the ground. He leaves, imagining that her body will be found by the police, who will assume that she was the killer. In a final twist, however, the mortally wounded Countess appears at the salon as Morlachi is preparing to make his getaway and shoots him dead before succumbing herself to the injuries she sustained in her fall.

From the standpoint of the traditional detective story, there are multiple problems with the ending of *Blood and Black Lace*. In the first place, it denies the efficacy of conventional methods of detection. The mystery at the heart of Bava's film is never solved by Inspector Silvestri or any of the other characters. The attempts made by the police to uncover the identity of the murderer are completely ineffectual, and the killers are never brought to justice. More important, Bava does not allow viewers the opportunity to crack the case on their own. Although he finally unmasks the murderers for us, we are unable to deduce their identity ahead of time because, ignoring the rules of the traditional detective story, he offers no clues from which we might make such a deduction (aside from the fact that the murderers are among the sizable group of characters still alive at the end of the story). Last, it could be argued that even the solution Bava offers to the film's central mystery displays what Xavier Mendik calls "the *giallo*'s obsession with displacing the actual logic and mode of detection" (35) insofar as it emphasizes the "problematic that surrounds detection" by linking the "inability to successfully detect" with the "fundamental insecurity that surrounds identity" (ibid.). This linkage is made in two ways at the end of *Blood and Black Lace* – first, through the disclosure that the murders in the film have been perpetrated by two killers, not one; and, second, through the revelation that these crimes have been committed by a woman and a man. Because of the way in which it "transgresses the norms of gender expectation" (Mendik 35), the second discovery, especially, works to deprive us of the satisfaction we might otherwise derive from the solution provided by Bava. Rather than representing a comforting return to normalcy and an affirmation of the conventional methods of detection, the "solution" to the central mystery in this film represents a "decentering and chaotic admission of mystery, of nonsolution" (Tani 40). Like the twists, turns, and reversals that kink earlier portions of the narrative, the ending of the story – despite the questions that it answers – refuses us the luxury of a stable viewing position, encouraging us to adopt an unfixed, performative mode of spectatorship instead.

It is important to note, finally, that the potential for spectatorship-as-performance created by Bava's anti-detective story is amplified by the formal qualities of the movie. From the very beginning of *Blood and Black Lace,* Bava visually and aurally establishes a "delicate, self-aware tone" (Newman, "*Blood and Black Lace*" 22) that invites us to see our experience watching the film as a game in which we are able to adopt and discard different viewing positions at our pleasure. As Kim Newman observes, the movie's original opening credits sequence (which was altered for its theatrical run in the United States, but has since been restored on DVD) "introduces [Bava's] cast posed like mannequins in compositions that include wicker dummies, indicating that they are puppets rather than characters" (ibid.). The bold, non-naturalistic lighting used in this sequence, ranging from blood red to pale lavender to icy blue, heightens this impression, as does the playful nondiegetic music – a jazzy mambo score composed by Carlo Rustichelli. For Newman, the artificial way in which the characters are presented at the outset of the film is fitting because the director then "pulls them on strings through a plot so complex it is impossible to take them seriously" (ibid.). I would argue, however, that the message of the opening credits sequence is that the characters are puppets at the disposal not of the director, primarily, but of the viewer. Bava is encouraging us here to see them as masks to be tried on, worn for a time, and exchanged for others as we progress through the movie.

Following the opening credits, he pushes us to take this performative approach to spectatorship not only by exciting our sympathies for and suspicions about one character after another via the narrative, but also by prompting us – via the camerawork, editing, music, and other formal devices – to assume a variety of different, often highly unconventional points of view throughout the film. Significantly, the way in which he "deterritorializes" the spectator's gaze runs counter to the sort of "suturing" commonly practiced in mainstream cinema. Indeed, to borrow from Adam Knee, Bava's "literal diffusion of points of view (and point-of-view shots) . . . [and] presentation of events from a range of not always clearly defined and often novel vantage points" (224) is concordant with a "questioning of any normative perspective" (ibid.). Rather than seeking to place viewers as part of a predefined psychological or ideological system of subject positioning, he hopes to displace us, to prevent us from relating too closely with any one of the multitude of perspectives offered by the film. In this way, he reconfigures spectatorship as a type of performance, a process of "becoming Other" in which, to quote Gilles Deleuze and Félix Guattari, the "subject itself is not at the center . . . but on the periphery, with no fixed identity, forever decentered, *defined* by the states through which it passes" (*Anti-Oedipus* 20).

Bava's unconventional use of film form to intensify spectatorship-as-performance is perhaps most obviously on display in the murder set pieces that regularly punctuate *Blood and Black Lace*. Take, for example, a memorable scene in which one of the killers stalks and slays one of the models in an empty antiques shop into which she has slipped after hours. Bava creates here the same atmosphere of playful unreality that pervades the movie's opening credits sequence. The shadowy store, crammed with dusty curios – some of which, like a menacing suit of armor, seem to represent a tongue-in-cheek nod to creaky "old dark house" mysteries – is lit completely non-naturalistically. While the pulsing green glow that fills the shop finds tenuous motivation in a flashing neon sign outside (it reads "DANCING," neatly suggesting the performative sort of spectatorship Bava wishes to elicit from viewers), it is complemented by washes of red, blue, and lavender light that have little or no apparent diegetic basis. Like the opening credits, these images are accompanied by Rustichelli's mambo score, which further imbues the proceedings with an air of theatricality, inviting viewers to see the act of watching as a form of role-playing.

Bava also encourages performative spectatorship in this scene through his stylized, unorthodox approach to cinematography and editing. Keeping his camera constantly on the prowl and cutting unexpectedly from one perspective to another as the model apprehensively makes her way through the antiques shop, he robs us of any fixed viewing position; we must instead adopt a more nomadic mode of cinematic perception. We drift between alternating points of view – some of which clearly belong to a specific character or are clearly omniscient, and others of which are of a more ambiguous provenance – experiencing each, but allying ourselves definitively with none. Our gaze is deterritorialized even more radically when the hidden murderer suddenly attacks: the perspectives presented to us multiply vertiginously as Bava increases the pace of the editing and toys both with our perception of events (reversing the action onscreen at one point by shooting it in a mirror) and with our identification with the characters (filming the victim's death from her point of view – not the killer's – when she receives the final blow from the iron claw). What obtains here, in the words of Adam Knee, is "a sense of pleasure and excitement in a pure sensory, perspectival play partially rooted in ambiguity, an emphasis on sensual dynamics that begins to transcend stable . . . generic polarities of active/passive, sadistic/masochistic, stalker/stalked" (222). The look becomes "radically diffused, unmoored from classical subject/object positions" (ibid.), freeing viewers to regard those positions as postures to be assumed and abandoned at will rather than as stations to which they have been permanently assigned.

Finally, one could argue that the gruesome end met by the victim in this scene – rendered, like the other deaths depicted in the film, through the agency of gory makeup effects – itself fosters performative spectatorship. On one hand, it does so at the level of representation, insofar as it "destroys customary meanings and appearances, ruptures the surfaces of the flesh, and violates the organic integrity of the body" (Shaviro 101), demonstrating the fragility not only of the human form, but also of the social contract. As Isabel Cristina Pinedo writes, such carnage suggests, in a postmodern manner, that "violence is a constituent element of everyday life and the threat of violence is unremitting" (5), violating "our assumption that we live in a predictable, routinized world" (18). Significantly, however, because it is so extravagantly staged, ensuring "that what fascinates is not primarily the suffering of the victim but her or his bodily ruination" (19), it also disposes us to contemplate the prospect of social disintegration – like Bava's artful image of corporeal destruction – not with dread, but with pleasure. The "ruined-body-as-spectacle" (60) showcased in the scene effectively opens up opportunities for viewers to perform their resistance to the norms governing the body politic.

On the other hand, this carnage also fosters spectatorship-as-performance at the level of reception, insofar as it appeals to our own bodies in a visceral way, putting us "in direct contact with intensive, unrepresentable fluxes of corporeal sensation" (Shaviro 101) that are immediate and largely outside our conscious control. Like the narrative twist that reveals the true identity of the killers at the end of the film, Bava uses the ruined-body-as-spectacle here to emphasize the fundamental insecurity that surrounds identity, this time by highlighting the alien and frequently ungovernable nature of our embodied selves. Establishing a correspondence between the body on film and the body of the viewer – a dynamic feedback loop in which we are "caught up in an almost involuntary mimicry of the emotion or sensation of the body on the screen" (L. Williams, "Film Bodies" 704) – Bava "splits the [viewer's] body into fragments, fetishes, and other sites of libidinal playfulness" (Brottman 4). The literal body without organs on display in this scene and others in *Blood and Black Lace* metaphorically evokes what Deleuze and Guattari call the "Body without Organs," a set of practices designed to dismantle the self. Bava invites us to lose ourselves in the spectacle of corporeal destruction, to find in it "potential movements of deterritorialization, possible lines of flight, experience them, produce flow conjunctions here and there, [and] try out continuums of intensities segment by segment" (Deleuze and Guattari, *Thousand Plateaus* 161). By accepting his invitation, we exchange, in a temporary but powerful fashion, the "forms, functions, bonds, dominant and hierarchized organizations, [and] organized

The faceless killer strikes in one of the many murder scenes that punctuate *Blood and Black Lace* (Allied Artists). *Courtesy of Photofest*

transcendences" (159) of a conventional viewing experience for a mode of spectatorship that offers the possibility of postmodern reconfiguration.

In his book on the *giallo* film, Mikel J. Koven writes that the murder set pieces found in this genre of Euro horror "are often protracted, longer than they need to be to further the plot alone, and act as spectacles in themselves" (123), suggesting that "the 'plot' is merely a pretext on which to hang those thrills" (32). These scenes certainly represent privileged moments of "heightened spectacle and emotion" (Freeland 256) that can be viewed as "interruptions of plot – scenes that stop the action and introduce another sort of element, capitalizing on the power of the cinema to produce visual and aural spectacles of beauty or stunning power" (ibid.); however, I hope it is clear by now that *Blood and Black Lace* is not simply all "plotless shock and dismemberment." Bava's film is a carefully crafted anti-detective story, one whose postmodern challenges to the narrative conventions of the traditional detective story are calibrated to induce a performative approach to spectatorship among viewers. Moreover, while the movie's murder set pieces may be largely extraneous to its plot, they also complement it by intensifying the disorienting effect of the anti-detective story and encouraging, as the narrative itself does, spectatorship-as-performance. Seen in this light, *Blood and Black Lace* manifests a purpose not apparent from its sensationalistic title. The "aporia" fostered by the film – to appropriate the term coined by Jacques Derrida to describe the sense of vertigo one experiences when confronted with the endless and inescapable deferral of meaning within language systems – is intended to prompt the audience to adopt multiple viewing positions and experiment with different subjectivities in a fashion generally proscribed by mainstream cinema and the dominant social order. Its principal pleasures lie not in solving a mystery, but rather in surrendering oneself to it.

Significantly, *Blood and Black Lace* is not unique in this respect; in fact, it is representative of its genre. Contra Gary Needham's contention that the *giallo* film resists generic definition, I would argue that it is defined by its narrative debt to postwar Italian anti-detective fiction and by the characteristic way in which it uses formal devices to amplify the destabilizing, postmodern tendencies of this brand of fiction. As one fan puts it in a perceptive post on the cult movie website Eccentric Cinema: "Many years ago, when I first discovered the *giallo* sub-genre I was amazed by the stylish ways in which a rather plain mystery story could be re-energized and transformed. By simply applying some of the same writing tricks employed by more inventive authors and visualizing the murders as glossy set pieces, these films made figuring out whodunit almost irrelevant. In a *giallo*, the destination is never as important as the ride" (Barnett par. 3). This fan's commentary suggests that the central feature of the *giallo* film is the ride it offers viewers – not the kind of safely mainstream thrill ride offered by contemporary Hollywood blockbusters, but rather an intensely interactive experience that involves potentially transgressive acts of performative spectatorship by viewers. If such spectatorship-as-performance is characteristic of Euro horror cinema in general – the theory I put forward in the first part of this book – the *giallo* film has a unique way of evoking it. Initiating a "teasing, puzzle-like relationship" (Tani 45) between film and viewer, it engages us in a role-playing game with conceivably radical implications for our sense of ourselves and our notions about the nature of subjectivity in general.

This is particularly true with regard to the *giallo* film's postmodern treatment of sex roles and gender identity. As we saw in *Blood and Black Lace*, the *giallo* tends to explore the "fundamental insecurity that surrounds identity" (Mendik 35) in a manner that "transgresses the norms of gender expectation" (ibid.). It delights in provoking what Judith Butler famously dubbed "gender trouble": the recognition that gender is not simply a biological "fact," but also the effect of a "subtle and politically enforced performativity" (146), "an 'act,' as it were, that is open to splittings, self-parody, self-criticism, and those hyperbolic exhibitions of 'the natural' that, in their very exaggeration, reveal its fundamentally phantasmatic status" (146–147). Far from insisting on the gendered viewing positions that typically structure the conventional horror movie experience (the assaultive male point of view and the reactive female point of view), *giallo* films treat gender as provisional and "posthuman," as "always stitched, sutured, bloody at the seams, and completely beyond the limits and the reaches of an impotent humanism" (Halberstam 144). By denaturalizing gender – by making gender itself their central, unsolvable mystery – they provide a "framework for addressing gender behaviors as modes of performance" (Berenstein 232–233). And like other horror movies that offer "a space for an attraction to figures that revel in sex and gender fragmentation" (261), they allow viewers to experiment with "a more fluid and malleable range of social and sexual identities than they would in their everyday lives" (233), pushing them to "question the notion of an authentic spectating self" (ibid.). In my view, the *giallo* film's presentation of gender "as *effect,* that is, as *produced* or *generated*" (Butler 147), goes a long way toward explaining its cult popularity in the United States today. Fans have responded to the way in which it "opens up possibilities of 'agency' that are insidiously foreclosed by positions that take identity categories as foundational and fixed" (ibid.) in contemporary

American culture. Accordingly, I will spend the remainder of this case study examining how the *giallo* film prompts audiences to experiment with different gendered viewing positions and identities through its adherence to the postmodern principles of anti-detective cinema.

A review of some of the most popular and well-known *giallo* films reveals that they foster spectatorship-as-drag by deploying a variety of "local strategies for engaging the 'unnatural'" (Butler 149) in ways that "might lead to the denaturalization of gender as such" (ibid.). This is true even of *giallo* films that have a reputation for being deeply and unrepentantly misogynistic. Consider, for example, Lucio Fulci's *The New York Ripper*, a film in which a male killer devises spectacularly nasty methods of dispatching women – especially those whom he views as being "promiscuous": prostitutes, live sex show performers, swinging socialites with a taste for S&M, and so on. It has been reviled by critics as a "sadistic sex picture" (Hardy 382) whose "nauseatingly ultra-conservative viewpoint" is telegraphed by its "unnerving misogyny" (ibid.). To be sure, the movie features many scenes in which female characters are murdered in particularly graphic fashion, and it is the case that the violence in these scenes is explicitly occasioned by and directed at the victims' sex. It would be an error, however, to assume that Fulci shares the ripper's misogynistic point of view or intends for the audience to. Indeed, I would argue that the film actually represents a recognizably feminist effort to deconstruct the figure of the male killer and prompt the viewer to interrogate, in a performative act of spectatorship-as-drag, the sadistic male gaze.

Fulci seeks to accomplish this goal, first of all, by subjecting the audience to the very depictions of male-on-female violence that have made *The New York Ripper* so despised among critics. The aim of these images, which dwell in harrowing detail on the objectification and destruction of the female form, is not to titillate viewers, but rather to disturb and disgust them. Such a reaction is guaranteed partly by the extreme nature of the carnage onscreen. In one scene, the killer grinds a broken bottle between the legs of a live sex show performer he has trapped in a dressing room backstage, while in another he ties up a prostitute whose apartment he has invaded before using a razor blade first to disfigure her face and then to bisect one of her nipples. We see this violence in graphic close-ups that showcase very realistic makeup effects, helping to ensure that the overall effect is repulsive rather than appealing. In addition, Fulci inserts the viewer into these scenes via an unusual number of point-of-view shots taken from the perspective of the victims as they are being murdered. By aligning us with the women in this way, Fulci primes us to empathize with their terror and pain, making it less likely that we will regard their deaths with anything approaching exhilaration or approval. Conversely, by visually equating the killer's assault on his victims with an assault on the audience, Fulci helps ensure that we will regard the murderer in antagonistic rather than empathetic terms.

The director further reduces the likelihood that viewers might identify with the ripper by completely deglamorizing him. One of Fulci's most effective strategies for doing so is to have the killer (whose identity remains hidden until the end of the film) adopt a ludicrous disguised voice reminiscent of Donald Duck's. It could be argued that such a move adds insult to injury by injecting an element of farcical humor into graphic depictions of violence against women. As Koven observes, "One of the reasons Fulci's film remains controversial is that the absurdity of the disguised voice is juxtaposed with extremely misogynist and horrific violence" (102). I would suggest, though, that the incongruity of this juxtaposition actually serves to trivialize not the violence, but rather its perpetrator, who is marked by his voice as a pathetic, infantile figure. The fact that the killer quacks like a duck as he murders his victims is liable to alienate members of the audience who might otherwise be tempted to identify with his treatment of women. Indeed, it prompts us to contemplate the manner in which his misogyny has literally dehumanized him.

Another strategy Fulci uses to deglamorize the killer is to assign him, in the end, an identity and a motive that rob him of any remaining allure he might hold for viewers. The ripper turns out to be a handsome young physics professor and single father driven mad by the rare terminal illness afflicting his young daughter, a hospitalized amputee with whom he communicates over the phone using the voice of a duck, her favorite cartoon character. Enraged that she will never grow up to become a woman, he murders female victims who have – unfairly, in his view – achieved sexual maturity, taking the duck as the symbol of his avenging persona. As fan-scholar Stephen Thrower writes: "The psychological 'reason' for his crimes is as nauseating as his actions. Not for Fulci the Thomas Harris–style sympathy for a maniac's tortured inner turmoils. This killer is presuming to act as a sick-hearted proxy for his physically deformed daughter. . . . His daughter [meanwhile] gets no hospital visits from this monster, just phone-calls where he adopts the voice of a duck. . . . Even then he pours out his hatred and misogyny . . . into the uncomprehending ears of his lonely daughter" (227). Unlike Hannibal Lecter or other fictional serial killers whose misdeeds are romanticized, Fulci's ripper comes across as a total loser – a failed, impotent patriarch so blinded by anger and self-pity that he neglects to give his dying daughter what she needs most: the comfort of his presence. The director underlines this tragic irony in the final frames of the film, after the killer has been cornered and shot by police, by dissolving slowly from his daughter's pale, stricken face to the Manhattan skyline as she cries inconsolably in her hospital bed for her father. The disclosure of his identity and motive, as well as the consequences of his actions, more or less negates any appeal he might have had for viewers as a mysterious, apparently unstoppable force earlier in the movie. Fulci's deconstruction of the ripper effectively "denaturalizes" his sadistic male gaze, exposing its "fundamentally phantasmatic status" (Butler 147). At the same time, the film encourages the audience to adopt a more fluid, performative approach to spectatorship – one not limited to rigidly gendered male/female viewing positions. Ultimately, then, *The New York Ripper* represents not an "ultra-conservative" exercise in "unnerving misogyny," but rather a potentially radical text that seeks to reveal "the precariousness of Western patriarchal institutions and values" (Berenstein 262) by pushing them to their extremes.

The deconstruction of the male killer is not the only way in which the *giallo* provokes gender trouble, however; in many *giallo* films, a female protagonist serves as the catalyst. A prime example is Sergio Martino's *Tutti i colori del buio* (*All the Colors of the Dark*, 1972), which follows the efforts of a young woman named Jane (Edwige Fenech) to come to grips with a recent car accident that resulted in a tragic miscarriage and has prompted a series of nightmares in which she is stabbed to death by a sinister man with piercing blue eyes (Ivan Rassimov). When the man from her dreams begins to appear in her waking life, menacing her as she goes about her daily routines, Jane becomes determined to learn his identity despite the protestations of her skeptical lover, Richard (George Hilton), and psychiatrist, Dr. Burton (George Rigaud), who believe that she is suffering from paranoid delusions caused by the traumatic accident. Her investigations lead her to the discovery that the blue-eyed killer is the agent of a satanic cult that once counted her mother among its members and now wants to claim her as its next sacrificial victim. In the end, she seemingly manages to defeat both the killer and the cult's Manson-like leader (Julián Ugarte) with Richard's help. (Whether she actually does so is difficult to determine because of the intensely oneiric nature of the film, which constantly shifts back and forth between her reality and her fantasies.) She is still, however, left with the nagging sense that she is not in control of her own destiny: "Oh Richard, I'm frightened!," she exclaims as she stares down at the body of the slain cult leader. "I feel as if some strange force were controlling me!" On this plaintive and extremely inconclusive note, the ending credits roll.

The ironic truth, of course, is that Jane is *not* in control of her life: the satanic cult was merely the most extreme and visible manifestation of the patriarchal forces that shape her destiny. More hidden and insidious, Martino implies, is Richard himself, a crass lothario who throughout the entire film has been carrying on a secret affair with Jane's sister, Barbara (Nieves Navarro). As Koven observes, "[T]he actions of Jane's partner, Richard . . . begin to complicate the presumed polarity between 'good, normal people' and 'evil, wicked Satanists.' . . . The film vilifies witchcraft as an evil practice, but the actions of the supposedly heroic characters undercut that moral certainty" (113). Thus while on the surface *All the Colors of the Dark* might appear simply to resuscitate the familiar horror film trope of the woman-as-victim, in effect reaffirming the dominant patriarchal order, it actually (or also) does exactly the opposite. In the manner of contemporaneous psychological horror films like William Castle's *The Night Walker* (1964) and Roman Polanski's *Rosemary's Baby* (1968) – as well as certain horror-themed arthouse films of the period like Polanski's *Repulsion* (1965) and Robert Altman's *Images* (1972) – Martino's film uses the figure of the alienated modern woman as a means of exposing and challenging the ideological assumptions upon which the patriarchal order is founded. Such a move is rare in a genre that, as

Linda Williams writes, often "permits the expression of women's sexual potency and desire and . . . associates this desire with the autonomous act of looking" ("Woman Looks" 32), but does so "only to punish her for this very act, only to demonstrate how monstrous female desire can be" (33). *All the Colors of the Dark* and other *giallo* films featuring female protagonists stand as interesting exceptions to this rule, films that – while purporting merely to horrify or titillate – actually express a recognizably feminist point of view.

Conversely, it is also illuminating to consider the ways in which many *giallo* films deploy the figure of the female killer. In Emilio Miraglia's fascinating *La dama rossa uccide sette volte* (*The Red Queen Kills 7 Times*, 1972), the titular character provokes gender trouble by inviting viewers to adopt a sadistic *female* gaze. Miraglia's film tells the story of two young women, sisters, who have grown up as members of a cursed aristocratic family in Germany. Legend has it that, centuries earlier, the siblings' female ancestors – known only as the Red Queen and the Black Queen – harbored a deep resentment toward one another. After enduring years of torment at the hands of the Red Queen, the Black Queen finally killed her sister in her sleep. Exactly one year later, however, the Red Queen rose from her grave and murdered six innocent people before killing the Black Queen herself in revenge. Since that time, according to the legend, history has repeated over and over again: every hundred years, female descendants of the two sisters reenact the same sororicidal drama, ultimately resulting in the deaths of seven people at the hands of the reincarnated Red Queen.

As the film opens, this cycle seems to have been broken. Although the relationship between present-day sisters Kitty (Barbara Bouchet) and Evelyn (Carla Mancini) is hardly friendly, they are both apparently alive and well. Kitty works as a fashion photographer in their hometown, while Evelyn is said to be studying abroad in the United States. We soon discover, however, that Kitty accidentally killed her sister in a vicious fight at the family estate some time ago and has covered up the crime, with help from another sister, Franziska (Marina Malfatti), by hiding the body in the crypt below their gothic mansion. Soon a mysterious female figure dressed in a flowing red cloak and wielding a long knife – a woman whose white, mask-like features and terrifying, Medusan laugh bear a striking resemblance to Evelyn's – begins murdering people close to Kitty in a manner that suggests that the curse has struck again. In the end, Miraglia reveals that the truth is a little more complicated. Kitty learns that Evelyn was not her real sister; she was adopted at an early age by Kitty's grandfather and presented to Kitty as her sibling. Meanwhile, Kitty's real sister, Rosemary (Pia Giancaro), was raised outside the household as a stranger to her. These steps were taken by the family in order to protect the sisters from one another. Kitty also discovers that her older sister, Franziska, has known all along about the switch and has used this knowledge, as well as Kitty's belief in the curse, to try to cheat her out of her share of the family fortune. Sometime earlier, Franziska tracked down Rosemary and brainwashed her into believing that she was the reincarnated Red Queen. Since then, Rosemary had been an instrument of Franziska's criminal intent; dressed in a cape and mask, she murdered people close to Kitty at Franziska's behest and in accordance with the legend. For Kitty, these revelations almost come too late: in the final scenes of the film, after discovering that Franziska has murdered Rosemary in order to cover her tracks, Kitty is trapped by her older sister in a rapidly flooding catacomb. Before Kitty falls victim to Franziska's scheme, however, she is rescued and Franziska herself is killed.

One of the most remarkable aspects of *The Red Queen Kills 7 Times* is the potency of its larger-than-life female killers. Rosemary, as the Red Queen, makes an especially powerful impression in this regard. Decked out in a mask and billowing cape, and possessing uncanny abilities to strike without warning and to effortlessly elude capture, she is presented as an unstoppable force in the film – more superhero than villain. (Amusingly, the independent DVD company NoShame Films included a plastic figurine of the Red Queen in its 2006 box set of Miraglia's movie, highlighting her iconic status.) Compared to the nominal heroes of the film – the frigid, neurotic Kitty (who is, after all, a murderer herself) and her smarmy boyfriend, Martin (Ugo Pagliai), who has placed his unbalanced wife in a sanitarium so that he can pursue a relationship with Kitty – the Red Queen emerges as a more interesting and, in some ways, more sympathetic character. Her victims are either characters who richly deserve their fates – like Hans (Bruno Bertocci), the insufferable head of the fashion house where Kitty works, who is murdered while cruising a park for prostitutes – or characters who are onscreen so briefly that they barely have time to register with the audience. By selecting targets like these, the Red Queen becomes almost a righteous avenger in the film; indeed, the fact that most of her victims are connected in some way with an industry that objectifies women as a matter of commerce makes it possible to read her as a specter of feminist rage. It is also interesting to note the way in which Martino encourages the viewer to identify with her sadistic female gaze. In one of the movie's most memorable murder sequences, the Red Queen spies on Kitty during an outdoor fashion shoot and then kidnaps and kills her assistant, a young woman who has uncovered a clue about the Red Queen's secret identity. Significantly, much of this scene is filmed from the Red Queen's perspective as she peers through bushes at the fashion shoot, traps Kitty's assistant in the back of a van, drives the truck to a remote location, and finally murders her victim. Like the contrasts that Martino draws between the Red Queen and the other characters in the film, the extended point-of-view shots in this sequence prompt us to identify with the female killer and to embrace the threat she represents to the patriarchal social order.

Ultimately, the female killer in this *giallo* film and others bears a close resemblance to the femmes fatales of classic American film noir: the hard-bitten, tough-as-nails seductresses who, more often than not, lead the weaker, more impressionable male characters to their doom in such films as *Double Indemnity* (1944), *Detour* (1945), and *The Postman Always Rings Twice* (1946). It can be tempting to dismiss the femme fatale as a negative, reactionary stereotype born of a patriarchal and misogynistic society. However, while film noir can be read as being one of those "myths of the sexually aggressive woman ... [that] first allows sensuous expression of that idea and then destroys it" (Place 48), it is important to remember that the figure of the femme fatale allowed female spectators in the 1940s and 1950s the opportunity to identify with powerful female characters who operated outside the norms of "good girl" behavior. As Janey Place suggests, it is not "their inevitable demise we remember but rather their strong, dangerous and, above all, exciting sexuality" (48); thus, "the final 'lesson' of the myth often fades into the background and we retain the image of the erotic, strong, unrepressed (if destructive) woman" (ibid.). Indeed, she suggests that a "fuller explanation for the current surge of interest in film noir must acknowledge its uniquely sensual visual style which often overwhelms (or at least acts upon) the narrative so compellingly that it stands as the only period in American film in which women are deadly but sexy, exciting and strong" (68). In a similar fashion, I would argue that the wealth of charismatic female killers in *giallo* cinema at least partly accounts for the popularity of the genre among contemporary American viewers. Both the figure of the female protagonist in the *giallo* film and the figure of the female killer challenge pat notions about the role of women in horror cinema – indeed, the role of women in the dominant cinema generally – providing spectators with the rare and welcome opportunity to engage performatively with female characters who do not conform to socially prescribed gender identities.

Finally, it is important to note the way in which many *giallo* films use the figure of the male victim as a means of provoking gender trouble. Take the example of Aldo Lado's *La corta notte delle bambole di vetro* (*Short Night of Glass Dolls*, 1971), which tells the story of Gregory Moore (Jean Sorel), an American journalist living in Prague, whose apparently lifeless body is found by a groundskeeper in a city park at the beginning of the film. After he is transported to the local morgue, it becomes clear that Gregory is not dead, but in a state of total paralysis. While his body is completely immobilized, he regains consciousness and becomes all too aware of what is happening to him. He cannot remember, though, how he came to be in this condition and spends the rest of the movie desperately trying to reconstruct what has happened to him and to give his medical examiners some sign that he is still alive before it is too late. Eventually, through a series of flashbacks, Gregory and the audience are able to piece together his story. It turns out that the events of the film have been set in motion by the sudden disappearance of Gregory's young Czechoslovakian girlfriend, Mira (Barbara Bach), some weeks earlier. When Gregory realizes that the police are not especially interested in her case, he becomes determined to conduct his own investigation. He finds out that Mira is just the latest in a string of young women to go missing in Prague over the years and that a secret society to which members of the city's highest social and political circles belong is responsible for these disappearances. Ostensibly devoted to the appreciation of chamber music, the society is actually a satanic cult that sacrifices young women in orgiastic black masses in order to maintain the power of its initiates. Before Gregory can report his discoveries to the authorities, however, he is captured by the cult, whose leader paralyzes him with a spell. As the film ends, Gregory, who is now in full possession of his memory, slowly begins to regain control over his body. Unfortunately, his recovery comes too late: as he tries furiously to move or speak, his body is wheeled from the morgue into a medical classroom, where he is vivisected alive by the professor, an initiate of the cult, while a group of students and other members of the secret society look on.

Short Night of Glass Dolls has been read as an allegorical critique of the brutal social and political repression that took place in Czechoslovakia after the Soviet Union militarily reasserted its authority over the country in 1968 in response to the Prague Spring reforms. Andrew Syder convincingly argues, for instance, that the film "uses horror and *giallo* conventions as political metaphors for class oppression and the moral corruption of the social elite" (186): "The horror convention of being buried alive, for example, is used as a metaphor for the silencing of political dissidents; Moore begins the film as an apolitical, womanizing journalist, and the disappearance of his girlfriend prompts a political awakening that is met with a response from the social elite that both literally and figuratively puts him back to sleep" (187). While one of its aims may well be to demonstrate that "the ruling classes expend the bodies of the young as a fuel to maintain power" (Syder 187), *Short Night of Glass Dolls* also works to expose and challenge the ways in which the dominant patriarchal order sustains itself through the expenditure of female bodies, offering viewers the opportunity to identify against the male gaze that so often structures the horror film experience.

The film does so by deconstructing the figure of the traditional male protagonist, transforming him from an active subject into a passive object, from a hero into a victim. Like the male detectives in many other *giallo* films (*Blood and Black Lace,* for example), Gregory fails to measure up to the standard set by the super-sleuths in traditional detective fiction: Edgar Allan Poe's C. Auguste Dupin, Arthur Conan Doyle's Sherlock Holmes, Agatha Christie's Hercule Poirot. He simply does not possess the powers of observation and deductive reasoning necessary to solve the central mystery of the film before it is too late; indeed, by his obliviousness to the clues all around him and his susceptibility to deception, he demonstrates that he is singularly unequal to the task. What sets Gregory apart from the failed detectives in other *giallo* films is that his failure is made literal in the movie through his immobility. Laid out in the morgue, paralyzed – the pawn of forces beyond his understanding or control, unable to save himself much less his missing girlfriend – he is the very embodiment not only of incompetent detective work, but also of diminished masculinity. This last point is underscored by the film's casting: Gregory is played by Jean Sorel, who was at the time perhaps most widely known for his earlier role as Catherine Deneuve's cuckolded, wheelchair-bound husband in Luis Buñuel's *Belle de jour* (1967). It is also emphasized by the director's approach to composition and camerawork. For example, when Gregory is taken to the morgue at the beginning of the film, the camera pans across the room, past the nude corpse of a young woman, to the shrouded gurney where he lies, as the male attendants who have just finished undressing him itemize his possessions. The point of the shot could not, in my view, be clearer: Lado is visually suggesting an equivalency between Gregory and the dead woman – not only in terms of their similar conditions (his paralysis and her rigor mortis), but also in terms of their similar subject positioning. Gregory has come to occupy the place in horror movies (and cinema in general) typically held by female characters. Stripped of his agency, rendered a passive object of the other characters' gazes and ours, robbed of his voice and his mobility, he is not the master of the narrative, but rather its plaything.

To be sure, he does make an effort to reclaim his agency in the film. When he is cursorily examined by a doctor and a nurse before being taken to the morgue, for example, we listen to him plead with them in voice-over to notice that he is not dead ("Can't you tell that I'm alive? I've got to make them see! You! Listen to me! Look at me! Can't you hear me?"); the extreme close-up of his unmoving lips that accompanies the sound of his inner voice, however, serves to highlight the ineffectuality of his attempts at communication and to strengthen rather than mitigate our impression of his impotence. Even his efforts to reconstruct in his head what has happened to him are marked by failure: the flashbacks that gradually reveal his story are constantly interrupted by barrages of free-associative imagery meant to represent fragments of the past that still elude him. Of course, Gregory ultimately succeeds in combining all the pieces of the puzzle; when he does, though, it is only to (re)discover his inadequacy as a detective-hero. Far from rescuing his girlfriend and bringing her kidnappers to justice, he realizes in the end that he has fallen victim to his enemies and sealed his own fate.

I would argue that Lado's deconstruction of the traditional male protagonist in *Short Night of Glass Dolls* is similar to Fulci's deconstruction of the sadistic male killer in *The New York Ripper* insofar as both work to denaturalize gender and destabilize the viewing positions that tend to define the experience of watching horror cinema. By making it more difficult for us to identify with Gregory – by depriving us of the default male perspective from which we might otherwise experience the film – he prompts us to experiment with other viewing positions and gendered subjectivities. While *Short Night of Glass Dolls* does not offer us a central female point of view to adopt, as do *All the Colors of the Dark* and *The Red Queen Kills 7 Times*, it nevertheless seems clear to me that, like them, it offers "something more than the conventional sex-role and gender options available to men and women in American patriarchy" (Berenstein 261). This does not necessarily mean that these films should be considered feminist by design. The opportunity for spectatorship-as-drag they offer is arguably just a by-product of their effort to play postmodern variations on the detective story – to form a "teasing, puzzle-like relationship" (Tani 45) with the audience. At the same time, the fact that we need to be careful about seeing these films as *purposively* feminist should not prevent us from appreciating the ways in which they might be *effectively* feminist. To the extent that they encourage viewers to embrace the "decentering and chaotic admission of mystery, of non-solution" (40) by subverting "positions that take identity categories as foundational and fixed" (Butler 147), they expose gender as the effect of a "subtle and politically enforced performativity" (146) and prompt viewers to consider alternatives to the gender norms established by the dominant social order. Although the means they employ are very different, this is the goal of traditional, oppositional feminist cinema. One could even argue that the strategies that *giallo* employ to denaturalize gender are more effective, in terms of the potential scope of their impact, than those utilized in traditional feminist films because of the way in which *giallo* films marry gender trouble with the pleasures of a popular genre of cinema like horror.

Indeed, this argument has been made about the seminal *giallo* films directed by Dario Argento – *Deep Red*, *Tenebre* (1982), *Opera* (1987), and *Trauma* (1993), among them. Again, at first glance, it may appear that these movies offer abundant evidence that the *giallo* is inherently antifeminist. Like other examples of the genre, they frequently seem to revel in the gruesome murder of attractive women at the hands of sadistic killers. Argento's own reluctant attempts to explain why the spectacle of the ruined female body receives such attention in his films, moreover, suggest nothing in the way of feminist intent. Echoing the infamous assertion made by Edgar Allan Poe (one of Argento's self-proclaimed heroes) that "the death... of a beautiful woman is, unquestionably, the most poetical topic in the world" (Poe 535), he has said, "I like women, especially beautiful ones. If they have a good face and figure, I would much prefer to watch them being murdered than an ugly girl or man" (qtd. in Schoell 54). Furthermore, he has revealed that he uses his own hands as stand-ins when shooting the trademark close-ups of the murderer's black-gloved hands that appear in many of his films, admitting, "I love all my killers" (qtd. in McDonagh 245). Both Argento's films and his comments about them seem, in Leon Hunt's words, "to confirm everyone's worst fears about the horror film as a sadistic and misogynist treatment of violence rendered into ultrachic spectacle" ("A (Sadistic) Night" 325). Nevertheless, a growing number of critics have suggested that upon closer inspection, it becomes clear that Argento's *giallo* films in fact embrace what Halberstam calls the "queer tendency of [the] horror film," which "lies in its ability to reconfigure gender not simply through inversion but by literally creating new categories" (139).

While conceding that it "may be problematic to ascribe a progressive function to a series of texts that have so much invested in the detailing of violence toward women" (226), Adam Knee has convincingly demonstrated that Argento's films "consistently foreground ambiguities of gender and sexuality and repeatedly suggest the instability of power relations implied by the acts of looking and perceiving" (215). Knee points out that although "Argento's work does tend to have more female victims

... he nonetheless includes quite a few male victims and often dwells on their deaths at some length" (ibid.); furthermore, Knee suggests that it is "*by way of* a largely unprecedented violence to bodies male and female that Argento's films articulate their questioning of gendered binarisms: the body in question becomes the body destroyed, markers of difference reduced to meat" (226, emphasis in original). He reminds us that while the killer is almost always a man – albeit an infantilized one – in slasher movies, "Argento's killers, in their variety and obscurity, tend to frustrate most such generalizations about gender" (215):

> Indeed, while Argento tends to visually present his killer as a single hooded and cloaked figure, the killer often turns out to be bi-gendered and multiple-personed, a number of individuals acting as one. The individuals involved in murder are themselves often presented as ambiguous in both their gendered characteristics and their sexual preferences – although the actual identity of the killer is rarely made clear before the film's conclusion, so the spectator is always forced to guess at the killer's sex. (ibid.)

Accordingly, Knee asserts, "it becomes difficult simply to attribute the murder and violence in Argento's films to sadistic male agencies – or, for that matter, to males whose masculinity has been somehow qualified, as in many American slasher films" (216). As a result of this difficulty, all "traditional positions, former points of identification, are thrown into question, and any strict sense of 'otherness,' always important to the horror film, thereby becomes diffused as binary distinctions lose their applicability" (226). What remains, Knee writes, is a "sense of pleasure and excitement in a pure sensory, perspectival play partially rooted in ambiguity, an emphasis on sensual dynamics that begins to transcend stable gendered polarities of active/passive, sadistic/masochistic, stalker/stalked" (222). As we have already seen, this kind of "perspectival play" is not unique to Argento's *giallo* films; it is a defining feature of the *giallo* as a genre. It can be argued, however, that Argento's *giallo* films are even more aggressive than the movies already discussed in their attempts to destabilize the gendered viewing positions that often define the experience of watching horror cinema; indeed, I would suggest that, for Argento, provoking gender trouble is not a means to an end, as it perhaps is in most other *giallo* films, but rather the end itself. This certainly appears to be the case, for instance, in his earliest *giallo* and in one of his more recent: *L'uccello dalle piume di cristallo* (*The Bird with the Crystal Plumage*, 1970) and *La sindrome di Stendhal* (*The Stendhal Syndrome*, 1996).

Set in Rome, *The Bird with the Crystal Plumage* tells the story of an expatriate American writer, Sam Dalmas (Tony Musante), who one night witnesses an attempted murder taking place in the brightly lit foyer of an art gallery as he makes his way home. He attempts to intervene, only to become trapped between a set of locked glass doors and forced to watch helplessly as a figure dressed in black wounds a young woman and then flees as she lies bleeding on the floor. When the police, alerted by another passerby, finally arrive, the young woman – who is identified as the gallery owner's wife, Monica Ranieri (Eva Renzi) – is taken to the hospital, and Dalmas is questioned at length as a material witness. Inspector Morosini (Enrico Maria Salerno) believes that the assailant was the same person responsible for the recent, apparently motiveless murders of three other women in the area. Dalmas, however, cannot shake the feeling that there was "something wrong, something off" about what he saw. With the reluctant cooperation of his girlfriend, Julia (Suzy Kendall), he begins an independent investigation into the matter by interviewing witnesses to the three previous murders. At the scene of the first murder, an antiques store, Dalmas discovers that the victim, a female clerk, died soon after a customer purchased a painting depicting a brutal attack on a local girl that happened years earlier. His inquiries into the other murders soon draw the attention of the mysterious killer, who makes threatening telephone calls, warning Dalmas and Julia to leave the country or risk becoming the next victims. Just as the couple is preparing to take the killer's advice, though, a friend, Carlo (Raf Valenti), is able to identify a peculiar noise on a tape they made of one of the killer's telephone calls. It is the cry of a rare bird with "crystal" plumage found in only one Roman zoo, which happens to be located next to the apartment owned by the woman attacked at the gallery, Monica Ranieri, and her husband, Alberto (Umberto Raho), the gallery owner. Suspecting that Alberto is the killer, Dalmas, Carlo, and Julia lead the police to the Ranieris' apartment. When they arrive, they find Alberto and Monica locked in a fierce struggle; Monica breaks free and accuses Alberto of trying to kill her. In desperation, Alberto jumps out the window; before dying on the street below, he confesses to the recent serial murders. In the confusion that ensues, Julia, Carlo, and Monica disappear. Dalmas traces them to the art gallery where, to his shock, he finds Carlo murdered and Julia bound and gagged by the real killer, who turns out to be Monica Ranieri herself. Dalmas realizes, almost too late, that he misread the attempted murder he witnessed at the beginning of the film: he took Monica for the victim when in fact she was the aggressor. After being rescued at the last moment by Inspector Morosini, he learns that the female killer's rage was triggered by the sight of the painting in the antiques store, which depicted a brutal attack she suffered years before as a child. Ironically, in an act of psychological self-defense, she identified with the figure of the male attacker rather than with that of the young female victim, which led to a psychotic break and caused her to embark upon the spree of murders. The film ends as the shaken and injured Dalmas embraces his rescuer while the police lead the raving Monica Ranieri away.

The Bird with the Crystal Plumage has the reputation of being the most conventional and conservative of Argento's *giallo* films. Maitland McDonagh writes that it invites the spectator simply to "sit back and enjoy the passive titillation of a well-crafted mystery whose transgressions against the law, against religion, against conventional morality ... are confined to matters of plot and swiftly resolved" (19). Leon Hunt has argued that it represents the embodiment of what he sees as the *giallo* film's "relentless Oedipality" ("A (Sadistic) Night" 329). While this Oedipality is evident in Argento's other films – whose killers "are generally constructed as perverse in their reluctance or inability to undergo 'correct' heterosexual Oedipal trajectories" (ibid.) – it is, he claims, particularly egregious in *The Bird with the Crystal Plumage*'s "anxiously phallocentric" scenario (ibid.). Contrary to McDonagh's and Hunt's assessments of the film, however, I contend that *The Bird with the Crystal Plumage* not only avoids providing the viewer with the familiar comforts of the traditional detective story – such as a satisfying resolution to the central mystery it introduces – but also destabilizes rather than reinforces normative assumptions about gender. Moreover, I suggest, the destabilization of point of view and the destabilization of gender in the film are intimately connected, since "the literal diffusion of points of view (and point-of-view shots)" (Knee 224) is used both to "undermine assumptions that we place onto the thriller as a genre" (Needham, *"Bird"* 90) and to "underscor[e] the fragility of masculinity and femininity as normalised and fixed constructions" (92).

Consider, for example, the way in which Argento manages both to undercut the conventions of the traditional detective story and to provoke gender trouble by having the central male figure of the film, amateur sleuth Sam Dalmas, play the role traditionally reserved in murder mysteries for the female victim: a passive witness to events that are beyond his understanding or control. Dalmas's unconventional position in *The Bird with the Crystal Plumage* is made abundantly clear in the first few minutes of the film when, after a short expository scene that indicates his impotence as a writer (he reveals to Carlo that although he came to Italy to beat a case of writer's block, he has not written a line in two years), he is unable to intervene in or fully comprehend the attack he witnesses at the art gallery. The image of Dalmas trapped between the glass doors leading into and out of the gallery perfectly "enunciates the theme of entrapment, alienation, and the fragility of Dalmas' masculinity" (Needham, *"Bird"* 90). Isolated, exposed, and robbed of his voice (he has difficulty making his cries for help heard through the thick glass when another pedestrian wanders by), forced to watch but prevented from participating in the drama that unfolds before him, Dalmas is explicitly feminized. Furthermore, if, as Needham writes, he hopes "through his detective pursuits . . . to attain mastery and control over the situation" (92), he is sorely mistaken. Like Gregory Moore in *Short Night of Glass Dolls*, Dalmas is far from being the ideal male detective-hero; indeed, he is shown time and time again as being astonishingly inept in his investigations. Throughout the movie – when he wanders through a fog bank early in the film, stalked by an unseen assailant; when he is almost run down by the car of a hired assassin on a dimly lit cobblestone street; when he stumbles through the darkened gallery offices at the film's conclusion, unaware that his incapacitated girlfriend is lying on the floor a few feet away and that the murderer is watching him from the shadows – Argento demonstrates to viewers that Dalmas, in the manner of countless screen ingenues, is frequently in the dark and consequently often in danger and in need of rescue. It is fitting, then, that the climax of the film finds him trapped once again at the scene of the original crime – this time, under

Masculinity compromised: amateur sleuth Sam Dalmas is unmanned at the climax of *The Bird with the Crystal Plumage* (Universal Marion Corporation).
Courtesy of Jerry Ohlinger Archives

a jagged, monolithic piece of abstract sculpture – and at the mercy of the killer, who is preparing to deliver the coup de grâce when Inspector Morosini intervenes. The effect of having Dalmas play the role of the damsel in distress in *The Bird with the Crystal Plumage* is twofold. In the first place, it prevents viewers from deriving the same sort of satisfaction from the film that they would from a traditional detective story in which the heroic male detective, who is always one step ahead of both the killer and the police, demonstrates both his masculinity and his intellectual prowess (they often amount to the same thing in this genre) by solving the crime and getting his man. Second, it introduces a new kind of viewing pleasure by opening "a space for an attraction to figures that revel in sex and gender fragmentation" (Berenstein 261).

The same is true, I would argue, of Argento's use of the female killer in *The Bird with the Crystal Plumage*. If the director manages both to undercut the conventions of the traditional detective story and to provoke gender trouble by making his detective somewhat less than a man, he also does so by making his killer something more than a woman. From the opening sequence, in which we witness the murder of the killer's latest victim through the killer's eyes – a montage of point-of-view shots shows us the black-gloved killer composing a letter to the police on a typewriter, snapping voyeuristic photographs of a young woman, caressing a collection of long, phallic knives fetishistically laid out on red velvet – Argento carefully deploys the gender markers that are associated, both in horror cinema and in the criticism of it, with the male killer. In subsequent scenes, he reinforces the idea that the killer is a man by having the two male protagonists – Inspector Morosini (who early in the film puts together a lineup composed entirely of men for Dalmas to inspect) and Sam Dalmas (who suspects that Alberto Ranieri is the killer) – assume this as well. Thus when it is revealed at the conclusion of the film that the killer is a woman, Morosini, Dalmas, and the audience are forced to confront and reexamine the fact that we tend to rely upon fixed conceptions about gender that have little or no correlation to the complex and mutable reality of performed subjectivity. The mocking laughter Monica Ranieri unleashes in the face of Dalmas's (and our) astonishment at her "true identity" – as well as the further revelation that she is a female victim reenacting the role of a male killer – denies the efficacy of such conceptions, pointing the way to a more provisional understanding of gender identity. Once again, Argento twists the conventions of the traditional detective story in order to prompt our recognition that gender is not simply a biological fact, but also a performative act.

It could be argued that the subversion of gender in *The Bird with the Crystal Plumage* is only temporary and ultimately downplayed by the film's final scenes, which seem to reaffirm the dominant view of gender by simultaneously invoking and repressing "the nightmare image of the monstrous-feminine" (Creed 63). This seems to be the interpretation favored by Hunt and other critics of the film. What such a reading ignores, however, are the multiple ways in which Argento draws out and emphasizes the queer tendencies of the horror film. If his "opposition of an active and aggressive feminine with a passive and helpless masculine is used to undermine the assumptions that we place onto the thriller as a genre" (Needham, "*Bird*" 90), it also works to undermine the assumptions we have about gender – to reveal it as fluid rather than fixed, as performed rather than received.

The same is true of *The Stendhal Syndrome,* a *giallo* film directed by Argento over twenty-five years later, at a time when the form had been all but abandoned by European horror filmmakers. It tells the story of Assistant Inspector Anna Manni (Asia Argento), a young policewoman who works on an anti-rape team for the Roman authorities. At the opening of the film, we find her in Florence, following the trail of a serial rapist named Alfredo Grossi (Thomas Kretschmann). An anonymous tip has led her to the Uffizi Gallery, where she hopes to finally capture Grossi. As she searches for him among the crowds of tourists, however, she is gradually overwhelmed by the Stendhal syndrome: hallucinations and feelings of vertigo triggered by the legendary works of art – Uccello's *Battle of San Romano,* Botticelli's *Primavera* and *The Birth of Venus,* Caravaggio's *Medusa* – that surround her. Finally, standing before Bruegel's *Landscape with the Fall of Icarus,* she faints and in her delirium imagines that she has entered the painting. Later, as Anna is recovering in her hotel room, she is attacked by Grossi, who witnessed her episode at the museum. After brutally raping her, he kidnaps her and forces her to watch as he rapes and murders another woman. Anna manages to escape and returns to Rome to resume her law enforcement duties. She is plagued by the trauma she has suffered, however, and begins to behave erratically. She cuts her formerly long hair and responds to those around her – including her boyfriend, Marco (Marco Leonardi), another member of the anti-rape team – with hostility and aggression. Her superior, Chief Inspector Manetti (Luigi Diberti), convinces her to take a leave of absence, and she returns to her rural hometown to stay with her father and two brothers. This family idyll is shattered when Grossi, who has become obsessed with Anna's unusual susceptibility to art and believes that he shares a special bond with her because of it, discovers her whereabouts and kidnaps her a second time. Imprisoning her in a riverside culvert, he once again rapes and brutalizes her; this time, though, she manages to fight back, badly wounding Grossi and pushing him into the raging river. The police assume that he is dead and although Anna is not entirely convinced, she attempts to bring a sense of normalcy back to her life. She covers her short hair with a blonde wig, returns to work, sees a psychiatrist, and even begins dating Marie (Julien Lambroschini), a young French art student whom she meets in a bookstore. Before long, however, she becomes convinced that Grossi is still alive and determined to possess her once more. When Marie is murdered by a mysterious assailant, the police believe that she is right; shortly afterward, though, Grossi's bloated corpse is found in the river into which Anna pushed him weeks earlier. It becomes clear, ultimately, that the traumatized Anna has internalized Grossi's personality and is intent on carrying out his work after his death. In the film's final scenes, she murders her psychiatrist and Marco, who have discovered her secret, before being arrested by her former colleagues on the police force.

Like *The Bird with the Crystal Plumage*, *The Stendhal Syndrome* has not received the kind of attention it deserves. As Robert Daniel notes, it was "released to almost unanimous scorn" (231) at a time in Argento's career when interest in Euro horror cinema had declined dramatically and even many of his fans openly expressed doubt that he would ever again equal the landmark films he directed in the 1970s and early 1980s. Although *The Stendhal Syndrome* represents a departure from his previous work in some respects – a movement from the colorful, deliberately surreal mise-en-scène of *Deep Red* and *Suspiria* toward a more muted, realistic look, for example – it is remarkably similar to the earlier movies in terms of its efforts to provoke gender trouble. The most obvious way it does so, of course, is by emphasizing the transformation that Anna Manni undergoes in the film. When we first meet her, she is positioned in the way a female protagonist traditionally is in horror cinema. She is marked as overtly feminine through her makeup, her hairstyle (long, flowing), and her attire (blouse, skirt, purse). She is also marked as the victim, subject to the killer's sadistic male gaze. After she is attacked by Grossi the first time, however, her appearance and behavior change. In the hospital, she cuts her hair boyishly short with a pair of surgical scissors and begins dressing in slacks and blazers. The drastic change in her appearance is noticed and remarked upon both by her superior, Chief Inspector Manetti, and by one of her brothers, who teases her that she "look[s] like a boy." She also begins acting more aggressively. When her boyfriend tries to make love to her, she responds violently, throwing him against a wall and thrusting her pelvis against his backside, shouting, "You want to fuck me, huh? Now I'm fucking you!" Later, she tells her psychiatrist: "I wanted to fuck him like a man, the way men do it. The idea of being fucked disgusts me." When she returns to her hometown of Viterbo on enforced leave, she takes up boxing and delights in sparring with a male partner and getting her nose bloodied. Finally, she is able to turn the tables on Grossi by outwitting and killing him the second time he kidnaps her. Interestingly, in the wake of her victory over Grossi, she begins once more to dress and behave in a "feminine" fashion, wearing a long, blonde wig and a flowing, white sundress. This time, though, her femininity is a masquerade, a disguise assumed to hide the cold-blooded killer she is becoming. It enables her to carry out the murders of the men in her life – Marie, Marco, her psychiatrist – without being suspected by anyone, including the viewer. As he does in *The Bird with the Crystal Plumage*, then, Argento uses our assumptions about gender against us, both to prevent us from guessing the answer to the film's central mystery (who continues to stalk Anna if Grossi is dead?) and to exacerbate the queer tendencies of this horror film.

Critics have wondered if Argento's subversive treatment of the female protagonist in *The Stendhal Syndrome* is enough – in and of itself – to qualify the film as a true example of feminist horror cinema. Linda Schulte-Sasse writes:

> *The Stendhal Syndrome* is unique in the radicality with which it relates aesthetics, culture and violence, but also in its having a feminist dimension that critiques patriarchy.... Far from a "social action" film, however, *The Stendhal Syndrome* shows patriarchy as an all-consuming structure whose unequal power distribution can be eluded by no one. In responding to it with her own gendered aggression, the protagonist remains entrapped in its logic, repeating rather than escaping violence. (192)

This is certainly a valid point. As I argued in my discussions of *The Red Queen Kills 7 Times* and *The Bird with the Crystal Plumage*, though, I believe that it overlooks the potential for performative spectatorship inherent in the image of "the erotic, strong, unrepressed (if destructive) woman" (Place 48) – a potential that feminist theorists and critics have been quick to point out in the case of the femme fatale in film noir.

Moreover, it is important to note that deploying the female killer is not the only way in which *The Stendhal Syndrome* provokes gender trouble. It also does so through the unconventional depiction of its male characters. Marco, Anna's boyfriend and fellow detective, is explicitly feminized in the film: a sensitive, passive young man with "pretty boy" good looks, he is twice victimized by Anna, first when she throws him against the wall and roughly dry humps him from behind (he has to beg her to stop) and later when she murders him after he figures out that she is the killer. Marie, the young French art student whom Anna begins dating after she kills Grossi, is depicted in much the same fashion. Aside from the obvious feminine connotations of his name ("But – I thought that Marie was a woman's name," Anna says when she meets him. "Well, in French it isn't so exact," he replies. "It can be a man or a woman"), he, like Marco, is young, passive, and sensitive, with the same kind of androgynous appeal. He is happy to let Anna take the lead in their lovemaking, lying back obediently when she insists on undressing him. He is also, ultimately, the victim of her murderous impulses when she stalks and slays him in the museum where he works as a research assistant.

Even Grossi, the film's male killer, is portrayed unconventionally by Argento. Far from being brutish or physically imposing, Grossi, as played by Thomas Kretschmann, is something of a dandy and an aesthete. Slender, well groomed, and handsome, with dyed blond hair and an obsessive interest in art, he strikes one as being more metrosexual than alpha male. The hint of effeminacy built into his character is amplified by Argento in a scene in which Grossi, having kidnapped Anna for the second time, demonstrates how he lured her to the Uffizi Gallery earlier by using an electronic voice changer to pose as the anonymous female caller who tipped her off to his whereabouts. Finally, of course, Grossi is feminized when, in the tradition of rape revenge movies like Meir Zarchi's *I Spit on Your Grave* (1978) and Abel Ferrara's *Ms .45* (1981), he becomes the victim of the woman he has brutalized. In an extended sequence full of gory close-ups, Anna reduces Grossi to a bloody mess, stabbing him in the neck with a pair of bedsprings she has covertly taken from the mattress to which she has been tied, kicking him in the face, kneeing him repeatedly in the groin, jamming her finger into his right eye, shooting him in the stomach, and breaking his neck with the butt of his gun. Having thoroughly unmanned him, she contemptuously dumps his body in the river.

It is worth noting, too, that Argento makes it unusually difficult for us to identify with Grossi's sadistic male gaze in *The Stendhal Syndrome*. While a few of the film's murder scenes – like the one in which Grossi woos a woman in the street with a rose before strangling and shooting her – are filmed from his point of view and could be said to encourage the audience's identification with him, most work to distance us from the male killer, either by having us share the victim's perspective (as we do when Anna is raped by Grossi for the first time) or by having us share that of the killer at his most vulnerable moments (as we do after Anna partially blinds Grossi and he tries to fend her off by firing his gun wildly in all directions). The end result of all this, in my view, is actually to undercut the notion that the patriarchy is an "all-consuming structure whose unequal power distribution can be eluded by no one." By demonstrating that the gendered terms upon which the patriarchy's unequal power distribution is founded are fluid and ever-changing – that men are not always "men" and women are not always "women" – Argento exposes the phantasmal nature of the structure itself. Moreover, by encouraging spectators to operate in between the points of view represented in the film by its ambiguously gendered characters, he tries to ensure that even if Anna herself becomes trapped in the fallacious logic of this structure, the audience does not. He liberates us by "open[ing] up possibilities of 'agency' that are insidiously foreclosed by positions that take identity categories as foundational and fixed" (Butler 147). While this may not represent an example of filmmaking as social action, I would argue that it does represent a recognizably feminist move on the part of a director whose work is often unfairly dismissed as misogynistic.

One of the dominant themes of both *The Bird with the Crystal Plumage* and *The Stendhal Syndrome* is that art is dangerous. The brutal attack witnessed by Sam Dalmas at the beginning of the earlier film takes place in an art gallery that displays vaguely threatening pieces of abstract sculpture, including one prominently featured work that resembles the talon of a gigantic bird. The real danger posed by the sculptures is made clear at the climax of the film, when another piece – the jagged monolith – is used by the killer to immobilize Dalmas so that she can taunt him with her stiletto. In addition, Monica Ranieri's psychosis is triggered by a painting that reminds her of the near-fatal attack she suffered at the hands of a madman ten years before the events of the film take place. The danger of art is made equally palpable in *The Stendhal Syndrome*. Anna Manni finds herself at the mercy of great works of art, which bring on crippling bouts of vertigo and powerful hallucinations; her susceptibility to art in turn elicits the unwelcome interest of the male killer, who is himself obsessed with art.

At the same time, art is represented as being strangely liberating in both of these films. In *The Stendhal Syndrome*, especially, Argento seems to be at pains to emphasize its potentially wondrous, transformative nature. One thinks of the moment early in the film when Anna faints before Bruegel's *Landscape with the Fall of Icarus* in the Uffizi Gallery and imagines that she has entered the painting; swimming through its waters, a fallen Icarus, she encounters an enormous Pleistocene fish with an oddly human face, which she tenderly kisses. Or the moment, later in the film, when she fantasizes that she has stepped into the painting of a waterfall in the waiting room outside Chief Inspector Manetti's office and walked behind the curtain of falling water – through which she can dimly see the real world that she has left behind. In these scenes, Argento seems to be suggesting that, ideally, a work of art is neither merely a passive object of contemplation nor purely a force that acts – sometimes violently – upon spectators; rather, it is (or should be) an arena that provides the basis for an imaginative interaction between viewer and viewed, one that takes us outside of ourselves and offers us the opportunity to experiment with different perspectives and states of being. One can imagine him making the same argument about his own films. Indeed, I have tried to show that both *The Bird with the Crystal Plumage* and *The Stendhal Syndrome* are geared precisely toward offering us the chance to engage in this kind of performative spectatorship, particularly where gender role-playing is concerned. In their celebration of the "decentering and chaotic admission of mystery, of nonsolution" (Tani 40), these films expose gender as the effect of a "subtle and politically enforced performativity" (Butler 146) and encourage viewers to explore alternative gender identities, demonstrating the feminist potential of an allegedly anti-feminist body of work.

In closing, we should recall that such is the case not only with Argento's films in particular, but also with the *giallo* in general. It is a genre of Euro horror cinema that, in adopting (and adapting) the strategies of anti-detective fiction in a distinctive fashion, banishes "all fixed points of reference and self-reference, all lines of perspective, and all possibilities of stabilizing identification and objectification" (Shaviro 53), offering us an array of different opportunities for becoming Other. This is especially true where gender is concerned. By provoking gender trouble – by exposing gender "as *effect*, that is, as *produced* or *generated*" (Butler 147) and thereby "open[ing] up possibilities of 'agency' that are insidiously foreclosed by positions that take identity categories as foundational and fixed" (ibid.) – the *giallo* film encourages viewers to "identify with and desire against everyday modes of behavior and to play with the masks that Western culture asks us to treat as core identities" (Berenstein 262). This is a major characteristic of the genre, as I have argued. Far from being a vague, unquantifiable "conceptual category with highly moveable and permeable boundaries that shift around from year to year" (Needham, "Playing with Genre" 135), the *giallo* film defines itself through its rejection of the "forms, functions, bonds, dominant and hierarchized organizations, [and] organized transcendences" (Deleuze and Guattari, *Thousand Plateaus* 159) of the conventional viewing experience in favor of "potential movements of deterritorialization, possible lines of flight" (161) that ultimately "[throw] into question the notion of an authentic spectating self" (Berenstein 233). Like the dangerous, seductive works of art that populate Argento's films, *giallo* reaffirms the potentially radical, transformative nature of spectatorship, allowing us to adopt multiple viewing positions and experiment with a range of subjectivities generally proscribed by mainstream cinema and the dominant social order.

SEVEN

The Whip and the Body

THE S&M HORROR FILM

Mario Bava's kinky gothic melodrama *La frusta e il corpo* (*The Whip and the Body*, 1963) stars Christopher Lee as Kurt Menliff, a sadistic aristocrat who returns to his family's ancestral home after a period of banishment to reclaim his patrimony as the eldest son of the ailing Count Menliff (Gustavo De Nardo) and to prevent his younger brother, Christian (Tony Kendall), from marrying Nevenka (Daliah Lavi), Kurt's former lover. The sudden reappearance of Kurt, who was exiled by the Count years earlier, throws the Menliff household into turmoil. He terrorizes his family from the moment he arrives, badgering his dying father to write him back into his will and tempting Nevenka to resume their violent, sadomasochistic love affair. Kurt's reign of terror is brought to a shockingly abrupt conclusion when he is murdered one night by an unseen assailant. Each member of the family is a suspect in his murder, since they all had ample motive; questions of guilt and innocence are soon forgotten, though, as strange lights start to appear at night in the windows of the mausoleum where Kurt's body is interred and Nevenka begins to have visions of a ghostly Kurt entering her chambers to whip her as she lies in bed – visions that are seemingly proven real when muddy boot prints are found on the floor of her room in the morning. Finally, a desperate Christian, believing that his brother has indeed returned from the grave to further torment them, opens Kurt's coffin and burns the remains he finds there along with the infamous whip. As he is returning to the house, however, he notices a figure dressed in Kurt's clothes walking ahead of him. Christian confronts this mysterious person, only to find to his astonishment and horror that it is Nevenka. Fleeing from

Christian, she locks herself in a cell inside the mausoleum, where she speaks to Kurt as if he were alive, leading Christian and the audience to understand that she murdered Kurt in an outburst of violent passion and then, regretting her act, "absorbed" his personality and began to carry on a double life as "Kurt" and "Nevenka." As Christian watches helplessly, Nevenka embraces an invisible Kurt and cries, "I love you, Kurt, only you!" before stabbing herself to death with a dagger. In the final moments of the film, the director cuts to a shot of Kurt's corpse, still burning in the coffin, and – as the film's lush orchestral score swells – slowly zooms in to a close-up of his whip, which twists like a living thing as it is consumed by the flames.

The Whip and the Body interests me, first and foremost, because of the distinctive way in which it seeks to bridge the gap between two marginalized film genres: horror and pornography. There is no hardcore porn in Bava's film, just as there is little of the gore that would become de rigueur in horror movies in the decades that followed its release; however, in its frank dwelling upon the sadomasochistic relationship between Kurt and Nevenka, it does create a sort of eroticized violence – or violent eroticism – that is rare in the genre. Film theorists have often observed that despite obvious differences – as Isabel Cristina Pinedo succinctly sums it up, "pornography is the genre of the wet dream ... [while] horror is the genre of the wet death" (61) – horror and pornography have much in common. First, they share "the frankly avowed goal of physically *arousing* the audience" (Shaviro 100) with the "spectacle of a body caught in the grip of intense sensation or emotion" (L. Williams, "Film Bodies" 703). Moreover, both genres are accorded low cultural status because they "expose what is normally concealed or encased to reveal the hidden recesses of the body [onscreen]" (Pinedo 61) and because they "literally anchor desire and perception in the agitated and fragmented body [of the spectator]" (Shaviro 54). Despite the fact that horror and pornography have often been linked in theory, though, the two genres seldom seem to mix in practice.

While several kinds of horror hybrids are widely accepted – horror/comedies like *Abbott and Costello Meet Frankenstein* (1948) and *Scary Movie* (2000), sci-fi/horror films such as *It! The Terror from Beyond Space* (1958) and *Alien,* and even horror/musicals like *The Rocky Horror Picture*

Show and *Sweeney Todd: The Demon Barber of Fleet Street* (2007) – the horror/porn film is not one of them. For all the nudity to be found in horror cinema, sex itself is almost invariably sublimated in the genre, where violence typically acts as a displacement of or substitution for carnal acts. As Carol J. Clover points out, while modern horror movies can be seen as "encroaching vigorously on the pornographic" (21), they also work to preserve a distinction between sex and violence by representing them "not [as] concomitants but [as] alternatives, the one as much a substitute for and a prelude to the other as the teenage horror film is a substitute for and a prelude to the 'adult' film (or the meat movie a substitute for and prelude to the skin flick)" (29). Conversely, violence has almost always been sublimated in pornography. That is, although a certain kind of ideological violence – the subordination of women in the name of the dominant patriarchal order – may be the driving force behind much of the sex that occurs in pornography, as anti-porn feminists like Andrea Dworkin and Catharine A. MacKinnon have contended, the genre contains little of the kind of literal, physical violence that we associate with modern horror cinema. On the surface, anyway, pornography is "far less violent than run-of-the-mill popular culture" (Kipnis 8). The fascinating implication here is that films that mix sex and violence are more or less taboo, even within the two most disreputable genres of cinema. If horror and pornography can be characterized as "*systems* of excess" (L. Williams, "Film Bodies" 702, emphasis mine), then horror/porn like that found in *The Whip and the Body* evidently constitutes a form of uncodified, unregulated excess that is completely beyond the pale.

Much of the transgressiveness of Bava's film stems from the way in which it blends horror with a relatively marginalized genre of pornography: S&M. Linda Williams has offered an explanation for S&M's liminality in her writing on sex in cinema. It has often been assumed by critics that S&M films – especially S&M films that seem, like *The Whip and the Body*, to eroticize the violent subjugation of women at the hands of men – merely reflect the fundamentally sadistic and misogynistic nature of patriarchal power and pleasure. Williams argues, however, that this is not the case – even with regard to male-on-female S&M – because in the sadomasochistic scenario, "violence is depicted not as actual coercion but as a highly ritualized game in which the participants consent to play predetermined roles of dominance and submission" (*Hard Core* 18). For this reason, "it is not easy to assign fixed gender roles [in S&M]" (L. Williams, *Screening Sex* 220); indeed, S&M "bring[s] focus to abruptly shifting sexual roles understood *as* roles and to sex understood as a scene of erotic possibilities tinged with threats of violence more than as a straightforward event" (235). Thus in S&M, sex "[can] no longer be reduced to the simple positions of penetrator and penetrated or to clear outcomes of climactic fulfillment" (ibid.); instead, the emphasis is on role-playing and on the elaboration of fantasy itself. And, as Williams notes, "fantasy is not about a subject who pursues and then gets, or does not get, the object," but rather "about desire's setting, about being caught up 'in the sequence of images' with no fixed position in them" (ibid.). While Williams cautions that S&M is "not a form that, even at its most aesthetic and playful, challenges male dominance" (*Hard Core* 225), she nevertheless speculates:

> The rise of sadomasochism in the full variety of its forms may very well indicate some partial yet important challenges to patriarchal power and pleasure in the genre of film pornography. S/M's emphasis on oscillating positions over strict sexual identities and its extension of sexual norms to include sadomasochistic play and fantasy suggest a rising regime of relative differentiations over absolute difference. Some of the apocalyptic force of much sadomasochistic pornography undoubtedly derives from these challenges to phallic laws that stand for strict dichotomization. (226)

Seen from this perspective, S&M reveals the "unavoidable role of power in sex, gender, and sexual representations" (228) while at the same time demonstrating that, although it is perhaps unavoidable in such representations, power is transferable and can be appropriated in ways that undermine the patriarchal dichotomization and hierarchization of sex and gender identities onscreen. It is perhaps not surprising, then, that S&M has been marginalized within pornography – a genre that has often manifested a decided interest in preserving the patriarchal status quo.

Above and beyond simply highlighting the instability of sex and gender roles at the level of representation, however, Williams writes that S&M cinema also gives viewers the unique opportunity to performatively explore a range of sexual identities in a fashion generally proscribed by mainstream cinema and the dominant social order. Because S&M "keeps in play the oscillation between active and passive and male and female subject positions, rather than fixing one pole or the other as the essence of the viewer's experience" (L. Williams, *Hard Core* 217), it lends itself "to the destruction of identification and objectification, to the undermining of subjective stability, and to an affirmation of the multiple techniques that denaturalize (or de-Cartesianize) cinematic perception" (Shaviro 42). As such, it can be "enjoyed by male and female spectators alike who, for very different reasons owing to their different gendered identifications and object choices, find both power and pleasure in identifying not only with a sadist's control but also with a masochist's abandon" (L. Williams, *Hard Core* 216–217). It offers "one important way in which groups and individuals whose desires patriarchy has not recognized as legitimate can explore the mysterious conjunction of power and pleasure in intersubjective sexual relations" (217–218). Given that S&M demonstrates the capacity not only to deconstruct conventional sex and gender roles onscreen, but also to foster a performative viewing experience that allows for sexual role-playing on the part of the audience, its liminality in pornography seems even less surprising.

An examination of *The Whip and the Body* confirms Williams's observations about the S&M film: Bava's film aims to be radically destabilizing in its representation of sex and gender. Consider, for example, a remarkable scene near the beginning in which Kurt seeks out Nevenka, who, disturbed by his sudden reappearance, has ridden a horse down to the rocky coast below the Menliff castle. The director fades in on a shot of waves lapping at the beach as Carlo Rustichelli's feverishly romantic score plays. The camera pans left to reveal Nevenka sitting on a stone, lost in reverie as she idly traces figures in the sand with her riding crop. Suddenly, she jumps in surprise and there is a cut to a close-up of the crop, which has been caught under a heavy black boot. The camera tilts up the length of the owner's body to reveal a grim-faced Kurt. Nevenka rises unsteadily. "Are you afraid of me?," Kurt asks, his voice dripping with sarcasm. "You were fond of me once." "Yes, once," she replies. After a moment of charged silence, they kiss passionately. Nevenka breaks away almost immediately, however, her face twisting. She grabs the riding crop and strikes at Kurt, who tears it away. Crop in hand, he advances toward her; she backs away, falling prostrate over a boulder. The director then cuts to an imposing, low-angle point-of-view shot of Kurt, who towers above, a strange combination of anger, frustration, hesitancy, and desire contorting his features. He begins to hit Nevenka savagely with the crop. "You haven't changed, I see," he grates between strokes. "You always loved violence." She looks up at him, a mixture of pain and desire on her face; he kneels, tossing aside the crop, and they embrace. The film cuts to a close-up of the discarded riding crop lying in the sand. The camera tilts up and pans left to reveal Nevenka's neglected horse grazing on the beach in the distance. The screen fades to black.

On the surface, it might seem that this scene – and much of the rest of Bava's film – merely serves to reflect the sadistic imperatives of patriarchal power and pleasure through the symbolic deployment of male-on-female sadomasochistic imagery. If we scratch a little deeper, however, we can see that it actually deconstructs the notion that male-on-female sadomasochism invariably victimizes and objectifies the masochistic "bottom," who is supposedly stripped of her agency and made a plaything by the sadistic "top." Significantly, the scene described above shows that Nevenka is the instigator – if not the agent – of the violence presented: Kurt hits her with the crop not because he wants to, necessarily, but because she demands it. Nevenka insists on the pleasure of her own punishment and deliberately provokes him into providing it for her. In fact, she refuses to submit fully to his embrace until he first satisfies her masochistic desires. When the camera finally cuts away from the lovers to the close-up of the riding crop and then swivels to capture the distant, freely grazing horse, we are given to understand that any use value the crop might have had as an equestrian tool – and any symbolic value it might have had as a sign of phallic authority – has been effectively displaced by its utility as a sex toy and its legibility as a sign of Nevenka's power over Kurt. The scene demonstrates, in short, that it is Nevenka and not Kurt who has been, is, and will always be in control in their relationship.

And the rest of the film bears this out. When Nevenka murders Kurt in his bedroom on the evening following their secret reunion, her power over him is made explicit, as fan-scholar Troy Howarth suggests: "Effectively turning the tables on her dominating lover, Nevenka uses the knife, the symbol of Kurt's destructive sexuality, as a means [of] stifling his libido. In taking control of the phallic blade, Nevenka usurps Kurt's role as a sexual predator" (93). Moreover, when we later learn that it is the force of Nevenka's masochistic desire that resurrects Kurt after his death, we realize that the scenes in which his whip-wielding ghost apparently terrorizes her actually represent her own intensely gratifying sexual fantasies – a fact that seems obvious in retrospect not only because of Bava's bold, expressionistic use of color and sound in these scenes, but also because of Daliah Lavi's performance, which makes it clear that Nevenka's reaction to the whippings (in reality a form of auto-erotic self-flagellation) is "positively orgasmic" (Howarth 92). Finally, when Nevenka kills both "Kurt" and herself at the film's conclusion, she demonstrates not only her power over Kurt in life and in death (as well as her determination to carry on their relationship with or without him), but also her unwillingness to commit to a conventional sexual relationship with her husband-to-be, Christian – a point that is utterly lost on the new patriarch of the Menliff clan, who obtusely speculates after her death: "Yes, perhaps she was possessed. She was convinced that Kurt was alive. She killed herself thinking that she was killing him. Let's hope she's free of him forever." In short, by disrupting "popular conceptions that [the female bottom] is passive, subjugated, and exploited" (Ross 272) and by showing that "the [male] top's own sexual needs/desires are dependent on the pleasure experienced by the bottom, and may even be sacrificed in the process of pleasure giving" (ibid.), *The Whip and the Body* does a surprisingly good job of suggesting the opposite. In Linda Williams's words:

> Under a patriarchal double standard that has rigorously separated the sexually passive "good" girl from the sexually active "bad" girl, masochistic role-playing offers a way out of this dichotomy by combining the good girl with the bad: the passive "good" girl can prove to her witnesses (the super-ego who is her torturer) that she does not will the pleasure that she receives. Yet the sexually active "bad" girl enjoys this pleasure and has knowingly arranged to endure the pain that earns it. The cultural law which decides that some girls are good and others are bad is not defeated but within its terms pleasure has been negotiated and "paid for" with a pain that conditions it. The "bad" girl is punished, but in return she receives pleasure. ("Film Bodies" 709)

In this way, I would argue, Bava's film "recognizes the role of power in the woman's often circuitous route to pleasure, and in that recognition . . . may even represent for women a new consciousness about the unavoidable role of power in sex, gender, and sexual representations and of the importance of not viewing this power as fixed" (L. Williams, *Hard Core* 228).

In addition, it is important to point out that *The Whip and the Body* not only deconstructs conventional sex and gender roles at the level of representation, but also prompts the performative exploration of unconventional sexual identities at the level of spectatorship. Such spectatorship-as-performance is made possible by the way in which Bava uses mise-en-scène, editing, and sound to "denaturalize (or de-Cartesianize) cinematic perception" (Shaviro 42), denying us a stable viewing position from which to experience the film. This strategy is on vivid display in one of several scenes detailing Kurt's apparent return from the grave after his death at Nevenka's hands. On the evening following his funeral, she stands alone in her darkened bedroom, dressed in a nightgown and caressing herself slowly, seemingly in a trance. At first, Bava presents her in an ostensibly straightforward medium shot, facing us, as her hands roam absently over her breasts and throat – an erotic object for the viewer's gaze. Almost immediately, however, the camera pulls back to reveal that she is actually situated in front of a mirror, facing away from us, absorbed in her own reflection. This is a destabilizing move, robbing us of the illusion that we occupy a privileged position as spectators (our belief that her performance is for our benefit alone), while at the same time it affirms her subjectivity and her ownership of her image. Bava then complicates matters further by having Kurt's face suddenly appear behind Nevenka's in the glass, as if summoned by the power of her masturbatory reverie. This initiates a dizzying chain of gazes in which, thanks to the placement of the camera and the mirror, we watch Kurt watch Nevenka watching herself, then meet one another's looks while at the same time seeming to return ours. The effect is to profoundly confuse the issue of who is watching whom and to raise the question of which vantage point the viewer is "supposed" to adopt.

Judging from what follows, the answer is "all of them." Startled by the unexpected appearance of Kurt's reflection in the mirror, Nevenka slowly turns around to the plangent sounds of Rustichelli's ubiquitous score, a mixture of fear and desire on her face. Bava then initiates a shot–reverse shot sequence that shuttles the viewer back and forth between the two characters' perspectives for the remainder of the scene. First, we share Nevenka's point of view in a series of vertiginous close-ups of Kurt as he circles her, gradually closing in. Next, after Nevenka is driven by Kurt to her bed, we adopt his perspective as he brutally flogs her bare back. And the viewpoint continues to oscillate, keeping time with the rhythmic lashes of Kurt's whip: one moment, Kurt looms over us, whip raised, grinning sadistically; the next, we watch Nevenka writhe in pleasure and in pain under our lashes. Finally, in a remarkable close-up from Nevenka's vantage point, Kurt moves in for a passionate kiss – his face getting steadily nearer and larger, alternately lost in shadow and illuminated by washes of blue, green, and red lighting, his mouth opening in expectation until it seems as though he is about to swallow us whole – before the image becomes blurry and fades to black.

The blocking, camerawork, editing, lighting, and sound work together in this scene to emphasize the instability both of routine viewing positions and of conventional sex and gender roles. Far from insisting that spectators adopt Kurt's sadistic gaze (and endorse the patriarchal imperatives it might be said to represent), Bava keeps us oscillating between active and passive and male and female subject positions. He encourages us to play the role of sadist *and* masochist, opening up a range of possibilities for viewer identification and prompting recognition of the fluid nature of sexuality. *The Whip and the Body* does not merely involve the representation of alternative sexual identities; it also, potentially, involves the participation of the viewer in the production of these identities. As one fan puts it in a review posted on the website Classic-Horror: "The sheer eroticism of *The Whip and the Body* is elusive and difficult to properly describe in words. The entanglement of pain and pleasure, color and darkness, desire and loathing, ghostly apparitions and insane hallucinations is so intense that not one of those elements is truly distinct from the other. They all rush together in Bava's melting pot, where he creates a potent formula for raw sensuality that emanates from the screen and infects the audience" (Yapp par. 8). Ultimately, it is by "infecting" the audience in this fashion that *The Whip and the Body* offers "one important way in which groups and individuals whose desires patriarchy has not recognized as legitimate can explore the mysterious conjunction of power and pleasure in intersubjective sexual relations" (L. Williams,

Hard Core 217–218). If viewers "surrender to and revel in cinematic fascination" (Shaviro 64) of the sort engendered by the scene described above, they embrace a nomadic mode of spectatorship in which they are free to experience "a more fluid and malleable range of social and sexual identities than they would in their everyday lives" (Berenstein 233). As with other S&M movies, it is by "throw[ing] into question the notion of an authentic spectating self" (ibid.) that *The Whip and the Body* taps into "film's radical potential to subvert social hierarchies and decompose relations of power" (Shaviro 64).

It is, of course, precisely this radical potential that, according to Williams, has led to the marginalization of the S&M film in popular cinema. One might imagine, given the liminality of S&M, that *The Whip and the Body* represents something of an anomaly even within the disreputable canon of Euro horror cinema, but that is not the case. As we saw in the first part of this book, one of the most unique features of Euro horror is the way in which it mixes sex with violence, "crisscrossing . . . [the] boundaries" (Tohill and Tombs 6) between horror and pornography. Its distinctive conflation of horror and porn was partly motivated by the relaxation of film censorship in a number of European countries during the 1960s and 1970s; the advent of hardcore pornography, which occurred at roughly the same time, further encouraged genre filmmakers to explore the circumstances under which "the boundary between sex and horror [becomes] blurred" (ibid.). Euro horror directors "mov[ed] sideways in[to] the skin-flick market . . . in order to compete with the explicit attractions of porno" (5), looking for ways to use the horror elements from their previous movies "inside a more sex-oriented framework" (6). Tales of vampirism, necrophilia, and even zombieism became popular vehicles for erotic horror cinema, but perhaps the most popular were stories involving sadomasochism.

The Whip and the Body was one of the first Euro horror S&M films to hit theaters – along with Antonio Margheriti's *The Virgin of Nuremberg* (1963) and Massimo Pupillo's *Il boia scarlatto* (*Bloody Pit of Horror*, 1965) – and was therefore a novelty at the time of its release, but it was soon followed by dozens more. Though it takes many forms – including the kinky gothic melodrama, the Nazi sexploitation movie, the women-in-prison picture, the nunsploitation film, and the direct adaptation of works by the Marquis de Sade and Leopold von Sacher-Masoch – Euro horror S&M cinema typically centers on the crimes of a Sadeian figure (sometimes male, sometimes female; sometimes straight, sometimes queer) who forces an (often captive, occasionally willing) individual or group of individuals to participate in his or her violent sexual fantasies. And crucially, like *The Whip and the Body*, it offers viewers the unique opportunity to performatively explore a range of sexual identities in a fashion generally proscribed by mainstream cinema and the dominant social order. The remainder of this chapter will be devoted to examining the ways in which Euro horror S&M fosters such spectatorship-as-performance through its deconstruction of conventional sex and gender roles.

Although Bava was among the earliest directors of Euro horror S&M cinema, the most prolific has, without a doubt, been Jesús "Jess" Franco. Over the course of his astonishing fifty-year (and counting) career as a filmmaker, Franco has made almost two hundred movies, working under dozens of pseudonyms in as many countries. His films typically have been ultra-low-budget international co-productions, shot on the fly with small, multinational crews in a matter of weeks or even days, featuring over-the-hill or down-on-their-luck British and American stars – Christopher Lee, Jack Palance, and Dennis Price, among them – and actors that Franco himself has "discovered," such as Lina Romay, his wife and frequent directing partner. By turns insufferable and fascinating, ridiculous and sublime, these movies draw upon an unusual "hodgepodge of quickly tossed-off pornography, American pulp fiction influences, and sadomasochistic iconography" (Landis and Clifford 177–178) that the director has obsessively mined over the years. They also boast a style – portentous voice-over narration, a relentlessly zooming camera, prolonged (and sometimes faked) slow-motion sequences, a bold use of color, exotic location photography, and jazzy soundtracks are notable components – that is equally singular. Franco is credited with directing the first Spanish horror film, *Gritos en la noche* (*The Awful Dr. Orlof*, 1962) (Tohill and Tombs 84), and the first hardcore pornographic movie released in Spain, *Lilian, la virgen pervertida* (1983) (ibid. 124), and has worked in nearly every genre imaginable, from horror, porn, and action-adventure to spy thriller, comedy, and documentary. He is perhaps best known for his many S&M horror movies, particularly the series of films he made in the late 1960s and early 1970s that were directly inspired by the writings of the Marquis de Sade and Leopold von Sacher-Masoch. These films – including *Marquis de Sade: Justine* (1969), *Paroxismus* (*Venus in Furs*, 1969), *Juliette* (1970), *Eugenie* (*Eugenie . . . the Story of Her Journey into Perversion*, 1970), and *Eugénie* (*Eugenie de Sade*, 1974) – offer fascinating insight into the various ways in which Euro horror S&M cinema encourages spectatorship-as-performance by transgressing the norms of sex and gender representation.

Take, for example, *Eugenie de Sade*, a loose adaptation of Sade's 1795 novel, *Philosophy in the Bedroom*. It stars Soledad Miranda as the title character, a naïve teenage girl who has lived in a rustic lakeside home outside Berlin with her stepfather, Albert (Paul Muller), since her mother died shortly after she was born. Albert, whom she adores unreservedly, is a renowned writer of sadomasochistic literature obsessed with the notion of acting upon his sovereign desire to wield "ultimate power over human beings." The story revolves around Eugenie's gradual induction into Albert's "savagely beautiful but forbidden" world. At first, Eugenie, who has been secretly reading her way through his extensive library of erotic fiction, professes to share his lust for "power which comes through pleasure and giving pain, living each moment with intensity and awareness while [others] suffer," and she pledges complete obedience to him: "Your will, will be mine," she promises. "We'll act as one." They embark on a sadistic killing spree, which commences with the strangulation of a model they hire to pose for nude photographs while on a trip to Brussels and eventually includes the murder of almost a dozen people, many of them young male and female hitchhikers whom Albert and Eugenie lure back to their home. These murders mix sex with violence, beginning with erotic games and ending with the deaths of the victims, which in turn trigger Albert and Eugenie's barely suppressed, quasi-incestuous lust for one another. Eventually, however, she begins to have misgivings about her stepfather. Their relationship starts to fray when she discovers that her mother did not die in childbirth, as he has always told her, but was instead murdered by him in a jealous rage over an infidelity. And it deteriorates completely when she falls in love with a young jazz musician whom Albert has targeted as their next victim. When he becomes aware of Eugenie's feelings, Albert viciously kills her new boyfriend, mortally wounds her, and then commits suicide. Before she dies, Eugenie confesses her and her stepfather's crimes to Attila Tanner (Franco, in one of his trademark supporting roles), a journalist who wants to write a book about Albert's life and who has been trailing them throughout the film.

At first glance, *Eugenie de Sade,* like *The Whip and the Body,* may seem to validate the view that S & M cinema merely reflects the sadistic imperatives of patriarchal power and pleasure. After all, it focuses in queasy detail on the absolute contempt and cruelty with which Albert uses his mostly female victims – including his own wife and her daughter – as means to gratify his lust and establish his dominance. He is the embodiment of what Georges Bataille calls Sade's "sovereign man":

> The kind of sexual satisfaction that suits everyone is not for de Sade's fantastic characters. The kind he has in mind runs counter to the desires of other people (of almost all others, that is); they are to be victims, not partners. De Sade makes his heroes uniquely self-centered; the partners are denied any rights at all: this is the key to his system.... Communion between the participants is a limiting factor and it must be ruptured before the true violent nature of eroticism can be seen, whose translation into practice corresponds with the notion of the sovereign man. The man subject to no restraints of any kind falls on his victims with the devouring fury of a vicious hound. (167)

Is the presence of this figure in *Eugenie de Sade* sufficient cause to condemn the film as reactionary horror/porn? I would suggest that the key question here is not *whether* it depicts the sovereign man, but *how* it depicts him. Were Franco's film simply to revel in Albert's misdeeds, it might well be considered indefensible. In my view, though, this is not at all what it does. Instead of celebrating the sovereign man, *Eugenie de Sade* undercuts his authority at every turn, ultimately rendering him a pathetic, rather than a powerful, figure.

Franco deconstructs the Sadeian man in a number of ways. To begin with, as the title of the film implies, Albert's status as the central figure of the narrative is challenged by Eugenie. The entire story is told from her perspective; her almost constant voice-over narration guides our interpretation of the events we see onscreen and encourages us to identify primarily with her rather than with Albert. Moreover, Franco is at pains to emphasize Eugenie's pivotal role in the crimes devised by Albert. It is her coming-of-age and acquiescence to Albert's plans that serve as the catalyst for their crime spree, and it is her choice of the jazz musician over Albert that ends it. By the film's conclusion, Albert appears to be less a "uniquely self-centered" sovereign man than a middle-aged pervert whose sexual satisfaction is wholly subject to his stepdaughter's whims.

Franco deconstructs Albert's status as a Sadeian hero in another way as well – one that borrows from Michael Powell's controversial British horror film *Peeping Tom* (1960). *Peeping Tom* tells the story of Mark Lewis (Carl Boehm), a shy cinematographer who also happens to be a serial killer. Damaged by a childhood in which he was incessantly photographed and recorded by his father, a psychologist interested in the emotion of fear, Mark is driven to commit murders in which he films female victims with his camera as he impales them with a blade hidden in one of the legs of the tripod. He does not derive satisfaction or stimulation from these acts of murder, however; it is rather the act of watching the films of his murders in his private theater at home that is his obsession. In fact, he spends the majority of his time screening films – not only of his murders, but also of his childhood – as though it is only in the process of reviewing his life that he has any sense of control over it. Finally, when his tentative romance with a kind neighbor, Helen Stephens (Anna Massey), is threatened by his homicidal tendencies, Mark despairs of ever living an unmediated existence and, turning his camera on himself, ends his life the same way he has ended the lives of his female victims. *Peeping Tom* has often been regarded as profoundly anti-feminist because of the way in which it seems to invite the viewer to adopt the sadistic male perspective of Mark's movie camera. Carol J. Clover persuasively argues, however, that the film privileges not an assaultive gaze, but rather a "reactive" gaze, which is fundamentally passive and masochistic. It is ultimately this gaze that is associated with Mark, making him as much a victim as a killer: "If, in his capacity as . . . filmmaker, Mark is fighting for voyeuristic distance from the victim, he is in his capacity as . . . spectator not only failing to resist her embrace, but hurtling himself into it. Uniting with the victim position seems to be the point of his spectatorial enterprise, the shameful fantasy his home-studio has been constructed to fulfill" (Clover 179).

Albert occupies much the same position in *Eugenie de Sade* that Mark does in *Peeping Tom*. Like Mark, he obsessively films or photographs the murders that he and Eugenie commit. Although we never see him reviewing these souvenirs, the movie does begin with Franco's journalist in a screening room watching some of the snuff footage, and Albert's compulsion to record the killings suggests that he seeks the same kind of voyeuristic distance from them that Mark does. It is significant that during the first murder Albert and Eugenie carry out together – that of the nude model in Brussels – Albert is content to snap pictures passively while Eugenie does all the dirty work. Also, when Albert does participate in the killings – for example, in the opening scene – it is interesting to note that he actively plays to the camera (and to Eugenie, who is operating it), acknowledging his status as the object rather than the bearer of the gaze. Finally, of course, he embraces the role of the victim at the end of the film by committing suicide, just as Mark does in *Peeping Tom*. By having Albert frequently occupy the position of passive voyeur and masochistic victim in *Eugenie de Sade,* Franco effectively highlights the fluidity of power and the consequent instability of patriarchal authority in the sadomasochistic scenario.

This is also the case in his other, earlier adaptation of *Philosophy in the Bedroom, Eugenie . . . the Story of Her Journey into Perversion*. There, Franco tells the tale of another teenage Eugenie (Marie Liljedahl), who is gradually corrupted over the course of the film by two aristocratic members of a Sadeian cult, Marianne Saint-Ange (Maria Rohm) and her stepbrother, Mirvel (Jack Taylor). In the opening scenes of the movie, the beautiful but rapacious Marianne, reading Sade as she lounges about her luxurious apartment in a negligee, fantasizes about the ceremonial sacrifice of a young girl, imagining that she is the executioner who wields the fatal dagger, removes the victim's heart, and drinks her blood. As the story unfolds, we come to understand that Marianne's fantasy has been prompted by Eugenie, a teenager whom she and Mirvel met at a recent party on the Spanish coast. Powerfully drawn to her beauty and innocence, they have secretly courted her ever since, promising to reveal life's great secrets to her while all along planning her debauchment. Marianne seduces Eugenie's hapless father (Paul Muller, in a paternal role very different than the one he plays in *Eugenie de Sade*) in order to secure his assent to her proposal that Eugenie come for a weekend visit to the private island getaway she shares with her stepbrother; their black boatman, Augustin (Anney Kaplan); and their deaf-mute servant, Therese (Uta

Dahlberg). Once there, Eugenie is wined and dined by Marianne and Mirvel, and slowly drawn into their world of sex and violence. Her "education" begins on the afternoon of her arrival, when she is drugged by her hosts and forced to participate in a quasi-incestuous ménage à trois. The following day, the rest of the Sadeian cult, led by the sinister Dolmance (Christopher Lee), arrives and subjects Eugenie, who has once again been incapacitated with drugs, to ritualized torture. Because of her intoxication and subsequent inability to ascertain whether either of these incidents actually occurred, Eugenie is disposed to regard them both as dreams, "terrible . . . so cruel . . . but wonderful, too." Soon afterward, though, she witnesses Mirvel in the act of murdering Therese and is then forced to kill him when he attempts to rape her. Surprisingly, Marianne is pleased by this turn of events, and we discover that, jealous of Mirvel's attraction to Eugenie, she has planned both of their deaths all along. Now that her stepbrother is out of the way, she hopes to sacrifice Eugenie in the same sort of ceremony she imagined at the outset of the film. Her scheme is foiled by Dolmance, however, who, following the perverse dictates of his Sadeian philosophy, makes Marianne the sacrificial victim instead; Eugenie delivers the coup de grâce with an enthusiasm that suggests she has learned much from her captors – and then Dolmance abandons the young girl to her fate. In a final twist, however, Franco cuts from Eugenie's frantic attempts to escape the island to a scene in which Marianne, staring pensively out her apartment window, takes a call from Eugenie about their impending weekend rendezvous. The scene is identical to one at the beginning the film, suggesting either that Marianne has daydreamed all of the ensuing events or that the characters are caught in a narrative loop that will play out the story again and again.

Like Franco's later adaptation of *Philosophy in the Bedroom, Eugenie . . . the Story of Her Journey into Perversion* demonstrates that the S&M horror film does not merely reflect the sadistic imperatives of patriarchal power and pleasure. Indeed, it confirms British novelist Angela Carter's observation that "however phallocentric the notion of sexuality implicit in Sade's pornography may be," aggression functions "in a serial fashion, now me, now you, and the cock, the phallus, the scepter of virility which is not a state-in-itself . . . but a modality . . . [is] passed from man to woman, woman to man, man to man, woman to woman, back and forth, as in a parlour game" (145). Certainly there is something of a power shift that takes place in the film as Eugenie is schooled in sadomasochism by Marianne and Mirvel. Although she is disturbed by what she remembers of her "dreams" after emerging from the narcotic haze that shrouds her S&M sessions, she is also clearly aroused by them. "Maybe you'll dream again tonight," Marianne suggests to her knowingly at one point. "I hope not – or do I?" is the telling response. There is even an implication that Eugenie has entertained fantasies about such activities before meeting the two cultists; she tells them that her experiences on the island are like a "dream I've had so many times before." By the end of the film, it is obvious that she has learned her lessons all too well. Rather than serving as Marianne and Mirvel's sacrificial victim, she becomes their executioner. She takes particular pleasure in Marianne's death, teasing her with passionate kisses before plunging a gigantic pair of scissors into her chest, removing her heart, and drinking her blood – a neat reversal of Marianne's fantasy earlier in the film, suggesting the ease with which the bottom can become the top and vice versa in the sadomasochistic scenario. It is important to point out, too, that viewers are primed to identify with Eugenie's empowerment. During the scene in which a drugged Eugenie is first ravished by Marianne and Mirvel, we adopt the perspective not of sadistic libertines, but rather of their household servants, Augustin and Therese, who, horrified but powerless to intervene, watch the proceedings from hiding spots behind the furniture. Like Eugenie, they are merely Marianne and Mirvel's playthings and Franco's camerawork and editing link us to them. Later in the film, when Marianne is killed by Eugenie as we look on with Augustin and the members of the Sadeian cult, we are invited to share vicariously in their sense of triumph over her. Far from reinforcing the notion that power relations are fixed and immutable, *Eugenie ... the Story of Her Journey into Perversion* reminds us how quickly they can shift, and even reverse themselves, in S&M.

Of course, the "scepter of virility" is passed to Marianne once more at the end of the film, thanks to Franco's last-minute narrative twist. This is all part of the ongoing "parlour game" Carter describes, however, and should be read as such rather than as a reinscription of the status quo. Indeed, it is important to recognize the transgressive nature of Marianne's character as a sovereign woman in the first place. Carter writes that Sade's work is significant for women "because of his refusal to see female sexuality in relation to its reproductive function" (1). Rather than being bound to the traditional role of wife or mother, women in Sade's fiction enjoy the same opportunities for power and pleasure as men do; gender is presented less as a defining physical characteristic than as an abstract concept that can be transcended. Thus in *Juliette; or, Vice Amply Rewarded*, written by Sade between 1797 and 1801: "The life of Juliette proposes a method of profane mastery of the instruments of power. She is a woman who acts according to the precepts and also the practice[s] of a man's world and so she does not suffer. Instead, she causes suffering" (Carter 79). In doing so, Carter argues, she becomes the equal of Sade's sovereign man: "Sade regularly subsumes women to the general class of the weak and therefore the exploited, and so he sees femininity as a mode of experience that transcends gender. Feminine impotence is a quality of the poor, regardless of sex. Juliette is an exception; by the force of her will, she will become a Nietzschian superwoman, which is to say, a woman who has transcended her gender but not the contradictions inherent in it" (86). This is an apt description of Marianne in *Eugenie . . . the Story of Her Journey into Perversion* as well. In some ways, she is the pivotal figure of the film, despite its title. It is surely significant that she – not Eugenie, Mirvel, or Dolmance – is the first character we see in the movie and, after Franco turns the clock back at the end, the last. Her fantasies and will-to-power drive the narrative and ultimately seem to render her impervious to death. Beautiful, imperious, seductive, and cruel, she represents every bit as much a challenge to the phallocentric social order as Eugenie does, albeit in a slightly different way. Rather than exposing the sadism of patriarchal power and pleasure through her victimhood, the way that the nominal heroines of both of Franco's adaptations of *Philosophy in the Bedroom* finally do, Marianne seizes that power and pleasure for herself, demonstrating without a doubt that they are up for grabs. She may be a distant figure in the movie, one whose perspective we do not share as much as Eugenie's, but she also stands as a potent example of the way in which S&M horror can tap into "film's radical potential to subvert social hierarchies and decompose relations of power" (Shaviro 64).

The same could be said of the sovereign woman at the center of Franco's *Succubus* (1968). Although this film is not directly based on one of Sade's novels, it is clearly inspired by his work: in addition to invoking his name several times, it revolves around a dominatrix who, like Juliette, exhibits a "profane mastery of the instruments of power." The movie's narrative is difficult to summarize succinctly, since it blends fantasy and reality in a surreal fashion that borrows heavily from contemporaneous art cinema – a debt that Franco openly acknowledges by having his characters discuss Luis Buñuel, Jean-Luc Godard, and Fritz Lang and by paying explicit homage to Jean Cocteau's *Orphée* (*Orpheus*, 1950), Federico Fellini's *La dolce vita*, Alain Resnais's *L'année dernière à Marienbad* (*Last Year at Marienbad*, 1961), and other key films of the period. It stars Janine Reynaud as Lorna Green, an actress who, as the story begins, is working at a nightclub in Lisbon where she plays a dominatrix in an S&M show designed by her boyfriend, an American producer named Bill (Jack Taylor). While they seem relatively happy together, she refuses to talk with him about her past, which has created a certain emotional distance between them. Matters are not helped by the fact that Lorna is often approached by strange men who behave as if they are former intimates of hers and call her "Countess." She rejects the title and tells Bill she has never met these men before, but privately she is not so sure. Her grasp of who she is has also been challenged by bizarre, recurring dreams that plague her sleep. In these dreams, she is a commanding, aristocratic woman who resides in an ancient white castle on the seashore and has apparently led many past lives in different places around the world. In each life, her existence has been devoted to actually committing the acts of eroticized violence that she simulates onstage in her current role as an actress, suggesting that her true identity is that of an immortal succubus – an evil female spirit who derives sexual pleasure from torturing and murdering men. Her smug psychiatrist, Ralf Drawes (Adrian Hoven), deems these dreams to be evidence of schizophrenic tendencies, but their veracity is seemingly confirmed by the presence of a mysterious, Mephistophelean man named Pierce (Michel Lemoine), who shadows Lorna throughout the movie, appearing both in her waking life and in her dream world. Moreover, the victims she claims in her dreams begin turning up dead in reality. As the boundary between Lorna's fantasies and reality grows progressively more porous, Bill begins to withdraw from her, finally leaving Lisbon for Berlin, where he intends to produce another show. He is unable to get her out of his mind, though, and is almost glad when she suddenly appears at his apartment in Germany. "Will you always stay?," he asks her. "I will stay until the end," she assures him, somewhat ominously. Indeed, it is not long before Bill, fearing more than desiring Lorna, seeks to rid himself of her for good. Back in Lisbon, he makes a deal with the elusive Pierce to have her killed. Bill puts Lorna into a trance during a rehearsal for the S&M show, causing her to actually murder her co-stars; when she subsequently flees the nightclub, Pierce is waiting to gun her down. The plan seems to work. Later, however, when Bill returns home, Lorna is inexplicably waiting for him. She seduces her dazed former lover with ease and then stabs him in the back of the neck as he embraces her. Afterward, Pierce drives her to the white castle from her dreams, telling her that her work is finished and that it is time for her to sleep once more.

Lorna emerges as a complex character in *Succubus*. On the one hand, her fate and her actions do not seem to be completely within her control. In the opening scene of the film, as she performs her S&M act at the nightclub in Lisbon, we see Pierce in the audience watching and hear his voice on the soundtrack: "I have done well. She is perfect. A disciple that mirrors my own image: the essence of evil, a devil on Earth." Having introduced the possibility that Pierce is a satanic figure and that Lorna is his creation, Franco proceeds to tease the viewer periodically with clues that this is the case. As noted above, Pierce appears throughout the movie, often in the scenes when Lorna commits her murders; in fact, his appearance often seems to precipitate these crimes. At one point, Franco photographs him posing next to a collection of classic movie monster figurines on the fireplace mantel in Bill's Berlin apartment, perhaps suggesting that Pierce is the true villain of the film. Finally, at the end of the movie, Pierce refers to Lorna as "Faustine," linking her to Faust, the German folkloric character who sold his soul to the devil in exchange for earthly power and pleasure. These clues point us toward a portrait of Lorna as a puppet of the devilish Pierce and seem to confirm Angela

Carter's observation that a dominatrix is "not cruel for her own sake, or for her own gratification" (21) – she is "most truly subservient when most apparently dominant" (ibid.).

On the other hand, Franco also offers hints that there is more to Lorna than this. To begin with, Pierce is often presented as her lackey rather than her master. We see him driving her around in a black Cadillac at various points in the movie – scenes that recall Heurtebise's chauffeuring of the deadly Princess in her Rolls Royce in *Orpheus*; at the conclusion of the film, he protects her from Bill's murderous scheme and pledges to guard her sleep. Moreover, Lorna seems to have her own agenda in *Succubus*. In an early dream sequence, she contemplates the figure of Pandora – "Pandora opened her forbidden box of evils," she muses in voice-over, "and cursed all men thereafter: vengeance!" – simultaneously recasting the first woman in Greek mythology as an avatar of feminist rage and inviting viewers to consider the parallels between Pandora and herself. The notion that Lorna is the latest incarnation of an age-old female spirit dedicated to violently redressing the power imbalance between the genders is lent credence not only by the past lives she has apparently led, but also by the single-minded purpose of those lives – an intentionality that prompts Bill to remark in one scene that she behaves as if she were "following a master blueprint lodged somewhere in her memory." Pierce seems to affirm this reading of Lorna when, after returning her to her castle at the end of the film, he intones in voice-over: "She loved the games men played with death when death must win, as though the slain man's blood and breath revived [her]."

Ultimately, it is as though Franco offers two competing portraits of the character: one in which she is the master and one in which she is the slave. The way in which the movie "blur[s] the boundaries between fiction and reality, perversion and playfulness" (Tohill and Tombs 94) makes it difficult to determine which is the truer. Phil Hardy points out that despite the blurring of "the borderlines between the various levels of the narrative" (191), we are left with a powerful impression of Lorna as "an oneiric creature condensing desire and death into a single figure" (191). Clothed in a form-fitting black jumpsuit as she puts her co-stars through their paces in the S&M show or in a flowing crimson robe as she strides purposefully through the streets of Lisbon (the impressive cos-

Theater of cruelty: Janine Reynaud performs the role of the Sadeian woman in *Succubus* (Trans American Films). *Courtesy of Jerry Ohlinger Archives*

tumes were created especially for the character by fashion designer Karl Lagerfeld), she cuts an imposing and attractive figure, offering, perhaps against the grain of the movie itself, a powerful point of identification for audiences. Like Marianne in *Eugenie ... the Story of Her Journey into Perversion,* she represents – at least at certain moments in the film – a genuine challenge to phallocentrism, a sovereign woman who offers the viewer the opportunity to performatively test the boundaries of normative sex and gender roles.

Finally, it is important to note that Franco's S&M horror films from this period encourage the viewer's performative exploration of sex and gender identity not only through their exploration of female sadism, but also through their exploration of male masochism. A key example in this regard is *Venus in Furs,* Franco's very loose adaptation of Leopold von Sacher-Masoch's 1870 novel of the same title. In this film, former teen idol James Darren plays Jimmy Logan, a jazz trumpeter whose life spirals out of control after he witnesses, but does nothing to stop, the sexual torture and murder of a beautiful young woman named Wanda Reed (Maria Rohm) by three of her acquaintances – Ahmed (Klaus Kinski), a millionaire playboy; Kapp (Dennis Price), an art dealer; and Olga (Margaret Lee), a fashion photographer – at a jet-set party in Istanbul. Wracked by guilt and unable to make music, Jimmy sequesters himself in his seaside bungalow after the crime. He cannot get Wanda out of his mind, even imagining that he sees her mutilated body wash up on the beach outside his home. Fleeing Istanbul in a desperate bid to forget her, he arrives in Rio during Carnival season and finds solace in the arms of Rita (Barbara McNair), a black nightclub singer who encourages him to take up the trumpet again. Before long, however, he finds himself haunted by Wanda once more. Seemingly alive, she shows up at one of his gigs dressed in luxurious furs and draws him into an obsessive sexual relationship that overshadows his love for music and for Rita. At the same time, Wanda begins appearing to the three individuals who murdered her, seducing them and claiming their lives in return, one by one. She and Jimmy eventually find themselves back in Istanbul, where, after she completes her revenge by torturing and killing Ahmed, the police track them down. Jimmy attempts to protect Wanda by taking her on the run, but when they seek refuge in a local church, she disappears. Frantically searching the grounds for her, he stumbles across her trademark furs draped at the foot of the grave where she was buried after her murder. In the final scene of the film, Jimmy has retreated once more to his seaside bungalow, where he again spots a body floating in the surf.

When he turns it over, he discovers that it is his own corpse. Franco zooms out, leaving Jimmy a small and powerless figure dwarfed by his surroundings, before fading to black.

Like *Eugenie . . . the Story of Her Journey into Perversion* and *Succubus*, *Venus in Furs* can be viewed in part as a celebration of the sovereign woman; Franco leaves no doubt that the beautiful and remorseless Wanda is the dominant figure in this film. She even has her own theme song, which Barbara McNair performs in a fantastic music video–like number as the ending credits roll. Ultimately, however, the movie focuses less on the suffering inflicted by Wanda than it does on the torment endured by Jimmy. It is his masochistic relationship with her that offers viewers perhaps the most unique opportunity for spectatorship-as-performance in the movie. For Gilles Deleuze, masochism represents a radical challenge to phallocentrism social order because of its insistence upon the supremacy of the mother figure. The masochist, he writes, "experiences the symbolic order as an intermaternal order in which the mother represents the law under certain prescribed conditions; she generates the symbolism through which the masochist expresses himself" (63). By fashioning the mother into the new representative of the symbolic law, the masochist banishes the father; indeed, when the masochist is beaten by the mother figure, it is understood that "what is beaten, humiliated and ridiculed in him is the image and the likeness of the father, and the possibility of the father's aggressive return. *It is not a child but a father that is being beaten.* The masochist thus liberates himself in preparation for a rebirth in which the father will have no part" (66). Rather than a simple reversal of the phallocentric order, then – a rejection of the "reality" of paternal law in favor of the "fantasy" of maternal law – masochism represents an effort to transcend the dialectical Oedipal relationship completely: "In masochism the masculine impulse is embodied in the role of the son, while the feminine impulse is projected in the role of the mother; but in point of fact the two impulses constitute one single figure; femininity is posited as lacking in nothing and placed alongside a virility suspended in disavowal. . . . We might say that the masochist is [a] hermaphrodite" (68). It is the emergence of this "new sexless man" (33) – born in an "atmosphere of suffocation and suspense" (25), taking pleasure in his repeated humiliation at the hands of a fetishized mother figure – as well as the novel viewing position such a figure offers to spectators, that interests Franco most in *Venus in Furs*.

The director invokes Deleuze's "new sexless man" in a number of ways in the film. Narratively, of course, it revolves around Jimmy's helpless obsession with Wanda and punishment at her hands; even its plot structure – which circles back to the beginning of the story at the end, suggesting that it can be seen as "an endlessly unresolved dream" (O'Brien 182) – reflects his masochistic desire to prolong the agony of his relationship with her, to escape, as he puts it, "from the real world into a dream world that [he] never want[s] to end." Franco also uses symbolism to emphasize that Jimmy has surrendered the prerogatives traditionally associated with masculinity in this relationship. At the beginning of the movie, we discover that in the wake of Wanda's murder he buried his horn in the sand – an apt, if obvious, metaphor for his disavowal of the phallus and one that Franco deploys throughout the film, linking Jimmy's (in)ability to perform musically with the ebb and flow of his association with her. More artful, perhaps, is the way in which the director represents Jimmy's masochism using camerawork, editing, sound, and other formal techniques. Certainly the manner in which he photographs Maria Rohm in the role of Wanda – in repeated low-angle shots, tilting slowly up the length of her body, which is fabulously decked out each time in silver heels, glittering hose and garter belt, black underwear, lush white furs, and a variety of different wigs – invites the viewer to see her as the fetishistic Jimmy does: as a dominant female figure supremely worthy of worship. The way that slow motion is used in the film is noteworthy as well. In the scenes where Jimmy pursues Wanda, such as the penultimate scene in the church cemetery in Istanbul, Franco slows the images down (and often brightly tints them as well), highlighting both the fantastical nature of their relationship and the atmosphere of sustained masochistic suspense in which it flourishes. A similar effect is achieved through Franco's extensive use of discontinuity editing, which returns us again and again to the same images as the movie unfolds: Wanda's mutilated corpse, the crashing surf, Jimmy's slow-motion sprint down the beach, and so on. Finally, Jimmy's omnipresent voice-over narration, especially his obsessive musings on the nature of his relationship

The emergence of the "new sexless man": abject masochism in *Venus in Furs* (American International Pictures). *Courtesy of Photofest*

with Wanda – "I was hypnotized," he rhapsodizes in one typical moment of introspection, "I was trapped in a whirlpool that kept sucking me in deeper and deeper" – vividly underscores his masochistic desire for her. More to the point, it, along with the other formal techniques, also invites the viewer to identify with Jimmy, to share that desire. The film is geared not only toward representing the "new sexless man," but also toward transforming us into him. Franco encourages the viewer to embrace "[m]ultiple, mobile spectatorial positions alternating identification and distanciation" (Studlar 192), reveling in what Gaylyn Studlar – describing the masochistic aesthetics of the films Josef von Sternberg made with Marlene Dietrich – has called the "visual pleasure of unpleasure." In the final analysis, then, it is the viewer who is being beaten, who is invited to surrender to the masochistic pleasures of *Venus in Furs*. Although this viewing position is diametrically opposed to the Sadeian perspective that viewers are often prompted to adopt (and sometimes to critique) in Franco's other S&M horror adaptations of the late 1960s and early 1970s, it epitomizes the kind of sexual role-playing that defines each of the movies discussed above and links those movies to other key examples of Euro horror S&M cinema.

My discussion of Euro horror S&M has, to this point, focused mostly on the heterosexual sadomasochistic scenario; it is important to note, however, that queer S&M – particularly lesbian S&M – is regularly featured in these films as well. Accordingly, I will end this case study with an examination of how two specific types of queer Euro horror S&M, the women-in-prison film and the nunsploitation film, can be said, because of their central investment in lesbian S&M imagery, to create what Alexander Doty refers to as a "queer zone" (9): a space "between the norms that regulate gender and sexuality" (Ross 271) opened up by "the theatrical agency of queer performativity, the campy dramatization of leathered queerness" (ibid.). The images associated with lesbian S&M – "the whips, chains, handcuffs, needles, razors, and other instruments; the bodies bound, gagged, tied, and suspended; the humiliating postures of the submissives; the military garb" (Hart 49) – have often been read negatively by both straight and queer critics as "a copy, an iconic representation" (ibid.) of the oppressive power structures informing the dominant heteronormative order. As Lynda Hart writes, however: "If we think of the erotic interplay of lesbian s/m as resignifications that are no doubt enabled by certain heterosexual or homosexual models but at the same time dissonant displacements of them, we might move toward a better understanding of their erotic dynamics" (49–50). Indeed, I will argue that the spectacle of lesbian S&M in Euro horror cinema "exposes the naturalized status of femininity (and masculinity) in ways that disrupt the power of heterosexualizing law" (Ross 271). At the same time, I will attempt to show that, like straight S&M, queer S&M in Euro horror cinema fosters "identificatory performativity" (Farmer 29), allowing spectators the opportunity to experiment with alternative viewing positions and sexual identities. I hope to demonstrate how queer Euro horror S&M invokes "those complex circumstances in texts, spectators, and production that resist easy categorization, but that definitely escape or defy the heteronormative" (Doty 7).

Let us begin with a consideration of Euro horror women-in-prison cinema. On the surface, it might be difficult to see how these movies challenge heteronormativity. As Judith Mayne has observed, the women-in-prison film – which originated in Hollywood during the studio era with social problem pictures like *Ladies of the Big House* (1931), *Caged* (1950), and *House of Women* (1962) – can seem to confirm homophobic stereotypes of lesbianism. She summarizes the genre formula as follows:

> A young woman either participated unknowingly in a crime; or participated in a crime because she was madly in love with a man who is a murderer or a thief; or didn't really participate in a crime but just happened to be in the wrong place at the wrong time; or is framed for a crime she didn't commit. She is sent to prison. There she encounters women (often in the requisite shower scene) who challenge her, try to seduce her, and make her life miserable. They include the prison warden, who is either kind and helpful or bitter and vindictive; the guard(s), who are also either kind or bitter, depending on the character of the warden; and of course the other prisoners. Among the prisoners, certain types are almost always present: a butch lesbian, an older mother-figure, a mentally disturbed woman, several prostitutes.... The heroine discovers that crime and corruption are going on in the prison.... By the end of the film the heroine has learned bitter lessons about life; she is no longer innocent. She leaves the prison but is destined for a life of crime (especially if she committed no crime to begin with); or is determined to get her sisters out of jail; or has learned her lesson and is determined to become a good, normal woman. Often as she leaves the jail another young, innocent victim arrives. (*Framed* 115–116)

The problem with such a formula, from the standpoint of queer theory, is that it "connects criminality and lesbianism, to the extent that the women in prison are made to seem more susceptible to lesbianism" (128). More or less implicit in classical Hollywood women-in-prison movies, this connection is totally explicit in the Euro horror women-in-prison films that began to emerge in the late 1960s, following the release of Jess Franco's *Der heiße Tod* (*99 Women*, 1969) and Narciso Ibáñez Serrador's *La residencia* (*The House That Screamed*, 1969). If the former "merely [hint] at the unhealthy atmosphere and the links between sadism, dehumanisation and power" (Tohill and Tombs 115), the latter offer "pretty much a catalogue of depravity" (117), (re)presenting the women's prison as

> a dehumanising hellhole, governed by perverts, lesbians and slimeballs. Prisoners are merely numbers, objects to be used and abused by the lowgrades who wield power. The camp commander is always a crop wielding dyke, the prison doctor a spineless impotent dupe. Together they corrupt the prisoners and play cruel sadomasochistic games. Their power is absolute. They take life

> and answer to no one. The authorities are implicitly in on the game, they don't care what happens to society's flotsam, all they care about is law, order and the status quo. Life is routine and doomed in a woman's prison. Escape is impossible and ends in futility, death and more gruesome incarceration. (109)

From this description, it seems clear that the Euro horror women-in-prison film equates lesbians with "perverts" and "slimeballs," and lesbian S&M with corruption and depravity. One might be forgiven for dismissing it – and its American cousin – as homophobic garbage that works to perpetuate the discriminatory ideology informing many of the images of queerness found in horror cinema.

This would be a mistake, however. As Mayne points out, while there is much to deplore in the American women-in-prison film – "in the sense that scenes of rape and torture are staples of the genre, and no matter how campy the films are, they still play on the helplessness and victimization of women" (*Framed* 115) – there is also much to appreciate, "in the sense that these films offer spectacles of female bonding, female rage, and female communities, with strong doses of camp and irony" (ibid.). The same could be said of Euro horror women-in-prison movies. In the first place, like earlier Hollywood women-in-prison films, they offer "images of women who are socially transgressive and active sexually and who must be chained and punished for violating patriarchal law and social order [that] can, for the female spectator, be quite inspiring at certain moments" (Zalcock 34). As Bev Zalcock notes, images of women who are "caged and chained, menacing and monstrous, husband killers, dykes, violent, rowdy and sexually active" (32) might seem to promise "a wet dream for a male spectator but they ... also always [represent] his worst nightmare, the castrating female" (ibid.). At the same time, they hint at the intriguing possibility of a nurturing, queer sisterhood of women that might exist as a refuge from the inequities of a male-dominated, heterocentric world. It is also important to recognize that like the Hollywood women-in-prison film, the Euro horror women-in-prison film undercuts and even subverts its own heteronormative tendencies with camp and irony, distancing viewers from the story and revealing its own representations of gender and sex to be fictive constructions rather than any sort of reality. Finally, Mayne finds the women-in-prison film compelling because it "does not just portray the 'objectification' of the female body as it has been theorized in feminist Film Studies . . . [but also is] predicated on the possibility that women observe other women" (*Framed* 117):

> Sometimes the notion of patriarchal authority is rendered oxymoronic in the women-in-prison film, for frequently the bastions of male superiority in the films are buffoons who are unable to shoot straight, for example, and especially whose sexual desire for the inmates renders them foolish and vulnerable.
> Indeed, what is quite striking about the women-in-prison genre is how marginal male figures really are to so many of the plots, and how thoroughly surveillance involves women watching other women, women objectifying other women. And the women-in-prison genre is one of the few established genres where lesbianism is not an afterthought or an anomaly. (117–118)

This holds equally true for Euro horror women-in-prison movies, which not only privilege the lesbian gaze, but also invite viewers to adopt it themselves. These films effectively seek to queer the act of spectatorship. Far from simply playing on homophobic stereotypes, Euro horror women-in-prison cinema "exposes the naturalized status of femininity (and masculinity) in ways that disrupt the power of heterosexualizing law" (Ross 271), while opening up a queer zone that offers an alternative to the dominant heteronormative order.

Take the case of one celebrated Euro horror women-in-prison film: Jess Franco's *Sadomania* (1981). It tells the story of a young, newly married couple, Olga (Uta Koepke) and Michael (Ángel Caballero), who are driving along the Spanish coast on their honeymoon when they decide to pull over to the side of the road for a quickie – despite the prominence of a nearby sign reading: "White Hacienda. Rehabilitation Center for Delinquent Women. No Trespassing." Their lovemaking is soon interrupted by a coterie of topless, rifle-toting female guards who take them captive and escort them to the office of the White Hacienda's sadistic bisexual warden, Magda (Ajita Wilson). Magda summarily declares that while Michael is free to go, Olga must remain at the prison until she serves out a sentence of indeterminate length as punishment for her encroachment onto its grounds. Once admitted into the White Hacienda, Olga undergoes the requisite abuse at the hands of Magda and the guards – whose favorite sport is to set prisoners loose in the surrounding swamp and then hunt them with guns – and bonds with her fellow inmates, most of whom are "confirmed lesbians" and unapologetically queer. She soon learns that the prison serves as a front for a white slave ring run by gay slave trader Lucas (played by Franco), and supported by Magda and Governor Mendoza (Antonio Mayans), a corrupt local official. When one of Olga's cellmates, Tara (Ursula Buchfellner), is sold to Lucas by the governor's wife because "it gives her a thrill," Olga formulates an escape plan with the help of her husband, who has been able to make contact with her from the outside. Together, they succeed in freeing the rest of the female prisoners and capturing Magda, whom they force to enter the swamp surrounding the White Hacienda. The film ends with the striking image of a nude and defiant Magda wading into the treacherous, alligator-filled waters.

Sadomania creates an unrepentantly queer economy of pleasure via its depiction of the lesbian S&M underworld of the White Hacienda. The subversive nature of the prison is made abundantly clear in the opening scenes of the film when Olga and Michael are arrested essentially for attempting to commit a heterosexual act on its grounds. Such heteronormativity is not permitted in this queer zone, as Magda's imperious response to Michael's protests in the face of his wife's sentencing makes clear: "Silence! . . . I'm not talking to you. . . . The Hacienda Blanca is a prison. [But] [i]t's not for you men. It's a women's camp. . . . I'm afraid the honeymoon is over." It is even implied that Olga's incarceration will put her heterosexuality at risk – and that this might not be such a bad thing. As Magda offhandedly suggests: "Who knows, Olga – you might like it here." Indeed, it is not long before Olga finds her sexual identity being tested. One of her cellmates, nicknamed Coñito (Andrea Guzon), propositions her after a long, hot afternoon working in the prison quarry: "What you need is a wet tongue on your body – that'll cool you off!" "That's all you lesbians think about, isn't it?," Olga snaps back. "Don't knock it if you haven't tried it," Coñito replies mildly. Later in the film, Coñito mocks Olga's heterocentric assumptions when Olga expresses her concern over Tara's forced visit to Mendoza's mansion for a session of kinky sex with the governor and his wife: "I'm just thinking of what they're doing to Tara. It must be horrible." "Are you kidding?," Coñito replies incredulously. "She's being wined and dined by the governor and eaten by his lovely wife!" Gradually, Olga's immersion in this environment breaks down her socially ingrained resistance to the notion of sexual experimentation. When she finally surrenders to Coñito's advances,

Franco adds a delicious note of irony to the eroticism of their sexual encounter by cutting away from their passionate lovemaking to a haggard Michael voicing his worst fear about his new wife's fate in the prison to a sympathetic listener: "I only hope they haven't killed her."

The irony of his heterocentric assumptions is compounded in a subsequent scene when he attempts to infiltrate the White Hacienda and rescue Olga, only to be captured by Magda, who ridicules his melodramatic straightness: "Well. What a surprise. The hero returns to rescue the princess from the evil dragon." In the context of Franco's queer S&M film, the prison's sadistic warden is not the villain, but rather a transgressive heroine who, as played by black transsexual adult film star Ajita Wilson, literally embodies "a challenge to easy notions of binarity, putting into question the categories of 'female' and 'male,' whether they are considered essential or constructed, biological or cultural" (Garber 10), while standing as the symbol of an alternative culture predicated on a recognition of the fluid nature of sexual roles and sexual identity. Michael, in contrast, emerges as a clueless agent of the dominant, heteronormative social order. Given that Franco cast himself in the part of the movie's gay slave trader – in one scene he is shown being happily buggered by a brawny, mustachioed black man (Ajita Wilson, in male drag) – it is not difficult to guess where his sympathies lie. And even though the film seems to end conventionally, with the defeat of Magda at the hands of Olga and Michael, it is telling that the formerly square, completely straight couple invites Coñito to accompany them on their future travels; their new three-way relationship testifies to the transformative potential of the queer zone to which they have been exposed. Moreover, it is significant that the last thing we see in the movie is the imperious and impenitent Magda slogging determinedly into the swamp, wearing nothing but a pair of leather chaps – a potent reminder and reaffirmation of the enduring power of unreformed queerness.

Franco is not content with merely representing the queer economy of pleasure over which Magda presides in *Sadomania*, however; he also encourages the audience to share in it by queering the act of spectatorship itself, by destabilizing the heteronormative male gaze and introducing ways of seeing that run counter to it. This process is apparent, for instance, in the scene in which Tara is brought to Governor Mendoza's mansion and forced to participate in sex games devised by him and his wife, Loba (Gina Janssen). On a narrative level, this scene is fascinating because although it quickly becomes clear that the couple's intention is to use Tara as a means of spicing up their own sex life – Mendoza is impotent and hopes to achieve a state of arousal with Tara so that he can make love with his wife and satisfy her wish for a child – her presence in their bedroom has the opposite effect. The governor is unable to perform and leaves the two women alone together: "I can't do it! I can't do it!," he sobs to Loba as he withdraws. "It's no good – you can give her a lot more pleasure than I can!" This indeed turns out to be the case, as is amply demonstrated by what follows. What makes this scene especially memorable, however, is how Franco shoots and edits it. First, he assiduously avoids cultivating the kind of heteronormative male gaze associated with straight porn. This is especially true at the beginning and the end of the scene, when Tara and Loba are having sex. Rather than fetishizing their lovemaking with leering close-ups, he films it obliquely – in reflections in mirrors with segmented glass, pulling in and out of focus – making it difficult for the viewer to see exactly what is going on (though the soundtrack leaves no doubt that the women are enjoying one another). At the same time, he privileges a queer gaze through his editing, which utilizes eyeline match cuts to link desiring female subjects with the female objects of their desire. Refusing to allow us to impose our own look, Franco instead invites us to see through their eyes, to share their look. In this way, the scene not only furthers the film's narrative motif of heterosexual coitus interruptus (the only time we see an act of heterosexual intercourse consummated is when Magda forces herself on a captive Michael in order to publicly humiliate him), it also contributes to the sustained effort on the part of the director to disrupt the heteronormative male gaze using purely cinematic devices. By celebrating "the theatrical agency of queer performativity, the campy dramatization of leathered queerness" (Ross 271), *Sadomania* succeeds in "open[ing] up spaces between the norms that regulate gender and sexuality" (ibid.) and giving viewers the chance to explore alternative sexual roles and identities.

The nunsploitation film, another popular form of queer Euro horror S&M cinema, offers similar opportunities for spectatorship-as-performance to viewers. Unlike the women-in-prison film, nunsploitation has its roots in European cinema, dating at least as far back as Benjamin Christensen's bizarre, unforgettable *Häxan* (1922) – which features a vignette about a possessed nun who triggers an outbreak of sexual hysteria in a convent – and possibly as far back as Georges Méliès's *Le diable au couvent* (*The Devil in a Convent*, 1899), according to fan-scholar Steve Fentone (25). It also owes a great deal to later, postwar art films like Michael Powell and Emeric Pressburger's *Black Narcissus* (1947) and Jacques Rivette's *La religieuse* (1966). In the early 1970s, the nunsploitation film emerged as a widely popular genre, energized by several key cinematic, literary, and historical catalysts: a wave of highbrow European sex comedies, including Pier Paolo Pasolini's *Il Decameron* (*The Decameron*, 1971) and *I racconti di Canterbury* (*The Canterbury Tales*, 1972); the international *succès de scandale* of *The Devils* (1971), Ken Russell's no-holds-barred adaptation of the Aldous Huxley novel about a nun's sexual obsession with a priest; and a renewed public interest in the story of the nun of Monza, an actual historical figure from the seventeenth century who, after being forced into a convent by her aristocratic family, defied her vows by having two children with a male lover and was punished by the Inquisition for it (Nakahara 127–128). Underlying these factors, of course, was the cultural fascination with sin and sexual transgression characteristic of the heavily Roman Catholic countries in which nunsploitation cinema first appeared – especially Italy, which produced Eriprando Visconti's *La monaca di Monza* (*The Awful Story of the Nun of Monza*, 1969), Mariano Laurenti's *La bella Antonia, prima Monica e poi Dimonia* (*Naughty Nun*, 1972), Domenico Paolella's *The Nuns of St. Archangel*, and other early examples of the genre.

The specificity of these influences might seem to mark off the nunsploitation film as an entirely unique form of Euro horror cinema; however, it has much in common with the women-in-prison film. To begin with, the narrative formula is more or less the same. As Bev Zalcock writes:

> Heavy manners and bad habits: sadomasochism, lesbianism, even Satanism are constant features of European nunsploitation films. Like the WIP [women-in-prison] genre to which it is closely related, nunsploitation boasts stock characters in endlessly reworked scenarios. Nun narratives usually feature an

innocent, a novice, who has arrived at the convent under duress, having been forced to take the veil by her family (or, in particular, her father). As such, the convent represents a prison, and its strict regime a form of prolonged torture . . . [presided over by] [t]he sexually frustrated and thus demented Mother Superior . . . [a] first cousin to the predatory matron of the WIP film, stalking the corridors for her prey. (148)

The nunsploitation film, like the women-in-prison film, establishes a space that operates as a queer zone. In the same fashion as the women's prison, the convent hints at the intriguing possibility of a nurturing, queer sisterhood of women that might exist as a refuge from the inequities of a male-dominated, heterocentric world. Moreover, the nunsploitation film "exposes the naturalized status of femininity (and masculinity) in ways that disrupt the power of heterosexualizing law" (ibid.). Like the women-in-prison film, it deconstructs the heterosexual norm, substituting an unrepentantly queer economy of pleasure in its place. Finally, the nunsploitation film works to queer the act of spectatorship itself. It encourages viewers to performatively adopt a queer gaze in the same way that the women-in-prison film does, using cinematic devices to subvert the male heteronormative gaze and introduce unconventional viewing positions that allow for the exploration of alternative sexual roles and identities. In all of these ways, the nunsploitation film emerges as a sister genre to the women-in-prison film, one that has just as much as its sibling to tell us about the radical potential of queer Euro horror S&M cinema.

Consider one key example of nunsploitation cinema: Joe D'Amato's *Immagini di un convento* (*Images in a Convent*, 1979). The film opens with the nuns at the Santa Fiora convent scrambling to prepare for a visit from a local cardinal. The beautiful, imperious Sister Marta (Marina Hedman) directs the elderly groundskeeper to make sure that there will be enough fresh fruit for His Eminence to eat; the groundskeeper shows her a dead rabbit he has found, hinting ominously that its torn, bloody corpse is a sign that the convent is cursed by an evil spirit housed in the strange, satyr-like statue that stands in the garden. Sister Marta dismisses his warnings as superstition, but subsequent events seem to bear them out. The visiting cardinal informs Santa Fiora's Mother Superior, Sister Angela (Aïché Nana), that a recently deceased nobleman stipulated in his will that a substantial portion of his wealth would pass to the church if his daughter, Isabella (Paola Senatore), were allowed to enter the convent as protection from her rapacious uncle's advances. Although Sister Angela objects to Isabella taking the vows "with no authentic call," she ultimately bows to the cardinal's will and agrees to accept Isabella into the cloister. Upon Isabella's arrival, however, it quickly becomes clear that she has no intention of living as a nun; indeed, it is revealed that, far from being an innocent victim of her uncle, she enthusiastically engaged in an incestuous affair with him and is fully committed to doing whatever it takes to escape the convent and be reunited with him. Her opportunity arrives when a handsome young man, Guido Bencio (Angelo Arquilla), is injured in a fight with the brigands that infest the local forests and is brought to Santa Fiora to recuperate. Meanwhile, as Isabella tries to figure out how to involve Guido in her escape plans, the nuns at the convent, already unsettled by recent developments, begin to fall under the spell of the mysterious statue in the garden, committing ever more lewd and outrageous acts. A lustful young novice, Sister Lacinia (Paola Maiolini), sneaks into Isabella's cell while she is sleeping and fondles her as Isabella dreams of sex with her uncle. Afterward, Sister Lacinia is caught in the hallway by Sister Marta, who whips her mercilessly as punishment and then tenderly licks the bloody gashes on her back before going down on her. Their sadomasochistic lesbian relationship intensifies as time goes on, and other nuns are overcome with erotic fervor as well, masturbating in their cells or pleasuring one another with homemade wooden dildos. A bewildered Sister Angela discovers that the convent was built over the ruins of an ancient pagan temple, of which the satyr-like statue in the garden is the last surviving remnant; the unholy deity of this temple, embodied in the statue, is responsible for the queer havoc wreaked on Santa Fiora. Desperate for help, Sister Angela sends for Padre Arnaldo (Donald O'Brien), an exorcist who may be able to rid the nunnery of this evil influence. But he finds that he is no match for the power of the sexual hysteria that has consumed Santa Fiora. Isabella, who has seduced Guido in order to secure his help in her planned escape, murders her new lover in an apparent fit of madness, while the nuns whom Padre Arnaldo has come to save taunt him from their cells in various states of undress before surrounding him, stripping him naked, and sexually humiliating him. In the final moments of the film, as the victory of pagan sexuality over repressive Christianity is made complete, D'Amato suddenly cuts back to the opening scene between Sister Marta and the groundskeeper, suggesting, as Franco does in *Eugenie ... the Story of Her Journey into Perversion* and *Venus in Furs*, that the events of the story will play out over and over again in an endless narrative loop.

The first thing to note about *Images in a Convent* is that it creates the same kind of queer zone that we find in *Sadomania*. Like the White Hacienda, Santa Fiora represents a space outside the heteronormative social order, a queer sisterhood that has deliberately cut itself off from the straight world and has no interest in its doings. As Sister Angela tells the visiting cardinal at the beginning of the film, "We try not to let news from the outside reach us." Within the convent, lesbianism, not heterosexuality, is the norm. Apart from church leaders, the nuns view men with suspicion and distrust. Sister Angela is not pleased about having to take in the straight Isabella, who has "no authentic call" to join the order. Of the dozen or so sex scenes in the film, only five feature heterosexual intercourse – and they do not present it in a flattering light. Straight sex is depicted as incestuous in the early scene in which Isabella has an erotic dream about her uncle as she sleeps in her cell (D'Amato further undercuts the heteronormativity of the scene by demonstrating through the editing that Isabella is sexually responding not to the dream image of her uncle primarily, but to the real caresses of Sister Lacinia, who has snuck into Isabella's bed). Heterosexual intercourse is then presented as rape in several scenes. Guido attempts to force himself on Sister Angela during his stay at the convent and later, in the film's most brutal and disturbing sequence, Sister Marta is waylaid and raped by two brigands as she makes her way to town to retrieve Padre Arnaldo. Finally, straight sex is depicted as psychotic at the end of the movie, when Isabella seduces Guido only to murder him immediately afterward. In contrast, D'Amato portrays lesbian sex in a decidedly positive light, characterizing it as passionate, pleasurable, and fulfilling – in short, everything that heterosexual intercourse is not. In scene after scene, as nuns kiss and fondle one another, play with improvised sex toys, and make love in a variety of different positions, the film lends lesbianism the kind of powerful erotic charge and allure that it consistently denies heterosexuality. Even the lesbian S&M scenes, violent though they are, end with the affirmation of a romantic bond between the partners – a bond that is almost entirely missing in the straight sex scenes. Through such means, D'Amato effectively queers the convent, transforming it from a space associated with the heterosexualizing law of patriarchal religious authority to a zone safely outside the norms that govern gender and sexuality. Of course, Santa Fiora is nominally under the control of the church, as the film's opening scene makes clear, but *only* nominally. The defeat and humiliation of Padre Arnaldo at the end of *Images in a Convent* highlights the limits of repressive heteronormativity; indeed, the way in which the final scene brings us back to the beginning of the story suggests that the lesbian desire invoked by the movie is ultimately impossible not only to exorcise, but also to contain narratively.

Like *Sadomania,* D'Amato's film works both to narratively transform a typically repressive and normalizing institution into a liberated (and liberating) queer zone, and to queer the act of spectatorship itself. Some critics have argued that the nunsploitation film actually invites an objectifying, voyeuristic gaze by offering up "the more deviant and excessive strands of renegade sisterhood" (Zalcock 148) for the spectator's viewing pleasure. In her reading of the genre, for example, Tamao Nakahara argues that movies like *Images in a Convent* "are pleasurable because they set up the repression/transgression structure and the voyeuristic 'ethnographic' lens around a stage on which anything that appears is constructed to horrify and excite us, and to excite us because it horrifies us" (132):

> With the fantastical ethnographic touch borrowed from Mondo films of the uncivilised within our civilised world, nunsploitation films display the nuns as the primitive within our modern culture. They are represented as caged tribeswomen who follow their own rules, power structures, and rituals that are not always comprehensible to "logical Western man." Once the camera enters the forbidden space of the cloister, it presents a freak show in which the unruly girls behave like primitives, expose their breasts, battle over convent hierarchy and partake in bizarre ritual whippings, all under the roof of the Church-sanctioned nunnery. (133)

I suggest, however, that the nunsploitation film is closer to the women-in-prison film than it is to the ethnographic film, in that it "does not just portray the 'objectification' of the female body as it has been theorized in feminist Film Studies ... [but also is] predicated on the possibility that women observe other women" (Mayne, *Framed* 117). In my view, movies like *Images in a Convent* deconstruct the disciplinary, heteronormative gaze Nakahara describes, privileging in its place a queer gaze attuned to the pleasures of lesbian S&M. In doing so, they foster the same kind of "identificatory performativity" (Farmer 29) as the Euro horror women-in-prison film. Take, for example, the scene in D'Amato's film when Sister Marta whips Sister Lacinia after discovering the highly aroused novice in the hallway outside Isabella's cell at night. Taking an approach reminiscent of the one adopted by Bava in *The Whip and the Body*, the director initiates a shot–reverse shot sequence that shuttles the viewer back and forth between the two characters' perspectives during the scene. First, we share Sister Lacinia's point of view as she cowers on the ground, looking back over her shoulder at Sister Marta, who towers over her, whip upraised; then we share Sister Marta's perspective as she brings the lash down on Sister Lacinia's bare back, drawing cries of pleasure and pain from her. And the viewpoint continues to oscillate, keeping time with the lashes of Sister Marta's whip: one minute the nun looms over us, whip raised, lust contorting her features; the next, we watch the novice writhe and moan under our punishment. The cinematography and editing in this scene prompt the spectator to behave not as a voyeur, but as a participant. We watch the lesbian sadomasochism depicted here (and the passionate lesbian lovemaking that follows) with a queer eye – a gaze in tune with "the theatrical agency of queer performativity, the campy dramatization of leathered queerness" (Ross 271). From this perspective, the renegade nuns onscreen are not ethnographic Others, but "us." *Images in a Convent* is constructed not as a "cinematic peep show and freak show" (Nakahara 132), but as an interactive viewing experience that gives spectators the chance to explore alternative sexual roles and identities. Ultimately, it is this sort of spectatorship-as-performance, in addition to a capacity for subverting sex and gender norms, that demonstrates the kinship between the nunsploitation and women-in-prison films, as well as the relationship between these two genres and the Euro horror S&M movies discussed earlier.

Many of the Euro horror S&M films covered in this case study emphasize the theatrical, performative nature of the sadomasochistic scenario. In *The Whip and the Body*, we believe that Nevenka is a victim of the ghostly Kurt's sadism until we discover that she took on his role as sadist after his death so she could prolong the masochistic pleasure she takes in being beaten. In *Eugenie . . . the Story of Her Journey into Perversion,* we see the Sadeian cult led by Dolmance flog a drugged Eugenie with whips, only to find out later that they were made of wool and dipped in red dye to leave what only *looked* like bloody gashes on her body. In *Succubus,* we are fooled into thinking that the sadistic sexual torture we see at the beginning of the film is real, when in fact it turns out to be a staged performance. This is not to say there are no scenes of genuine violence in these films; plainly, that is not the case. Rather, it is to point out that the S&M in these movies is often playful, blurring the line between fantasy and reality, pleasure and pain, in a teasing, tongue-in-cheek fashion. As Linda Williams puts it, the violence is depicted "as a highly ritualized game in which the participants consent to play predetermined roles of dominance and submission" (*Hard Core* 18). I hope it is clear by now that the ludic violence of the Euro horror S&M film has much in common with that of the *giallo*. While they tell very different kinds of stories, both of these types of Euro horror cinema invite us to approach film spectatorship as a form of play or performance in which we are free to try on and act out different sex and gender roles. By accepting this invitation, we replace the conventional cinematic experience and its fixed viewing positions with something closer to spectatorship-as-drag. In short, through their postmodern treatment of sex and gender, the Euro horror S&M film and the *giallo* film enable us to engage in a process of becoming Other. I will turn now to a final case study that considers how two other forms of Euro horror cinema accomplish the same thing through their treatment of race.

EIGHT

Cannibal Apocalypse

CANNIBAL AND ZOMBIE FILMS

Antonio Margheriti's *Apocalypse domani* (*Cannibal Apocalypse*, 1980) tells the story of retired Green Beret captain Norman Hopper (John Saxon), who attempts to settle back into life in suburban Atlanta after serving in the Vietnam War, only to find that he is suffering not only from post-traumatic stress disorder, but also from a contagious virus that is slowly changing him into a bloodthirsty cannibal. The film opens with a flashback sequence detailing a wartime mission he led to rescue a pair of American POWs held captive at a North Vietnamese village. His unit storms the village and locates the two soldiers, Charlie Bukowski (Giovanni Lombardo Radice) and Tom Thompson (Tony King), who are imprisoned in a pit. Recognizing Bukowski as a hometown acquaintance, Norman drops to his knees and extends his hand to help the men out. As his eyes adjust to the gloom, however, he is horrified to see that they are busy feasting on the corpse of a young Vietnamese woman who fell into the pit with them during the firefight. Before Norman has time to react, Thompson lunges toward him and takes a bite out of his arm. The flashback ends, and Norman is back in the United States after his tour of duty, unable to adjust to life at home. He is emotionally distant from his wife, Jane (Elizabeth Turner), suffers from terrible nightmares, and battles an almost uncontrollable craving for human flesh. This craving – which family friend and psychiatrist Dr. Mendez (Ramiro Oliveros) variously describes to Jane as a "contagious illness that manifests itself as a form of rabies" and a "biological mutation due to a psychic alteration" – only grows more powerful when the supposedly cured Bukowski is released from a nearby mental hospital and insinuates himself into Norman's life. Norman finds himself opening his refrigerator in the middle of the night to stare hungrily at a slab of raw meat that has begun to drip bloody juices onto the shelf below. During a guilty tryst with Mary (Cinzia De Carolis), a rebellious teenage girl who lives next door with her aunt and younger brother, he cannot keep himself from biting her leg in the throes of passion. Even when Bukowski is recommitted after a violent confrontation with the police at a local flea market, Norman cannot rein in his cannibalistic impulses. Ironically, it is when he visits the hospital where both Bukowski and Thompson are being held, desperate for treatment, that he finally surrenders to his urges, feasting on a lab technician and helping a nurse named Helen (May Heatherly), who has also been infected by the cannibal virus, to free his former army buddies. In a climax that recalls the ending of Carol Reed's postwar thriller *The Third Man* (1949), the quartet of runaway cannibals are pursued by the police through the sewers of Atlanta, where they are gunned down one by one until only Norman survives. He returns home and dresses in formal military attire before shooting his wife – who has been infected by Dr. Mendez, a victim of nurse Helen – and then himself. Arriving belatedly, the police pronounce the strange case closed. In a twist ending, however, it is revealed that Norman's teenage neighbor, Mary, and her younger brother have both contracted the contagious cannibal virus and are feeding on the flesh of their aunt, whom they have murdered and stored in their fridge.

My interest in *Cannibal Apocalypse* stems, first and foremost, from its direct engagement with issues of race. As a number of film scholars have noted, one of the most distinctive features of Western horror cinema, past and present, is its whiteness. Broadly speaking, the genre has been shaped by white filmmakers, dominated by the racial imagery of white people, and marketed to white audiences. As such, it is deeply implicated in a larger white discourse that "implacably reduces the non-white subject to being a function of the white subject, not allowing her/him space or autonomy, permitting neither the recognition of similarities nor the acceptance of differences except as a means of knowing the white self" (Dyer 13). This is certainly true of many classic horror movies made in Hollywood during the studio era – such as *The Mask of Fu Manchu* (1932), *King Kong* (1933), *Captive Wild Woman* (1943), and *Cobra Woman*

(1944) – which represent non-white characters as the embodiment of evil or subhuman savagery against which the symbolic purity and transcendence of whiteness is measured. One could say the same of more recent popular horror movies like *The Mummy* (1999), *Exorcist: The Beginning* (2004), *The Skeleton Key* (2005), and *Turistas* (2006). It is also important to note that in addition to the many horror films that explicitly Other the non-white subject, there have been far more that normalize whiteness by simply erasing the non-white subject entirely. Taken together, these movies paint a portrait of a genre that plays a major role in buttressing the racial hierarchy that informs the dominant social order.

There have, of course, been challenges to the hegemony of whiteness in horror cinema. The independently produced "race horror" movies of the 1930s and 1940s – *Drums o' Voodoo* (1934), *Ouanga* (1936), *The Devil's Daughter* (1939), and *Son of Ingagi* (1940), among them – feature mostly black or all-black casts, were occasionally directed by black filmmakers, and could be said to represent an attempt to make the genre relevant for African American audiences; a similar argument could be made about 1970s blaxploitation horror movies like *Blacula* (1972), *Ganja and Hess* (1973), *Abby* (1974), and *Sugar Hill* (1974). These films find contemporary equivalents in the thriving direct-to-video black horror market, which has turned out hundreds of titles, including *Crazy as Hell* (2002), *Vampz* (2004), *Hood of the Living Dead* (2005), and *Holla* (2006). In Hollywood, meanwhile, so-called color-blind casting has resulted in the greater visibility of non-white actors in popular horror movie franchises: *Jason X* (2001), *Halloween: Resurrection* (2002), AVP: *Alien vs. Predator* (2004), and *Saw IV* (2007), for example. We have even seen a few non-white actors in lead roles in mainstream genre films – such as *Queen of the Damned* (2002), *Gothika* (2003), *Snakes on a Plane* (2006), and *I Am Legend* (2007) – and the occasional emergence of non-white horror stars such as Wesley Snipes in the *Blade* series or Tony Todd in the *Candyman* series. One might also point to the contributions to Hollywood horror made by non-white directors like Kasi Lemmons, M. Night Shyamalan, Albert and Allen Hughes, Tarsem Singh, Guillermo Del Toro, Takashi Shimizu, and Ernest R. Dickerson. Finally, greater attention has been given to issues of race in such mainstream horror films as *Bones* (2001), *Land of the Dead* (2005), *Primeval* (2007), and *The Ruins* (2008). Despite these noteworthy exceptions, though, horror in the United States remains a largely white enterprise, one in which the raced subject and the subject of race are, to borrow a term coined by Mas'ud Zavarzadeh, "de-narrated." Or as Mark H. Harris, freelance entertainment writer and creator of the website BlackHorrorMovies, puts it: "While the marginalization of [non-white] actors in other genres translates into undeveloped characters and storylines, in horror, it translates into something more concrete: death. Usually the painful kind" (par. 1).

As Isabel Cristina Pinedo notes, however, race is "a *structuring absence* in the milieu of the contemporary horror film where monsters, victims, and heroes are predominantly white, a racially unmarked category" (111, emphasis mine). In other words, even when it is marginalized or de-narrated in horror cinema, race continues to inform and shape the films from which it has been excluded. Richard Dyer makes a similar argument in *White*, a groundbreaking study of the racial imagery of white people in Western visual culture that compellingly dissects the "invisibility" of whiteness by analyzing the way in which whiteness has reproduced itself as "neutral and unsituated – human not raced" (4). Observing that "as long as whiteness is felt to be the human condition, then it alone both defines normality and fully inhabits it" (9), he seeks to make whiteness visible, or "strange," again by exposing the paradoxical foundation upon which white identity is constructed:

> [It is a] vividly corporeal cosmology that most values transcendence of the body; a notion of being at once a sort of race and the human race, an individual and a universal subject; a commitment to heterosexuality that, for whiteness to be affirmed, entails men fighting against sexual desires and women having none; a stress on the display of spirit while maintaining a position of invisibility; in short, a need always to be everything and nothing, literally overwhelmingly present and yet apparently absent, both alive and dead. (39)

Interestingly, Dyer ends his study of whiteness by writing about the images of white death found in horror cinema. While he acknowledges that "horror as a genre does seem, despite some interesting exceptions, to be a white genre in the West" (210), he raises the possibility that the popularity of horror among white audiences stems not only from their perception of themselves both as "dead and as bringers of death" (ibid.), but also from the fact that the genre provides "a cultural space that makes bearable for whites the exploration of the association of whiteness with death" (ibid.). Dyer is intrigued by this idea, for "if the white association with death is the logical outcome of the way in which whites have had power, then perhaps recognition of our deathliness may be the one thing that will make us relinquish it" (208).

The virtue of *Cannibal Apocalypse,* in my view, is that it *explicitly* makes the association between whiteness and death that is only implicitly acknowledged in the Anglo American horror films that Dyer discusses. From the opening scenes of the film – the flashback sequence in which Norman and his Green Beret team rescue Bukowski and Thompson from their North Vietnamese captors – Margheriti confronts and explores the deathliness of whiteness. In images that are clearly meant to recall the infamous 1968 My Lai massacre, we see the American soldiers systematically burning the village and shooting even its most defenseless inhabitants. When a young North Vietnamese woman who has been set on fire with a flamethrower falls into the pit where Bukowski and Thompson are being held and is immediately devoured by them, it becomes clear that – unlike such celebrated Hollywood Vietnam War movies as *Apocalypse Now* (1979), *Platoon* (1986), and *Full Metal Jacket* (1987) – this film aims to lay bare the neocolonial impetus behind the conflict in Vietnam, using cannibalism as a metaphor to explore the seemingly boundless appetite for imperialist expansion exhibited by "white culture" (that is, the culture of whiteness described by Dyer). Crucially, Margheriti suggests that the cannibal virus with which these men have been infected is not a consequence but the cause of the war; its origins lie not in their bloody tour of duty, but in the society that produced them. It is for this reason that the bulk of the film takes place in suburban Atlanta rather than in Vietnam. By setting the story in the United States, the director is able to demonstrate that there is nothing particularly extraordinary about Norman and his cannibalistic friends: they are not anomalous, but representative, members of white culture. In fact, if anything, they are presented in a more sympathetic light than most of the other characters we encounter in *Cannibal Apocalypse,* including the creepy Dr. Mendez, who puts the moves on Norman's wife when Norman is not around; the rowdy biker gang that tangles with Bukowski in the flea market; and the bigoted police detective, Captain McCoy (Wallace Wilkinson), who, when he arrives on the scene of Bukowski's standoff with the police, impatiently demands of one of his officers: "Is he a subversive, a queer, a black, a Commie, or a Muslim fanatic – what the hell is he?" The only difference between these characters and the rampaging war veterans is that they are not literally cannibals – yet. It is only a matter of time before their participation in white culture also manifests as a craving for human flesh.

Indeed, there is seemingly no one left to resist the growing cannibal catastrophe in the film. Its non-white characters – Dr. Mendez (the Latino psychiatrist) and Tom Thompson (the black POW), both of whom help to spread the deadly virus – are shown to be totally complicit with the white power structure that is the source of the contagion. Even the movie's young white characters – in a possible reference to the collapse of the counterculture movement following the end of the Vietnam War – offer little in the way of resistance, as its ironic twist ending makes abundantly clear. After the police discover the bodies of Norman, Jane, and Dr. Mendez in the Hopper home, the director cuts to a long shot of the exterior of the house, featuring Captain McCoy and one of his officers. The officer asks, "Should I call the coroner, Chief?" McCoy answers with gruff assurance, "Yeah. And tell him this nightmare's fuckin' over." The film then cuts to a medium shot of Mary – the teenage neighbor whom Norman bit during a romantic encounter earlier in the film – and her younger brother watching the police from their kitchen window. The camera slowly zooms past them to focus on the refrigerator in the background of the shot, revealing that the door is open and a human hand is hanging out. "Will they look for Aunt Tina?," Mary's younger brother asks. Margheriti cuts to a long shot of the police deputy talking to the coroner on his patrol car radio and then back to Mary and her brother. They look at one another for a moment and then back at the police, chewing slowly as the final credits roll.

In the final analysis, *Cannibal Apocalypse* makes explicit not only the deathliness of whiteness, but also the way in which it will eventually collapse under the weight of its own moral bankruptcy. Far from emphasizing the physical rehabilitation of the returning veterans and the spiritual regeneration of the country following the Vietnam War in the manner of Hollywood films like *The Deer Hunter* (1978), *Coming Home*

(1978), and *Born on the Fourth of July* (1989), Margheriti's movie imagines an apocalyptic postcolonial scenario in which white culture, in the wake of America's failed attempt at neocolonial conquest in Southeast Asia (carried out under the guise of the Cold War fight against Communism), is finally doomed to consume itself as it has consumed so many other cultures.

Cannibal Apocalypse is not content merely to deconstruct whiteness at the level of narrative, however; it also seeks to disrupt the normative white gaze at the level of spectatorship by encouraging us to adopt viewing positions that allow for experimentation with alternative racial roles and identities. This invitation to spectatorship-as-performance is first extended in the opening scenes of the film. After presenting stock Vietnam War era footage of army helicopters flying over the jungle on military maneuvers, Margheriti cuts to a foreboding low-angle shot of the North Vietnamese village where the POWs are being held. His handheld camera captures shaky images of its inhabitants going about their daily routines when they suddenly hear the sound of approaching choppers. Shouting warnings to one another, they rush their children indoors and prepare their meager defenses. Ultimately, of course, they are no match for the Green Beret team led by Norman and are massacred in the sequence that follows. However, because we are shown the firefight from the villagers' point of view from the beginning, we are inclined to mourn rather than celebrate their demise. Indeed, it is almost impossible not to sympathize with them as the director shows the invading American soldiers acting brutally. These disturbing images effectively prompt us to identify performatively with the Asian "villains" and against the putative white "heroes" of the film.

Margheriti's disruption of the normative white gaze continues even after the story moves to Atlanta, albeit in a different register. There, he invites us to participate in the destruction of a white culture obsessed with war, conquest, and death by encouraging us to adopt the perspective of the cannibalistic veterans. Take, for example, the scene in which Bukowski wanders into a movie theater after being released from the mental hospital. The theater is showing a World War II film entitled *From Hell to Victory* to an appreciative audience, including a young couple who trigger Bukowski's cannibalistic urges when, apparently aroused by the carnage depicted onscreen, they begin to make out in the row in front of him. As Bukowski's bloodlust builds, Margheriti expertly cuts between his watching eyes, his view of the war movie onscreen, and his view of the couple necking in front of him. The sequence works not only to highlight the deep-seated, even erotic, attraction to violence Bukowski shares with the rest of the audience for *From Hell to Victory* – and with white culture in general – but also to intensify our excitement at the prospect of Bukowski claiming a victim and thereby spreading the contagion that will eventually lead to the apocalyptic end of the dominant social order. While the director does not provide a non-white point of identification here, as he does in the opening scenes of the film, he does once again prompt us to performatively adopt a viewing position that challenges the normative white gaze. From this perspective, we can recognize the sadistic and voyeuristic bent of that gaze and contemplate the possibility – the necessity – of dismantling it. Finally, then, *Cannibal Apocalypse* is as much about offering alternative modes of seeing, where race is concerned, as it is about offering alternative representations of race. For both of these reasons, it is a rarity in a genre that all too often attempts to avoid the question of race altogether.

As unique as *Cannibal Apocalypse* is, however, it is important to note that it is not alone among Euro horror movies in its attention to race. It actually draws upon two related and very popular types of Euro horror cinema to perform its critique of whiteness: the cannibal film and the zombie film. Unlike most modern horror movies, which tend to pass over matters of race and imperialism in silence, Euro horror cannibal and zombie films address these issues head-on. In the case of the Euro horror cannibal film, this means a return to the colonial origins of the cannibal. Recent Western horror cinema has manifested a veritable obsession with cannibalism; however, it is the spectacle of white cannibalism and the figure of the white cannibal – embodied most famously by Hannibal Lecter in a series of movies based on the work of novelist Thomas Harris – that have dominated the genre. This denotes a shift away from past representations of cannibalism in Western science, literature, and cinema, where the specter of the non-white cannibal served as a justification for the annexation and colonization of Other(ed) lands and bodies; unfortunately, it does not signify a shift away from the racism and imperialism that motivated such images – just a displacement of these attitudes. The displacement at work in modern horror cinema is not evident in the Euro horror cannibal film; there, the focus is almost always on non-white cannibalism. Critically, the figure of the non-white cannibal emerges in these movies not as a sign of white racism and imperialism, primarily, but rather as a means of deconstructing the dynamics of cannibalistic consumption at play in the historical relationship between colonizer and colonized. The figure of the zombie operates in a similar fashion in Euro horror cinema. While the majority of contemporary Western zombie films have dealt only with white zombies – zombies removed from the imperialist mythology that gave rise to them – Euro horror zombie movies often are concerned explicitly with the colonial origins of the zombie. They initiate a postcolonial counter-discourse that once again deconstructs the historical relationship between colonizer and colonized in an effort to interrogate the racist and imperialist attitudes informing colonialism. The apocalyptic postcolonialism of the Euro horror cannibal and zombie films does not just operate at the level of narrative, however; it also operates at the level of spectatorship. These movies open up ways of seeing that cut against the grain of the normative white gaze frequently invoked by Western horror cinema, offering viewers the opportunity to adopt differently raced viewing positions and experiment with a range of racial identities. It is, perhaps more than anything else, this capacity to foster spectatorship-as-performance that makes them, like the *giallo* and S&M horror films discussed in the previous two chapters, exemplary forms of Euro horror cinema.

The Euro horror cannibal film typically revolves around the story of white adventurers in the jungles of South America or Southeast Asia who run afoul of indigenous cannibalistic tribes and, when not slaughtered and eaten outright, undergo various forms of torture, humiliation, or initiation at the tribe's hands before escaping. This narrative formula is not exactly new: it recalls old Hollywood jungle adventure films from *Trader Horn* (1931) and *Tarzan the Ape Man* (1932) to *King Solomon's Mines* (1950) and *The Naked Prey* (1966), as well as early exotic exploitation movies like *Ingagi* (1930), *Gow the Killer* (1931), and *Angkor* (1935). Euro horror cannibal films were also partly inspired by Italian mondo films like *Mondo cane* (1962) and *Africa addio* (1966), which offer pseudodocumentary accounts of "titillating" and "bizarre" cultural practices from all over the world – but particularly from "primitive" non-white societies in Third World countries. To these influences, early cannibal films such as Umberto Lenzi's *Il paese del sesso selvaggio* (*Man from Deep River,* 1972), Ruggero Deodato's *Jungle Holocaust,* and Sergio Martino's *La montagna del dio cannibale* (*The Mountain of the Cannibal God,* 1978) added the kind of extreme gore and sexual violence that had become de rigueur in Euro horror cinema by that point, as well as a tone of brutal, dog-eat-dog nihilism, establishing a genre that quickly became notorious even among hardcore fans of Euro horror cinema. As Bill Landis and Michelle Clifford write in their appreciation of the grindhouse movies that played in theaters in New York City's Times Square during the 1970s and 1980s:

> Italy's most dubious horror achievement was birthing the cannibal vomitorium genre. These are among the most appallingly violent movies ever made, a deranged hybrid of giallo melodramatics and Mondo movie disgust. The violence promised by the zombie movies is delivered in amplified spades, and sometimes can be shockingly real. The films' subplots about Westerners lost in the jungle are mere frameworks for some of the most grotesque outbursts of violence ever recorded on film. Cannibal movies take you on a carnival ride to hell, where scenes of actual animal abuse alternate with hideous simulations of natives dining on other human beings. . . . [They] are among the most morally reprehensible of all exploitation [films]. (205)

The notoriety of Euro horror cannibal movies rests on more than just their stomach-churning scenes of actual and simulated violence, however; it also stems from their perceived racism. By reveling in "hideous simulations of natives dining on other human beings," they threaten to reduce the non-white subject to something less than human – an amoral, man-eating animal. On the other hand, by focusing on the heroic attempts of American or European adventurers to "tame" the jungle and its inhabitants, they seem to designate the white subject as something more than human – a morally advanced, spiritual being. The result, arguably, is a form of racial Othering in which the non-white subject serves as little more than proof of the innate superiority of whiteness.

Euro horror cannibal cinema abounds with apparent examples of such racial Othering. In *Mountain of the Cannibal God,* for example, Ursula Andress plays a woman who puts together an expedition to find her husband, an explorer who has gone missing in the jungles of New Guinea; when her search party reaches the island mountain of the film's title, it is captured by a tribe of indigenous cannibals whose savagery seems designed to highlight the racial superiority of the white characters. Jess Franco's *Mondo cannibale* (*Cannibals*, 1980) tells the story of a white researcher whose young daughter is kidnapped by cannibals during a scientific voyage down the Amazon River; certain that she is still alive, he returns years later in an attempt to rescue her from the natives, but discovers that she has been made their queen. Recycling the colonialist character of the white jungle goddess found in classical Hollywood films like *She* (1935) and *Blonde Savage* (1947), the film appears to "inscribe the White female imperialist as a figure of mastery... who embodies White female supremacy" (G. A. Foster 44–45). Meanwhile, in Umberto Lenzi's *Cannibal Ferox,* a white graduate student and her friends set off into the Amazonian rainforest on a mission to prove that cannibalism is a myth that was invented to justify the imperialist conquest of South America, only to be taken prisoner and gruesomely tortured by a tribe of cannibals who are all too real. Even more explicitly than the two movies discussed above, Lenzi's film seems to reject the postcolonial thesis that cannibalism has for centuries served as a justification for white imperialism, "proving" instead that the racist view of non-Western cultures as savage and primitive is supported by scientific and historical fact. All of these films, though, give the impression of seeking to Other the non-white subject, while at the same time normalizing whiteness, via the figure of the cannibal. On the surface, anyway, they demonstrate little, if any, interest in offering a postcolonial critique of race and imperialism.

In other words, there appears to be nothing to distinguish the images found in Euro horror cannibal movies from earlier representations of cannibalism in Western cinema. As Peter Hulme and others working in the field of Postcolonial Studies have shown, "cannibalism" – as a rhetorical trope divorced from any sort of empirical reality – was deployed by imperial powers in the West as early as the fifteenth century as a rationale for their subjugation and "civilization" of the New World. It was perhaps never deployed more intensively, however, than during the first half of the twentieth century, a time when these empires were desper-

White adventuress Ursula Andress surrounded by cannibals in *The Mountain of the Cannibal God* (New Line Cinema). *Courtesy of Jerry Ohlinger Archives*

ately trying to maintain control over their increasingly restive colonies. The new medium of cinema was key to this effort. In early ethnographic documentaries, filmmakers retraced the footsteps of the colonizers in order to capture "authentic" images of the colonized – that is, images that served to reinforce the link between racial Otherness and primitive savagery forged long before in the Western consciousness. These images frequently involved the figure of the cannibal. Travelogues such as those produced by Martin and Osa Johnson – *Cannibals of the South Seas* (1912), *Among the Cannibal Isles of the South Pacific* (1918), and *Head Hunters of the South Seas* (1922), for example – obsessively stage what Hulme has called the "primal scene of 'cannibalism'" (2) in order to represent racial Otherness "as exotic and uncontrollable" (G. A. Foster 158). The same is true of early narrative films, including such silent comedies as *King of the Cannibal Islands* (1908), *Queenie and the Cannibal* (1912), and *Canning the Cannibal King* (1917), as well as animated shorts like *On the Cannibal Isle*

(1916) and *Cannibal Capers* (1930). While our first instinct might be to preserve a distinction between the cinema of "fact" and the cinema of "fiction," Gwendolyn Audrey Foster has shown that early narrative films like these actually represent "an extension of the ethnographic practice of denial of subjectivity, and the privileging of the gaze of the captor over the 'primitive,' 'exotic,' 'sexual,' backwards, and romantic savage" (3). Both served imperialist interests not only by facilitating the dissemination of the centuries-old, racist trope of cannibalism, but also by inviting what Fatimah Tobing Rony calls "fascinating cannibalism": in this case, the cannibalism practiced by "the consumers of the images of the bodies – as well as actual bodies on display – of native peoples offered up by popular media and science" (10). More important, both helped to inaugurate an enduring line of cinema in which "the viewer/maker seeks to 'capture' the dark continent, and the Black body, defining Whiteness against the backdrop of this simulacrum of the dark body" (G. A. Foster 2). This line of cinema includes the classical Hollywood jungle adventures and exotic exploitation movies mentioned earlier – movies like Columbia's serial film *Cannibal Attack* (1954) and the independently produced shockumentary *Cannibal Island* (1956) – which make explicit use of the figure of the non-white cannibal in order "to focus on difference, to emphasize Otherness" (Schaefer 269). It would also seem to include the Euro horror cannibal cinema, given the obvious debt that genre owes to these kinds of films. I will argue in the pages that follow, however, that this is not the case – that Euro horror cannibal movies actually work in many ways against the racist and imperialist agenda motivating earlier cinematic representations of cannibalism. In order to understand how they do so, we first need to take a look at the transformation that the figure of the cannibal has undergone in contemporary Hollywood cinema.

Although films about cannibalism are arguably more prevalent today than ever before, they no longer revolve around the figure of the non-white cannibal; instead, they take white cannibalism as their subject. Hollywood movies like *Wrong Turn* (2003), *Sin City* (2005), *Black Christmas* (2006), *The Hills Have Eyes* (2006), *The Texas Chainsaw Massacre: The Beginning* (2006), and *Sweeney Todd: The Demon Barber of Fleet Street* revel in the spectacle of white people eating human flesh. Indeed, the white cannibal has emerged as something of a cult hero in contemporary American cinema. This is nowhere more apparent than in the pop culture canonization of Hannibal Lecter, the urbane psychiatrist and bloodthirsty cannibal who has appeared in a series of films based on the novels of Thomas Harris: *Manhunter* (1986), *The Silence of the Lambs* (1991), *Hannibal* (2001), *Red Dragon* (2002), and *Hannibal Rising* (2007). An initial indication of Lecter's popularity came in early 1992, when Anthony Hopkins, the actor who has played the character in all but two of the films listed above, won an Oscar for his role in *The Silence of the Lambs* – an almost unheard-of feat for a performer in a horror film. Further confirmation came a decade later, with the astonishing commercial success of *Hannibal*, Ridley Scott's much-anticipated sequel to *The Silence of the Lambs*. The gory, ultraviolent *Hannibal* earned over $58 million during its first weekend in domestic release – at that time a record opening weekend for an R-rated film and the third-largest opening weekend ever, after Steven Spielberg's *The Lost World: Jurassic Park* (1997) and George Lucas's *Star Wars Episode I: The Phantom Menace* (1999) ("Box Office" pars. 1–3). It played in theaters for twenty-six weeks in the United States, where it grossed over $165 million in box-office receipts ("Hannibal" par. 1). CBS responded to the public's enthusiasm for *Hannibal* by acquiring exclusive television broadcast rights to the film, which the network ran, recut with additional footage not included in the theatrical version, as a four-hour television miniseries during the November 2003 sweeps. And predictably, a sequel to *Hannibal* was immediately rushed into production with Hopkins again in the lead role. Released just a year after Scott's film, *Red Dragon* – a remake of the original Hannibal Lecter movie, *Manhunter*, which featured Brian Cox as the character rather than Hopkins – was specifically designed to satisfy the public's demand to know more about Lecter's early anthropophagic exploits. The same is true of *Hannibal Rising*, which offers a triumphant account of Lecter's transformation from a World War II orphan into a cannibalistic avenger who hunts down and eats the Nazi collaborators responsible for his family's demise. The apotheosis of Hannibal Lecter – his evolution from a minor character in *Manhunter* to a major character in *The Silence of the Lambs* to the central character in *Hannibal*, *Red Dragon*, and *Hannibal Rising* – stands as possibly the most powerful testament to the contemporary American fascination with white cannibalism. But what are we to make of this fascination? If Mark Seltzer is correct in his sobering assertion that the "spectacular public representation of violated bodies ... has come to function as a way of imagining and situating our notions of public, social, and collective identity" (21), what does the seeming ubiquity of white cannibalism in recent Hollywood movies say about us at the beginning of the twenty-first century?

Some critics have interpreted the privileged place of the white cannibal in contemporary pop culture as a positive indication that, in Maggie Kilgour's words: "The man-eating myth is still with us, but now explicitly revealed to be a story about *ourselves,* not others" (247). Since – unlike their "primitive" and "savage" antecedents – cannibals today are "sited by Western subjects *among themselves* rather than in a distant 'other' world" (Bartolovich 234), cannibalism, it has been suggested, might now function as a "means of satire, a trope with which we parody more idealised myths about ourselves" (Kilgour 241). Crystal Bartolovich contends, for example, that the pervasiveness of white cannibalism in mainstream films can be read as "one of the morbid symptoms of capitalist appetite in crisis" (234); for her, the white cannibal is the villainous embodiment of a key socioeconomic dilemma of our time: the "desire for infinite (capitalist) consumption and its impossibility" (232). Bartolovich's account of the "cultural logic of late cannibalism" (her witty repurposing of Fredric Jameson's famous phrase) is intriguing; however, it is also flawed in my view, given that white cannibals like Hannibal Lecter are more often than not portrayed sympathetically, even heroically, in contemporary cinema – not vilified or parodied as symptoms of postmodern malaise. I take the valorization of white cannibalism in recent Hollywood movies as a sign that a solution to the socioeconomic dilemma Bartolovich describes has already been negotiated: a solution that involves the simultaneous reinvocation and disavowal of racial Otherness in response to the "problematic" factors limiting white consumption. It seems to me that Hollywood has symbolically reclaimed and "de-raced" cannibalism because on some level Americans recognize its relation to our public, social, and collective identity as a late capitalist culture of whiteness that, having exhausted its own resources, has turned to the business of eating the Other.

In other words, the omnipresence of white cannibals – and the near absence of non-white cannibals – in contemporary American cinema should not be taken as a sign that the project of imperialism has finally been deconstructed and abandoned, but rather as evidence that it has been reinvented and perfected to the point of near transparency. The prevailing cannibal chic that has elevated Hannibal Lecter to the level of pop culture icon stands as an example of what Jean Baudrillard calls "antiethnology" – paradoxically, "the pure form of triumphal ethnology, under the sign of dead differences, and . . . the resurrection of differences" (8). In *Simulacra and Simulation,* Baudrillard explains: "As ethnology collapses in its classical institution, it survives in an antiethnology whose task it is to reinject the difference fiction, the Savage fiction, everywhere, to conceal that it is this world, ours, which has again become savage in its way, that is to say, which is devastated by difference and death" (9). Accordingly, he argues, it is "very naïve to look for ethnology in the Savages or in some Third World – it is here, everywhere, in the metropolises, in the White community, in a world completely catalogued and analyzed, then *artificially resurrected under the auspices of the real*" (8). Following Baudrillard, I suggest that the ubiquity of white cannibals in recent Hollywood movies is a symptom of the reinjection of the "difference fiction," an emblem of both the endemic denial of cultural difference and, simultaneously, the affirmation of that difference. This paradoxical play of denial and affirmation informs the neoimperialist project of globalization, in which First World multinational corporations, deploying the rhetoric of global unity and the rhetoric of Western superiority in equal measure, create and exploit Third World markets. White cannibalism, in short, has become one of the most visible signs of our effort to make the world safe for Western trade by commercially (re)colonizing those domains that the West could not subjugate militarily or politically in the twentieth century.

In order to resist the antiethnological impulse in twenty-first-century American pop culture and the project of cultural imperialism it both reflects and reinforces, it is necessary to create images and narratives that somehow lay bare the dynamics of cannibalistic consumption at play in the contemporary relationship between colonizer and colonized. One strategy for doing so would be to produce works of experimental ethnography that subvert and radically reinvent the language of classical ethnographic cinema. Catherine Russell associates the "decolonization of ethnographic film" with the "experimental critique of realist film languages – both narrative and documentary – and the development of new forms of audiovisual representation" (25). Writing along similar lines, Jay Ruby argues: "Ethnographic filmmakers must disassociate themselves from ... naïve realism and produce films that will become viewed as the filmmakers' construction of the social construction of the actuality of the people portrayed – an interpretation of someone else's interpretation" (275). This theory of ethnographic self-reflexivity has been put into practice by Trinh T. Minh-ha, who rejects the notion of "speaking for" or "speaking about" Others in ethnographic cinema, and instead searches in films like *Reassemblage* (1983) and *The Fourth Dimension* (2001) for a means of "speaking that does not objectify, does not point to an object as if it is distant from the speaking subject or absent from the speaking place. A speaking that reflects on itself and can come very close to a subject without, however, seizing or claiming it" (218). In the same spirit, Dennis O'Rourke deconstructs the myth of the "primitive" Other as cannibal in his film *Cannibal Tours* (1989). Documenting the encounters between wealthy white tourists traveling up the Sepik River in Papua New Guinea and the supposedly cannibalistic indigenous people whom they have paid to see, O'Rourke demonstrates that, in fact, what "remains of the primitive world are ex-primitives, recently acculturated peoples lost in the industrial world, and another kind of ex-primitive, still going under the label 'primitive,' a kind of performative primitive" (MacCannell 100). It is the tourists, he shows, who are guilty of "cannibaliz[ing] the primitive" (113). Unlike Hollywood movies that revel in the spectacle of white cannibalism, then, experimental documentaries like *Cannibal Tours* effectively resist the antiethnological spirit of contemporary American pop culture, revealing exactly who is cannibalizing whom today. I argue, however, that they are not alone in doing so – that there exist other strategies for laying bare the dynamics of cannibalistic consumption at play in the neoimperialist relationship between the First World and the Third World, which have been deployed by films that might seem, at first glance, to be as far removed from those of the experimental documentaries as possible.

I am referring, of course, to Euro horror cannibal movies. I would like to demonstrate that, despite the reputation for unmitigated racism they have acquired, they distinguish themselves not only from earlier ethnographic and narrative films dealing with cannibalism, but also from contemporary Hollywood cannibal movies by the way in which they use the trope of cannibalism to deconstruct the myth of white superiority that has driven Western imperialism for centuries. This approach is visibly at work even in the notorious examples of Euro horror cannibal cinema described earlier. In *The Mountain of the Cannibal God*, for example, Martino reveals that, far from being motivated by the altruistic desire to rescue her husband from the cannibals who captured him, the white adventuress played by Ursula Andress is bent on exterminating the tribe so she can exploit uranium deposits that lie beneath the film's titular mountain. *Cannibal Ferox* likewise exposes the violence and duplicity of white imperialism by implicating its "heroes" in the South American drug trade and focusing in detail on their acts of cruelty against the indigenous population. When the natives retaliate by capturing, torturing, and eating them, the sole survivor – the graduate student who initially set out to expose the myth of cannibalism – covers up her friends' misdeeds by submitting a fraudulent thesis that "proves conclusively" that cannibals do not exist. Even *Cannibals,* which seems simply to revive the tired colonialist fantasy of the white jungle goddess, works to emphasize the link between whiteness and deathliness – largely by taking the cannibal film into the realm of parody. As one fan puts it, Franco's movie features "some of the most unconvincing cannibals you're ever likely to see! Seriously, the tribesmen speak English as well as ooga booga, are mostly white (this makes their fighting words like *'Death to the white invaders!'* seem quite comical) and sport distinctly European hairstyles and beer bellies, and their garish face paint actually makes them look more like rabid football fans dressed up for the grand final [sic] than a bunch of primitive savages" (Villinger par. 5). The unconvincingly "raced" cannibals in *Cannibals* prompt viewers to question not only the authenticity of these characters, but also the veracity of the broader myth from which they spring; through his parodic approach to filming cannibalism, Franco suggests, quite correctly, that anthropophagy has more to do with the racist projections of white culture than it does with the actual cultural practices of Amazonian tribes. Like *The Mountain of the Cannibal God* and *Cannibal Ferox*, then, *Cannibals* ultimately demonstrates that *we* are the cannibals, not the non-white colonial subjects to whom this epithet has historically been attached. Euro horror cannibal films do not merely deconstruct whiteness at the level of narrative, however. As my analysis of *Cannibal Apocalypse* indicates, they also seek to disrupt the normative white gaze at the level of spectatorship by encouraging viewers to adopt perspectives that allow for experimentation with alternative racial roles and identities. In effect, they invite us to identify against the colonizer and with the colonized – to recognize the true dynamics of cannibalistic consumption that continue to inform the relationship between East and West, and to relish the reversal of those dynamics. For all of these reasons, Euro horror cannibal cinema warrants the same kind of serious consideration accorded to experimental ethnography; against all odds, these films demonstrate the same kind of capacity to interrogate white racism and imperialism.

A prime example in this regard is Ruggero Deodato's *Cannibal Holocaust*, perhaps the most infamous Euro horror cannibal movie ever made. The film's narrative breaks down into two main parts. The first half of the story deals with an expedition launched by noted NYU anthropologist Harold Monroe (Robert Kerman) to find a crew of documentary filmmakers that recently disappeared while on assignment in the Amazon jungle. With the help of a guide, Monroe retraces the filmmakers' footsteps, pushing farther and farther into the "green inferno," until he uncovers evidence that they died at the hands of the Yanomamo, a fearsome tribe of cannibals. Soon afterward, the expedition makes contact with the Yanomamo and Monroe is able to use his knowledge as an anthropologist to overcome their intense distrust of outsiders; he is initiated into the tribe and then led to a clearing where the bones and equipment of the missing filmmakers have been arranged into a totemic shrine. Sifting through the debris, he finds sealed cans containing the film they shot before their deaths and brings it back to New York for inspection by the television executives for whom the filmmakers were working. The second half of the movie, anticipating later horror films like *The Blair Witch Project* (1999) and *Paranormal Activity* (2007), revolves around a screening of the recovered footage. It reveals that the dead filmmakers – Alan Yates (Gabriel Yorke), Faye Daniels (Francesca Ciardi), Jack Anders (Perry Pirkanen), and Mark Tomaso (Luca Giorgio Barbareschi) – committed shocking atrocities in pursuit of their "documentary" about life in the Amazon. Ensconced in a private screening room at the television studio, Monroe and the executives watch with mounting horror as Yates and his crew film themselves casually mutilating and killing animals, raping native women, and burning villages – all in order to create a sensationalistic story for their movie. Finally, the Yanomamo tribe takes revenge by cornering, torturing, killing, and eating the filmmakers; the last thing captured by the white filmmakers' camera is their own gruesome death. When the final reel ends, the executives decide to bury the film in their archives and Monroe leaves the television studio in a daze, wondering "who the *real* cannibals are."

That question is central to *Cannibal Holocaust* and is raised by Deodato from the beginning of the film. In the opening scene, a white television reporter standing atop the Empire State Building solemnly advises the viewer that although "we are already on the threshold of conquering our galaxy ... man seems to ignore the fact that on this very planet there are still people living in the Stone Age and practicing cannibalism – primitive tribes isolated in a ruthless and hostile environment where the prevailing law is survival of the fittest." "[B]efore venturing into space," he concludes, "we should become more familiar with the planet we live on." As the reporter delivers this smug lecture, however, the director cuts not to the expected images of the "green inferno" and its "savage" inhabitants, but rather to a montage of shots showing the towering skyscrapers and crowded streets of New York City. The surprising counterpoint between image and sound here suggests that white culture is the real "ruthless and hostile environment" populated by cannibals.

The connection between whiteness and deathliness is cemented by the reprehensible behavior of Yates and his documentary crew. Although the director initially presents them as heroic white adventurers who set out to help "man" become "more familiar with the planet we live on" before they tragically went missing in the Amazon jungle, Deodato ultimately shows them to be sadistic psychopaths who will go to any lengths to satisfy the Western public's insatiable appetite for exotic images of the Other. Tellingly, the filmmakers feel compelled to manufacture these images, since the idea of racial Otherness they promote in their "documentaries" is just that – an idea, not reality. A key scene in this regard is the one in which Yates instructs his crew to burn to the ground a village inhabited by the peaceful Yacùmo tribe so they can simulate an attack by the Yanomamo for their movie. As they herd the bewildered Yacùmo into their huts at gunpoint and set fire to the thatched roofs – while Yates shouts excitedly into the camera, "In the jungle, it's the daily violence of the strong overcoming the weak!" – it becomes manifestly clear that the "savages" in *Cannibal Holocaust* are not the indigenous people whom Yates and his crew capture on film, but rather the white filmmakers themselves. Thus Monroe's question at the end of the movie – "I wonder who the *real* cannibals are?" – is answered before it is even asked: white Westerners are. Deodato shows these representatives of white culture as "dead and as bringers of death" (Dyer 210) not only because of their actual murderousness, but also because of the role they play in feeding the Western hunger for "images of the bodies ... of native peoples" (Rony 10).

Of course, not all of the cannibalism in *Cannibal Holocaust* is metaphorical. At the end of the film, Yates and his crew *are* literally eaten by the Yanomamo. To a certain extent, perhaps, this narrative twist undercuts Deodato's postcolonial critique of Western imperialism as inherently cannibalistic, reinscribing the centuries-old trope of the non-white colonial subject as cannibal. As Jay McRoy notes, "in both its representation of the indigenous population of South America as cannibalistic, and in its actual extermination of animal life for entertainment, the picture ultimately risks perpetuating the very ideologies it pretends to critique" (40). In other words, *Cannibal Holocaust* may well be "guilty of the transgressions which it seeks to condemn" (Fenton, Grainger, and Castoldi 65). In his comprehensive essay on the history of the movie, however, Andrew DeVos argues that to "understand such a complex and convoluted film requires dialectic, not diatribe, for *Cannibal Holocaust* is both trash and treasure" (95); indeed, it "is an intentionally contradictory film employing hypocritical methods to discuss paradoxical social, psychological, and moral issues, and thus deserves a contradictory reading. It blurs reality and fantasy and forces the viewer to sort out the difference and identify the savages on both sides of the screen" (ibid.). Certainly, there is a delicious irony in Deodato's reversal of the historical relationship between colonizer and colonized: the white Westerners who have been feeding off the indigenous population of South America for so long are themselves eaten. And there is no question how we feel about this. As one fan, Scott Ashlin, writes of the film on his movie review website: "By the time the cannibals get their hands on Yates, we're practically cheering for them" (par. 8). Rather than inviting us to identify with the white adventurers, the way that classical Hollywood jungle movies do, *Cannibal Holocaust* encourages us to identify with the non-white natives and to see their consumption of the documentary crew as a form of poetic justice. In this respect, it resembles certain examples of "Third Cinema" made in Brazil and other South American countries in the 1960s and 1970s as part of the tropicalist movement. Joaquim Pedro de Andrade's *Macunaíma* (1969) and Nelson Pereira dos Santos's *Como Era Gostoso o Meu Francês* (*How Tasty Was My Little Frenchman*, 1971) also use the figure of the non-white cannibal as a means of exposing and redressing the injustices of Western imperialism. Like De Andrade and Dos Santos, Deodato returns to the "primal scene of 'cannibalism'" (Hulme 2) not to resuscitate it as a colonialist trope, but rather to put it to a distinctly postcolonial use.

Cannibal Holocaust could be said to move beyond the postcolonial critique carried out by these tropicalist films insofar as it interrogates not only the concept of cannibalism, but also the primary means by which this concept has been promulgated over the last century: moving pictures. Speaking about his movie, Deodato has said: "At that time on the television we were always seeing death scenes . . . and my film was . . . a condemnation of a certain kind of journalism" (qtd. in Fenton, Grainger, and Castoldi 19). Harvey Fenton, Julian Grainger, and Gian Luca Castoldi see it as a response, more specifically, to the kind of exotic exploitation cinema popularized in Italy during the 1960s by the quasi-documentary mondo film:

> *Cannibal Holocaust* is the bastard son of the mondo genre. It seeks to critique the form and lambast the methods of its proponents. It questions the integrity of all

> involved in an industry which sells images of genuine pain, humiliation, torture and death, packaged for the consumer under the guise of "public interest" programming.... Were the film-makers really just innocent spectators, recording incidents in the real world as and when they happened? Or were they perhaps partly responsible for what they filmed, catalysts who precipitated events so that their camera lenses could capture sacred moments of life and death simply to fulfil [sic] the voracious demands of the commercial media machine? (64–65)

By raising these questions, Deodato engages in a "deconstruction of authenticity, a practice that posits so-called 'verist' or 'documentary' film-making as every bit as constructed and manipulative as any other cinematic tradition" (McRoy 40). He also calls to our attention to the way in which documentary cinema has supported the project of Western imperialism by depicting non-white people as primitive, savage Others. As McRoy points out, the look of Deodato's film recalls "mass media images from Vietnam, Africa, and other sites of brutal colonial aggression ... reveal[ing] Western culture as virulently imperialistic" (ibid.). In both of these respects, *Cannibal Holocaust* answers Jay Ruby's call for a brand of cinema that would "disassociate [itself] from ... naïve realism and produce films that will become viewed as the filmmakers' construction of the social construction of the actuality of the people portrayed" (275). The only difference between Deodato's film and the experimental ethnographic films Ruby applauds is that the former accomplishes the deconstruction of the normative white gaze through fictional rather than documentary means. By returning to the "last cannibal world" (to borrow the title of an earlier cannibal film made by Deodato), *Cannibal Holocaust* provides us with an alternate way of seeing, a viable framework for critiquing the antiethnological tendencies dominating contemporary American cinema, and "a cultural space that makes bearable for whites the exploration of the association of whiteness with death" (Dyer 210).

A similar argument could be made about the Euro horror zombie film. Although it has not received as much attention in Postcolonial Studies as cannibalism, zombieism has also served as a convenient justification for Western imperialism. The zombie, or *zombi*, originated as a figure in traditional West African Vodoun mythology, where it was represented not as the flesh-eating ghoul familiar to horror movie audiences today, but rather as a dead person reanimated and enslaved through sorcery. This figure found its way into Caribbean folklore as a result of the Atlantic slave trade, which brought, along with many captive West African peoples, West African religions like Vodoun to the West Indies. In the early twentieth century, however, the zombie was appropriated and repurposed by white culture. The English word "zombie," as a term for the living dead, first appeared in William Seabrook's bestselling 1929 travelogue, *The Magic Island* (Rhodes 81). *The Magic Island* gives a highly sensationalized and heavily fictionalized account of Haiti as "an impoverished land of throbbing drums, ruled by pretentious buffoons and populated by swamp doctors, licentious women, and children bred for the cauldron" (Davis 73). Of all the "bizarre" customs and "occult" practices detailed in the book, though, none captivated Western readers more than its lurid tales of zombieism. Playing on the white fascination with "black magic," these stories ultimately offered little more than a laughable caricature of life in Haiti. Wade Davis notes, however, that Seabrook's book and the many that followed it "served a specific political purpose. It was no coincidence that many of them appeared during the years of the American occupation (1915–1934), or that every marine above the rank of sergeant seemed to land a publishing contract. There were many of these books, and each one conveyed an important message to the American public: any country where such abominations took place could find its salvation only through military occupation" (73). Indeed, the figure of the zombie emerged at a pivotal time in the history of Western imperialism, when European empires were fighting to maintain control over their colonial holdings in the Caribbean and when the United States had embarked on its own imperialist adventures in the region, acquiring territories like Puerto Rico and the U.S. Virgin Islands and intervening militarily in the affairs of sovereign states like Cuba and Haiti. Like cannibalism, zombieism – as a rhetorical trope divorced from any sort of empirical reality – reduced the non-white colonial subject to a "primitive savage" in need of the civilizing influence of white culture, providing the West with a rationale for imperialist expansion and colonization. This rationale was especially important to the United States, which needed to legitimize its new efforts at empire building in the Caribbean. As Gary D. Rhodes writes, the depiction of zombieism in books like *The Magic Island* both "echoed and inspired dominant

U.S. prejudices" (70) about the non-white natives of the West Indies, demonstrating "their inferiority and inability to rule themselves" and helping America in "the late 19th and early 20th centuries move toward goals of geographical expansion and militant imperialism in competition with European countries" (ibid.). Robbed of its own life as an integral component of West African Vodoun, then, the zombie was resuscitated in the service of a colonial master and, like the cannibal, forced to labor as a symbol of imperial conquest.

What is interesting, given the colonialist roots of the zombie myth, is that so many American zombie movies revolve around the figure of the white zombie. This is especially true of twenty-first-century Hollywood films like *Resident Evil* (2002), *Dawn of the Dead* (2004), *Doom* (2005), the "Planet Terror" segment of *Grindhouse* (2007), *Quarantine* (2008), *Zombieland* (2009), and the upcoming *World War Z*. One might mention as well the hundreds of independent and straight-to-video zombie movies released in recent years, including *Zombiegeddon* (2003), *Zombie Honeymoon* (2004), *Zombie Strippers!* (2008), and *Zombie Apocalypse* (2011). It is also true, though, of the vast majority of zombie movies celebrated as classic examples of the genre. For example, George Romero's original "living dead" trilogy – *Night of the Living Dead* (1968), *Dawn of the Dead* (1978), and *Day of the Dead* (1985) – rewrites the mythology of the zombie with its apocalyptic stories of small bands of human survivors fending off an ever-growing horde of flesh-eating ghouls in rural and suburban America. The process of divorcing the figure of the zombie from its colonialist roots began even earlier, however, with such films as *King of the Zombies* (1941), *Zombies on Broadway* (1945), and *Zombies of Mora Tau* (1957). It is perhaps not surprising, therefore, that today – well over half a century later – zombieism is seldom associated with the colonial past. Instead, like cannibalism, it is typically read as a metaphor for the mindless consumerism and postmodern anxieties of the present. I want to suggest, against the grain of this reading, that the popularity of the white zombie in Anglo American culture signals the same kind of antiethnological displacement that the popularity of the white cannibal does – a simultaneous reinvocation and disavowal of the project of Western imperialism. It represents a reinjection of "the difference fiction, the Savage [*sic*] fiction, everywhere, to conceal that it is this world, ours, which has again become savage in its way, that is to say, which is devastated by difference and death" (Baudrillard 9). In other words, far from an attempt to critique the cultural logic of late capitalism, white zombieism is symptomatic of a capitulation to that logic. We have symbolically reclaimed and de-raced zombieism because on some level we recognize its relation to our public, social, and collective identity as a late capitalist culture of whiteness that, having exhausted its own resources, has turned to the business of eating the Other. Along with the white cannibal, the white zombie has become one of the most visible signs of our effort to make the world safe for Western trade by commercially (re)colonizing those domains that we could not subjugate politically in the twentieth century.

There have been exceptions to the rule of the white zombie in American horror movies. In fact, some of the original zombie movies, which appeared shortly after the first written accounts of zombieism, display recognizably postcolonial elements. In Victor Halperin's *White Zombie* (1932), for example, it is a villainous white hypnotist played by Bela Lugosi who transforms the black inhabitants of his island into zombies and puts them to work in a sugar mill. When he attempts to use his diabolical powers to enslave a young white woman, however, his reign of terror is brought to an end by her fiancé and a local missionary. Likewise, in Jacques Tourneur's *I Walked with a Zombie* (1943), "voodoo" is revealed to be a tool used by the matriarch of a dysfunctional family of white plantation owners to manage both the black islanders and her own wayward daughter-in-law; eventually, the islanders exert their own control over the film's zombies in an attempt to redress her misuse of their religion. In both of these movies, the colonialist myth of the zombie provides a vehicle for a contemplation of the evils of Western imperialism and the inevitability of its collapse. I will argue in the pages that follow that it is this kind of zombie cinema – rather than the white zombie movies discussed above – that has inspired the most intriguing Euro horror zombie films. Unlike their American counterparts, Euro horror zombie movies often concern themselves explicitly with the colonial origins of the zombie, deconstructing the historical relationship between colonizer and colonized in an effort to interrogate the racist and imperialist attitudes informing it. In these movies, the figure of the zombie emerges not as a symbol of postmodern angst, but as an agent of postcolonial rage – a monster whose virulent contagiousness threatens the destruction of the imperialist Western culture that produced it.

Not all Euro horror zombie films return us to the roots of the zombie myth, to be sure. Indeed, some of the most popular – Jorge Grau's *The Living Dead at Manchester Morgue,* Umberto Lenzi's *Nightmare City,* and Lucio Fulci's *The Beyond,* for example – resemble the bulk of American zombie movies in their focus on white zombieism. There are, however, a significant number of Euro horror zombie films that do engage with the mythology of the zombie in a recognizably postcolonial fashion. In Marino Girolami's *Zombi Holocaust* (*Zombie Holocaust,* 1980), an expedition to a remote Caribbean island encounters a mad white scientist, who has been performing experimental brain transplants on the indigenous population in order to turn them into zombie slaves. Claudio Fragasso's *Zombie 4: After Death* (1989) concerns a group of white scientists who subject the native population of another island to dangerous medical experiments in order to find a cure for cancer; this callous exploitation of the indigenous people angers a Vodoun priest, who calls forth the dead to avenge them. In Umberto Lenzi's *Black Demons* (1991), white tourists visiting Rio de Janeiro are made pawns in a Macumba ritual designed to call a group of former black slaves from their graves to wreak vengeance on the descendants of their old masters. Perhaps the most popular and important Euro horror zombie film to offer a critique of the colonialist zombie myth, however, is Lucio Fulci's *Zombie.*

The first real zombie movie made in Italy, *Zombie* was a huge commercial success – costing just 410 million lira (under $500,000), it grossed more than 3 billion lira ($30 million) worldwide (Thrower 16) – and inspired a wave of similarly themed Euro horror films in the early 1980s, including Fulci's own *Paura nella città dei morti viventi* (*City of the Living Dead,* 1980), Bruno Mattei's *Hell of the Living Dead* (1980), and Andrea Bianchi's *Le notti del terrore* (*Burial Ground,* 1981). It was especially popular on the grindhouse theater circuit in the United States. Heavily promoted by its American distributor – which played up the film's gory subject matter with a now-famous poster featuring a headshot of a rotting ghoul and the tagline "We Are Going to Eat You!" – it did brisk business at the box office and quickly attained cult status among aficionados of hardcore horror. As it has undergone remediation in the years since its theatrical release, migrating from celluloid to digital video, its reputation and following have steadily grown. Today, *Zombie* is available to

American viewers in three different DVD editions and on Blu-ray, and it is regarded by many horror fans as a bona fide genre classic. Perhaps the most telling sign of its entrance into the popular canon of horror cinema is the regularity with which it is referenced in contemporary American horror movies – including *Grindhouse,* Quentin Tarantino and Robert Rodriguez's double-feature homage to exploitation cinema of the 1970s and 1980s.

Zombie began as an attempt to cash in on the commercial success enjoyed by George Romero's *Dawn of the Dead* when it was released in Italy in September 1978 as *Zombi*. Romero's film generated $1 million in box-office receipts during the first month and a half of its lengthy theatrical run (Thrower 15), motivating producer Fabrizio De Angelis to hire Fulci to direct an unofficial sequel. The movie was shot in June and July 1979 and rushed into Italian cinemas by the end of August as *Zombi 2* in a brazen attempt to court fans of *Dawn of the Dead* (ibid. 16). (For the purposes of its theatrical debut in the United States the following year, its title was changed to *Zombie* to avoid confusion – and perhaps the possibility of a lawsuit on behalf of those who held the American rights to Romero's film.) Fulci's movie is not simply an opportunistic knockoff of *Dawn of the Dead*, however; even a cursory glance reveals that it differs radically from the film that inspired it. Unlike *Dawn of the Dead*, which concerns a zombie outbreak in Philadelphia that forces the heroes of the film to take refuge in a suburban shopping mall, *Zombie* locates its story squarely in the colonial domain, pitting the zombified victims – and perpetrators – of Western imperialism against the present-day white inhabitants of a former Caribbean colony. Moreover, it encourages viewers to identify performatively with the zombies as they consume those who have fed off the colonized Other for so long. Ultimately, *Zombie* is less a postmodern recycling than a postcolonial revision of *Dawn of the Dead,* one that borrows from Romero the conceit of "zombie flesh eaters" (the title Fulci's film was given in the United Kingdom), but also returns to the roots of the zombie myth in order to deconstruct it.

Zombie tells the story of a British reporter, the aptly named Peter West (Ian McCulloch), who works in Manhattan. At the beginning of the film, West teams up with Anne Bowles (Tisa Farrow), an American woman, to track down her father, an adventurer last seen sailing toward the small island of Matul in the West Indies. His boat has drifted into New York harbor, empty save for a bloodthirsty ghoul who bites one of the investigating harbor patrolmen before being shot and falling into the water. When Peter and Anne reach Matul in the company of Brian (Al Cliver) and Susan (Auretta Gay) – a vacationing white couple who provide transport from a neighboring island when the "superstitious" natives refuse to take Peter and Anne to Matul – they are horrified to discover that it has been overrun by the living dead. The corpses of former slaves and their masters have been brought back to life and are devouring the island's white inhabitants, the heedless beneficiaries of their ancestors' imperialism. Dr. Menard (Richard Johnson), Matul's resident British physician, believes that there is a scientific explanation for this phenomenon, but concedes that there have been rumors that an "evil witchdoctor" is responsible. The ominous beat of distant drums heard all over the island seems to confirm these reports. As the four unfortunate visitors try to avoid the voracious zombies – whose ranks are swelled in one memorable scene by the rotted remains of the Spanish conquistadores who originally "discovered" the island – it becomes clear that Menard and the other white islanders are helpless to stop the forces arrayed against them. After making a last stand in the ramshackle church that the doctor has converted into a laboratory and infirmary, Peter, Anne, and Brian are able to escape Matul in a boat. The film does not end there, however. By the next morning, Brian has died from a zombie bite he sustained on the island and Peter and Anne are forced to lock him in the hold. Soon they hear his reanimated corpse raging below deck. In an effort to drown out its inarticulate cries of rage and hunger, Peter turns on the ship's radio, only to hear the shrill voice of a New York City news anchor announcing that Manhattan too has fallen victim to the zombie contagion – thanks, presumably, to the harbor patrolman bitten at the beginning of the film. The final shot of the movie shows a long line of the living dead shambling over the Brooklyn Bridge and into the city.

On a narrative level, *Zombie* essentially dramatizes what Robin Wood has famously called the "return of the repressed" – the reemergence in horror cinema of those elements "that our civilization represses or oppresses" (171), and the subsequent disintegration of the dominant social order "as all it has repressed explodes and blows apart" (192). In

Fulci's film, the black zombie becomes the perfect embodiment of all that is repressed in the colonialist scenario, its return tapping into long-held white fears about the unmanageable nature of the colonial subject. If the figure of the zombie was originally deployed in an explicitly racist way as a justification for Western imperialism, it also existed, at the same time, as a source of considerable anxiety for white people. As fan-scholar Stephen Thrower notes of books like Seabrook's *The Magic Island:*

> There's almost a sadomasochistic quality to the fears expressed in these inflamed accounts of what the slave underclass were doing in their secret societies. Whilst Europeans may have held the upper hand in terms of fire-power and wealth, they were on shakier ground when it came to the realm of the symbolic, where the "native" appeared as a figure of awe and potency in the eyes of a decadent "civilised" class.... These black "devils" must have seemed appallingly committed, to observers who could feel their Judaeo-Christian beliefs crumbling under the onslaught of atheist malcontents. The voodoo energy witnessed could hardly be matched by the enervated tatters of Christian ritual. These fears of a secret energy, sullenly amassing itself beneath a tissue of subservience, present us with an image of the insecurities of power. (20)

From the moment of its creation, then, the figure of the zombie paradoxically represented both the inferiority and the indomitability of the colonized subject. Its myth embodied what Homi K. Bhabha refers to as the "ambivalence" of colonialist discourse – an irresolvable tension present in the colonizer's image of the colonized that ultimately makes mastery of the colonized untenable and presages the failure of Western imperialism. *Zombie* captures this sense of ambivalence in the images of the reanimated bodies of black islanders shuffling patiently and in ever greater numbers through the jungles of Matul, down the dusty streets of its villages, and finally to the barricaded church, which they assault in wave after wave to consume those who have fed off them with impunity for years. These images clearly speak to the postcolonial notion of past imperialist injustices, buried but not forgotten, returning to haunt the present. So too does the famous scene in which the white "heroes" of the film stumble across the conquistador graveyard while walking through the jungle. The spectacle of the four-hundred-year-old corpses of the original colonizers rising from the ground to terrorize their modern-day beneficiaries provides an ironic commentary on the circular and finally self-defeating nature of imperialist violence. Moreover, the final

An undead conquistador rises from the grave as an instrument of black postcolonial rage in *Zombie* (Jerry Gross Organization). *Courtesy of Jerry Ohlinger Archives*

apocalyptic shot of hordes of zombies entering New York City affirms in a postcolonial fashion that the repressed history of colonialism – the all too often unacknowledged fact that our civilization was built on the backs of Others – has the potential to return with a force sufficient to destroy all of Western culture, not just its far-flung outposts.

Zombie makes it clear that the institutions of white culture cannot provide a means of containing the elements it has suppressed once they have been unleashed. Western science, embodied in the film by Dr. Menard, is shown to be ineffectual. His stubborn refusal to recognize the validity of non-Western forms of knowledge – a refusal that is deeply rooted in his own sense of whiteness and masculinity – ultimately leads to his destruction. Consider the following exchange with his black assistant, Lucas (Dakar), regarding the origin and nature of the zombies that have begun appearing on Matul:

> MENARD You know what has caused all this? Is it voodoo?
>
> LUCAS Lucas not know nothing, mon. The father of my father always say when the earth spit out the dead, they will come back to suck the blood from the living.
>
> MENARD That's nonsense. That's just a stupid superstition.
>
> LUCAS [ironically] Yes, you are right, Doctor. You know many more things than Lucas.
>
> MENARD I don't believe that voodoo can bring the dead back to life!
>
> LUCAS And I don't believe that the dead be dead.

It is, of course, Lucas who ultimately proves to be correct, as Menard seems to acknowledge – but only partially and too late – toward the end of the film. After working in his laboratory for days, desperately searching for a scientific explanation for what he is witnessing, he modifies his views on zombieism somewhat: "As a man of science, I don't believe in voodooism. But the phenomenon defies logical explanation. I've attempted to apply the disciplines of bacteriology, biology, even of radiology. We've performed tests for epilepsy and for catalepsy. Nothing fits!" By showing us Menard's inadequacy in the face of this event he tries (but is unable) to quantify, Fulci deflates the great white imperial figure that often dominates the colonial scenario. Likewise, he demonstrates that Western religion has no power to stop the zombie onslaught, especially at the end of the movie when the living dead easily penetrate the old church where the main characters have taken shelter. Perhaps nothing short of an acknowledgment of and atonement for past wrongs would suffice to mitigate the rage that drives the zombies, and these are things that no one in the film thinks to offer.

This brings me to the second way in which *Zombie* communicates its postcolonial critique of Western racism and imperialism to viewers. Using a variety of formal means, Fulci encourages us to recognize and reject the flawed perspective of the film's nominal white heroes, while at the same time inviting us to performatively adopt the point of view of the living dead. I have already outlined one example of how he alerts us to the white characters' compromised vision: by emphasizing Dr.

Menard's failure to see and accept the true cause of the zombie outbreak on Matul. Fulci also draws our attention to their flawed perspective in a more visual and visceral fashion, however. Perhaps the best example of this is the scene in which Mrs. Menard (Olga Karlatos), who, like her husband, scoffs at the notion that the dead are rising from their graves because of black magic, is attacked by zombies in her bungalow. As she listens in her room for the sound of their approach, one of the ghouls smashes its arm through the door, grabs her by the back of the head, and slowly pulls her forward, forcing her toward a long splinter sticking out from the shattered wood. Then, in a shot reminiscent of the famous opening image from Luis Buñuel's surrealist masterpiece *Un chien andalou* (1929) – another film about the importance of rejecting conventional ways of seeing – Fulci shows us in graphic close-up the splinter piercing her right eyeball. The literal blinding of Mrs. Menard in this scene underscores the metaphorical blindness she shares with the film's other white characters and encourages the audience to look elsewhere for a more reliable point of view with which to identify.

Crucially, the point of view Fulci provides is that of the zombies. The film is regularly punctuated by "unclaimed" point-of-view shots accompanied by the sound of breathing on the soundtrack that are meant to represent the perspective of the living dead as they lurk behind trees or outside windows, preying on Matul's white inhabitants. This "zombie cam" is put to particularly effective use in the scene where the reanimated conquistadores attack the main characters in the jungle. Peter, Anne, Brian, and Susan stop to rest in a clearing, exhausted by their desperate flight from the zombies and unaware that they have chosen a centuries-old graveyard as their refuge. As they catch their breath and comfort one another, Peter and Anne share their first kiss; this romantic interlude is cut short, however, by the appearance of the undead conquistadores, whose moldering corpses begin to mushroom up from the ground. (It is significant that their appearance is seemingly triggered by the kiss that Peter and Anne share, as if the zombies are intent on killing off not only their white descendants, but also future generations of Western imperialists; in short, the attack can be read symbolically as an effort to prevent the reproduction of whiteness.) What is fascinating about this scene is that it is shot primarily from the zombies' point of view. As they rise from the ground, the camera repeatedly takes on their perspective – tilting slowly upward from a supine position, loose dirt falling away from the lens – as though we ourselves are returning to life. And when the film's most famous zombie – the one prominently featured on the movie poster, with the mottled skin, rotting teeth, and nest of worms writhing in one eye socket – struggles to its feet before the petrified Susan and takes a bite out of her throat, the camera looms over and lunges at her as though we are making the kill. Such moments prompt the viewer to identify with the zombies rather than the film's white protagonists. As the result of our performative spectatorship, we understand the forces driving the living dead far better than they do; indeed, we come to feel as though we are the ones being called upon to avenge the past injustices suffered by the victims of colonialism. And, ultimately, as we shuffle over the Brooklyn Bridge into Manhattan with the rest of the zombies, we can only view the collapse of white culture with satisfaction.

It is interesting to note, in closing, that cannibal and zombie films have occasioned more critical vituperation and legislative interdiction than any other kind of Euro horror cinema. *Cannibal Holocaust* alone has allegedly been banned at one time or another in over fifty different countries, including Italy, the United Kingdom, Australia, and New Zealand. Why? The answer, perhaps, seems obvious: Euro horror cannibal and zombie films have been heavily censored because of their graphic and disturbing violence, which many government officials have deemed unfit for public consumption and even morally suspect. (Ten days after its original theatrical release in Italy, prints of *Cannibal Holocaust* were seized and Deodato arrested when rumors surfaced that it was actually a snuff film whose onscreen acts of murder and cannibalism were genuine.) Such movies represent a prime example of what Mikita Brottman calls *cinéma vomitif*: a taboo-breaking cinema whose "ultimate aim is the arousal of strong sensations in the lower body – nausea, repulsion, weakness, faintness, and a loosening of bowel or bladder control – normally by way of graphic scenes featuring the by-products of bodily detritus: vomit, excrement, viscera, brain tissue, and so on" (11). The relentlessness with which they seek to "gross out" the viewer is surely one factor that has led to them being "ignored, banned, censored, rejected, repressed, dismissed, and reviled" (1). I suggest, however, that this only partially explains their marginal cultural status. The full explanation for the liminality of Euro horror cannibal and zombie movies has to take into account the fact that they address issues of race – a subject that is seldom overtly broached in Western horror cinema – in a recognizably counter-hegemonic, postcolonial fashion. I have attempted to show in this chapter that – unlike American cannibal and zombie films, which tend to focus exclusively on white cannibals and zombies – these movies concern themselves explicitly with the colonial origins of the cannibal and zombie myths, initiating a postcolonial counter-discourse that deconstructs the historical relationship between colonizer and colonized in an effort to interrogate the racist and imperialist attitudes informing it. It is at least partly for this reason, I would argue, that Euro horror cannibal and zombie films are so heavily censored. They interrogate the ways in which race serves as a powerful means of identifying, classifying, and hierarchizing human beings and as a convenient justification for imperialist expansion and colonialism. Moreover, they actively encourage us to identify with the viewpoint of their postcolonial monsters, offering the opportunity for a kind of spectatorship-as-performance that allows us to experiment with raced perspectives and identities in a fashion generally proscribed in mainstream cinema. Ultimately, then, Euro horror cannibal and zombie films demonstrate themselves to be not only a province of revolting bodies, but also bodies in revolt – a defining trait they share with the other genres of classic European horror cinema I have discussed.

CONCLUSION

From the Grindhouse to the Arthouse

THE LEGACY OF EURO HORROR CINEMA

As I noted in part 1 of this book, the golden age of Euro horror cinema more or less came to an end with the 1980s. By then, the economic, industrial, and cultural factors that had sustained the rampant production of European horror films for over three decades were simply no longer operant. In the first place, movie attendance had shrunk dramatically in Europe. According to Pierre Sorlin, three of the biggest Continental film industries – those in Germany, France, and Italy – had, by the 1980s, lost between one-half and three-fourths of the viewers they commanded at the peak of their power in the middle of the twentieth century (150). This precipitous decline in attendance was due in part to a series of economic crises Europe endured beginning in the 1970s that left people without money to spend on movies and led to theater closings across the Continent. It was also a product of changing cultural attitudes toward film as a form of entertainment. In the age of cable television and home video, going to the movies was just not as popular as it once had been. As Sorlin writes: "While cinema was the definitive art of 1950 it was a negligible social activity by 1990" (151). Furthermore, when Europeans did go to the movies, they now increasingly preferred imported Hollywood blockbusters to cheap genre fare made domestically. With investors leaving the film market in droves and international co-productions becoming more and more difficult to put together, Euro horror directors could not hope to compete against multimillion-dollar movies backed by huge corporations. On their home turf, then, they found themselves in a losing battle for a dwindling pool of viewers.

To make matters worse, their American audience had largely disappeared as well. By the end of the 1980s, Euro horror was no longer shown on network television in the United States, and the grindhouses and drive-ins that once were reliable venues for its exhibition had been mostly driven out of business by the explosive growth of multiplex theater chains. Many of these new theater chains were, in the wake of the widespread industry deregulation of the Reagan years, owned by or allied with the same multinational conglomerates that now ran the major Hollywood studios, making it all the more difficult for foreign films not produced or distributed by companies with corporate ties to receive a theatrical release in the United States. Essentially, the only way Euro horror directors could reach American viewers was through the home video and cable television markets – neither of which brought them the kind of audience they had been able to capture on network television and in theaters. This was ultimately a moot point, however, since the tastes of American viewers had changed significantly. Interest in dubbed or subtitled foreign fare, whether highbrow art films or lowbrow genre movies, had been almost completely eroded by Hollywood blockbuster cinema. At the same time, the crude, brutal, and often transgressive brand of horror popular in the 1960s and 1970s no longer held the same allure for audiences, who were now drawn to slicker, safer, and more mainstream genre films suffused with the kind of hip self-reflexivity and tongue-in-cheek humor that emerged with the *Nightmare on Elm Street* franchise in the 1980s and climaxed with the *Scream* series in the 1990s. To these viewers, Euro horror already seemed like a strange relic from another age. Even when Euro horror directors managed to get their films released on video or cable by jettisoning everything that made their work unique and by slavishly following popular trends in American horror – as Claudio Fragasso did with *Troll 2* – audiences in the United States were generally indifferent. Defeated, many of the filmmakers who had played key roles in shaping European horror over the previous three decades abandoned the genre, drifting into hackwork or jobs in television, or leaving the industry altogether. The classic era of Euro horror cinema was definitely over.

Of course, horror movies continued to be made in Europe. A few established Euro horror auteurs – such as Dario Argento, Jean Rollin, and Jess Franco – soldiered on, remaining active in the genre throughout the 1990s. Moreover, several new European horror films won widespread critical acclaim: *C'est arrivé près de chez vous* (*Man Bites Dog*, 1992), *Nattevagten* (*Nightwatch*, 1994), *Tesis* (*Thesis*, 1996), and *Insomnia* (1997), among them. These films seemed to promise a horror renaissance on the Continent, and something of a genre revival has taken place. The first decade of the twenty-first century saw a wave of horror movies emerge from France, Spain, Germany, and elsewhere in Europe, including *Les rivières pourpres* (*The Crimson Rivers*, 2000), *Promenons-nous dans les bois* (*Deep in the Woods*, 2000), *Anatomie* (*Anatomy*, 2000), *Le pacte des loups* (*Brotherhood of the Wolf*, 2001), *Belphégor – Le fantôme du Louvre* (*Belphégor: Phantom of the Louvre*, 2001), *Maléfique* (2002), *Darkness* (2002), *Haute tension* (*High Tension*, 2003), *Nochnoy dozor* (*Night Watch*, 2004), *Calvaire* (2004), *Antikörper* (*Antibodies*, 2005), *Frágiles* (*Fragile*, 2005), *H6: Diario de un asesino* (*H6: Diary of a Serial Killer*, 2005), *Sheitan* (2006), *Ils* (*Them*, 2006), *The Abandoned* (2006), *Frontière(s)* (*Frontier(s)*, 2007), *[Rec]* (2007), *El orfanato* (*The Orphanage*, 2007), *À l'intérieur* (*Inside*, 2007), *Kollegiet* (*Room 205*, 2007), *Sauna* (2008), *Martyrs* (2008), *Linkeroever* (*Left Bank*, 2008), *Låt den rätte komma in* (*Let the Right One In*, 2008), *Mutants* (2009), *Død snø* (*Dead Snow*, 2009), *Shadow* (2009), *The Human Centipede (First Sequence)* (2009), *Secuestrados* (*Kidnapped*, 2010), *Los ojos de Julia* (*Julia's Eyes*, 2010), *Trolljegeren* (*TrollHunter*, 2010), and *Srpski film* (*A Serbian Film*, 2010). Garnering international attention, critical accolades, and a loyal fan following both in Europe and in the United States, this new wave of genre cinema has put Europe definitively back on the horror map.

Significantly, however, contemporary European horror films are in many respects fundamentally different from the classic European movies discussed in this book. Most of the elements characteristic of Euro horror – especially the distinctive ways in which it invites spectatorship-as-performance – are notably absent in recent European horror cinema. It actually has more in common, both narratively and formally, with modern American horror cinema – with the movies of John Carpenter, George Romero, Wes Craven, Tobe Hooper, and their protégés – than it does with classic European horror cinema. In fact, contemporary European horror films often seem like little more than retreads of popular

American genre movies: *The Crimson Rivers*, for example, is obviously inspired by *Se7en* (1995), while *Antibodies* borrows heavily from *The Silence of the Lambs*, *H6: Diary of a Serial Killer* from *Henry: Portrait of a Serial Killer* (1986), and *Frontier(s)* from *The Texas Chain Saw Massacre* (1974). *Deep in the Woods* is closer to slasher movies like *Friday the 13th* (1980) and *Sleepaway Camp* (1983) than it is to *giallo* films like *Blood and Black Lace* and *The Bird with the Crystal Plumage*. The sexualized violence in *Calvaire* is more akin to that found in survival horror movies like *Deliverance* (1972) and *The Hills Have Eyes* (1977) than it is to that found in S&M horror films like *The Whip and the Body* and *Sadomania*. And *[Rec]* owes more to postmodern zombie movies like *Resident Evil* (2002) and *Dawn of the Dead* (2004) than it does to postcolonial zombie films like *Cannibal Apocalypse* and *Zombie*. Perhaps not surprising, given the way in which Hollywood movies have dominated the cinematic landscape in Europe since the 1980s, it would appear that the new generation of European horror directors grew up watching American genre films rather than Euro horror, and has set out to win recognition by mimicking them as closely as possible.

Neither the critical success of contemporary European horror cinema nor its uncanny resemblance to modern American horror has escaped the notice of corporate Hollywood, which has sought to capitalize on both. Indeed, contemporary European horror cinema has been embraced by the American film industry in a way that Euro horror never was. Almost all of the European horror movies mentioned above have been released on DVD in the United States, either by the major studios or by independent mini-majors like Lionsgate and the Weinstein Company. Several have even been given limited theatrical runs in the United States—a coup for a foreign film at a time when many of the current masterpieces of world cinema are unable to find their way into American theaters. Moreover, a number of contemporary European horror filmmakers have been hired to direct high-profile genre movies for the studios. French horror directors, in particular, have proven attractive to Hollywood: after shooting *The Crimson Rivers*, Mathieu Kassovitz was hired to helm *Gothika;* Christophe Gans was signed to direct *Silent Hill* (2006) following the release of *Brotherhood of the Wolf;* and after making *High Tension*, Alexandre Aja went on to direct *The Hills Have Eyes* (2006),

Mirrors (2008), and *Piranha* (2010). Finally, a number of recent European horror movies have been remade in the United States, including *Them*, which was refashioned into *The Strangers* (2008); *[Rec]*, which was recycled as *Quarantine*; and *Let the Right One In*, which was redone as *Let Me In* (2010). American remakes of *The Orphanage*, *Room 205*, *Martyrs*, and *TrollHunter* have also been announced, with more sure to follow. The intense interest shown by corporate Hollywood in contemporary European horror cinema speaks to the basic compatibility between it and modern American horror. While Euro horror movies distinguished themselves from American genre films by drawing on a range of uniquely Continental influences, the new wave of European horror cinema, having drawn much of its inspiration from modern American horror, seems to belong more to Hollywood than to Europe.

This is not to say that contemporary European horror movies are completely disconnected from the various national contexts that produced them. Take the example of French horror cinema. Guy Austin notes that it reflects the "economic and social malaise that France has been experiencing since the nineties" (144). In particular, films like *Sheitan*, *Frontier(s)*, and *Inside* plumb the horror of *la fracture sociale*, the growing gap between the haves and the have-nots in French society: the rich and the poor, the urban and the suburban, the naturalized white citizenry and the black and *beur* immigrant community. In *Sheitan*, a trio of working-class, ethnically diverse teens who are invited to the country estate of a wealthy young woman they meet at a discotheque find themselves in a fight for their lives with the mansion's bizarre inhabitants, including a maniacal satanist who works as the caretaker. *Frontier(s)* follows the fortunes of a band of Arab youths who commit a robbery in Paris during the chaos surrounding the election of a right-wing political candidate and hide out at a country inn afterward, only to discover that it is run by a family of murderous neo-Nazis. *Inside* tells the story of a young, pregnant widow who is terrorized in her home by a mysterious woman with designs on her unborn child while immigrant rioters clash violently with the police in the streets outside. Clearly, these films are rooted in fears and anxieties specific to contemporary French culture.

They are just as clearly rooted, however, in modern American horror cinema, taking their narrative and formal cues from landmark genre films like *Rosemary's Baby, The Texas Chain Saw Massacre,* and *Halloween* (1978), as well as from more recent movies like *Wrong Turn, Hostel,* and *When a Stranger Calls* (2006). Indeed, their culturally specific touches are far outweighed by the familiar American horror tropes they employ: satanic births, backwoods settings, monstrous families, people slaughtered like cattle, home invasions, teenagers in peril, gory scenes of torture, and so on. While it has not been completely deracinated, then, contemporary European horror cinema has been significantly Americanized, losing in the process much of what made Euro horror distinctive. This is true, I might add, even of new work by Euro horror directors like Dario Argento. Many fans have complained about the way in which Argento pictures such as *Nonhosonno* (*Sleepless*, 2001) and *Il cartaio* (*The Card Player*, 2004), unlike the inimitably surreal and sensationalistic *giallo* films of the classic phase of his career, are movies of "aggressive ordinariness" (Chaw par. 6) that "could have been directed and conceptualized by any direct–to–USA Network hack with a formula procedural screenplay and a cast of earnest unknowns" (ibid.). Given that the films not only of young European horror directors, but also of old masters like Argento bear such signs of Americanization, it is tempting to conclude that the Euro horror aesthetic is truly dead and gone.

Sadly, the few contemporary European horror movies that do take their inspiration from classic Euro horror cinema give us no reason to think otherwise: most are empty exercises in style, favoring pastiche and homage over a real engagement with the legacy of Euro horror. Several recent productions positioning themselves as "neo *giallo*" films are representative in this regard. *Amer,* an arty, erotic Belgian movie directed by Hélène Cattet and Bruno Forzani in 2009, is essentially a valentine to the *giallo* film, a compilation of its greatest hits. Cattet and Forzani's rather exiguous three-act story, which involves the psychosexual development of a young woman with ties to a sinister old house, is merely an excuse to rummage through the genre, recycling imagery from movies as diverse as Mario Bava's *Black Sabbath,* Dario Argento's *Suspiria,* Lucio Fulci's *Una lucertola con la pelle di donna* (*A Lizard in a Woman's Skin*, 1971), and Antonio Margheriti's *La morte negli occhi del gatto* (*Seven Deaths in the Cat's Eye*, 1973), and sampling the soundtracks of Sergio Martino's

La coda dello scorpione (*The Case of the Scorpion's Tail*, 1971) and Massimo Dallamano's *La polizia chiede aiuto* (*What Have They Done to Your Daughters?*, 1974), among other films. It is atmospheric and elegantly shot, but ultimately empty. Weaving an elaborate web of references, allusions, and quotations, it captures the surface look and feel of the *giallo* film, but overlooks the genre's central investment in identity play and performative spectatorship. The same is true of *Ubaldo Terzani Horror Show*, an Italian movie made by Gabriele Albanesi in 2010, and *Masks*, a German film shot by Andreas Marschall in 2011. *Ubaldo Terzani Horror Show*'s self-reflexive tale of a young horror director who has the opportunity to collaborate on a new screenplay with a famous but reclusive (and decidedly unbalanced) cult novelist owes more than a passing debt to Fulci's *Un gatto nel cervello* (*A Cat in the Brain*, 1990), and Albanesi never misses an opportunity to reference not only Fulci, but also Bava, Joe D'Amato, Michele Soavi, and a slew of other Euro horror auteurs. Likewise, *Masks* lifts its premise – a young girl enrolling at a private arts academy with a dark secret – straight from *Suspiria*, its moody ambience from Sergio Martino's *All the Colors of the Dark*, and its musical cues from Antonio Bido's *Il gatto dagli occhi di giada* (*Watch Me When I Kill*, 1977). Unfortunately, while *Ubaldo Terzani Horror Show* and *Masks* boast many of the superficial hallmarks of the *giallo* film, neither offers the kind of opportunities for spectatorship-as-performance that truly define the genre. Like *Amer*, they are all style and no substance; although they express an undeniable passion for *giallo* cinema, they do not evince a deep understanding of it.

I want to end this book, however, by suggesting that there is a brand of contemporary European cinema that can be viewed as a direct descendant of Euro horror. Interestingly, it is the work not of genre filmmakers, but rather of internationally celebrated arthouse auteurs. The first decade of the twenty-first century saw an explosion in the production of European art films that blended the highbrow with the lowbrow in a postmodern fashion, using graphic and unconventional depictions of sex and horror as a means of fostering spectatorship-as-performance. Martine Beugnet has alternately described this new type of art film as a "cinema of abjection" and a "cinema of sensation," observing:

> Transgression is the main principle, the thematic and aesthetic crossing of the frontier of the acceptable into the sphere of the abject. Some directors concentrate on taboo subjects (violent crimes, rape, incest), and draw on the conventions of genres such as gore and pornography, that have been marginalized by both mainstream and art cinema. Often, the body as flesh is the raw material of the filmmaking; assaulted, mutilated, violated, it becomes a war zone, symbolic of the attack that is supposedly performed by the same token on social, cultural, and cinematic conventions. Abjection, the violent repulsion against and expulsion of bodies felt as alien or threatening, also works as a metaphor for the processes of exclusion through which a social "body" seeks to "purify" itself. The cinema of abjection focuses precisely on those "aberrant" elements: criminals, psychopaths, monstrous beings or those perceived as such, creations of the very system that must eradicate them. ("French Cinema" 296–297)

Beugnet sees the cinema of abjection/sensation as a distinctly French phenomenon, citing films like Bruno Dumont's *L'humanité* (1999), Claire Denis's *Trouble Every Day*, Catherine Breillat's *À ma soeur! (Fat Girl*, 2001), and Gaspar Noé's *Irreversible* as key examples. In fact, however, it is more of a Continental trend that also includes such films as Michael Haneke's *Funny Games* (1997 and 2007), Giuseppe Tornatore's *La sconosciuta (The Unknown Woman*, 2006), Giorgos Lanthimos's *Kynodontas (Dogtooth*, 2009), Lars von Trier's *Antichrist*, and Pedro Almodóvar's *The Skin I Live In*. National origin is not what unites these movies, primarily; what unites them is the unique way in which they bring "art cinema to new heights of horror or graphic description" (Beugnet, *Cinema and Sensation* 16), deploying certain generic features – "technically, a limited array of pre-set narrative structures, moods and character identities" (131) – in order to "facilitate the emergence of cinematic becomings" (ibid.). Deconstructing "the conventional vision-knowledge-mastery paradigm" (68), Beugnet writes, the new "extreme" European art cinema makes possible "a relation where the spectator may surrender, at least partly, a sense of visual control for the possibility of a sensuous encounter with the film – where the subject affectively yields into its object" (ibid.). Significantly, Beugnet notes that there is nothing new about the cinema of abjection/sensation she delineates for us:

> There is a long, established practice of mixing "high" with "low" forms of popular expression and, in particular, of bringing elements of cinema's genres of "excess" into French art film, and it has been considered customary for its directors to venture into such transgressive territories. As such, the late work of

> Breillat, Denis, Dumont, [Philippe] Grandrieux or [Marina] de Van – to name but a few of the directors whose filmmaking looks toward pornography, horror or the violent thriller – does not establish a novel pattern but, on the contrary, arguably partakes in a long tradition of French artistic subversion. (34)

It is difficult to know exactly what artistic tradition Beugnet has in mind here (though she references at various points the work of Luis Buñuel, Dziga Vertov, and Alain Resnais), but classic Euro horror cinema certainly shares many characteristics with the extreme European art cinema she describes. Both mix art with horror, blending high and low culture in a recognizably postmodern fashion; both revel in postmodern excess and transgression; and both foster cinematic becomings in which the viewer can engage in potentially transformative acts of spectatorship-as-performance. Given these fundamental similarities, it does not seem unreasonable to suggest that contemporary extreme European art cinema is in some sense a reincarnation of Euro horror – that Euro horror's animating spirit has moved from the grindhouse to the arthouse.

In the interest of providing some support for this argument, let me offer a specific and compelling example of the connection between Euro horror and extreme European art cinema: Claire Denis's *Trouble Every Day*. One of the more memorable scandals to erupt at Cannes in recent years revolved around the premiere of Denis's film on the Croisette in 2001. Up until then, Denis had been a favorite at Cannes: her debut film, *Chocolat*, a masterpiece of postcolonial cinema, was nominated for the Palme d'Or in 1988; *J'ai pas sommeil* (*I Can't Sleep*), her haunting take on the "granny killer" murders that rocked Paris in the 1980s, was an official selection for the sidebar Un Certain Regard in 1994; and she was chosen to be a member of the Cinéfondation and Short Films Jury in 2000. The critical success of her then-latest film, *Beau travail* (1999), a loose adaptation of Herman Melville's *Billy Budd* set at a French Foreign Legion outpost in East Africa and rendered in images of hallucinatory beauty, had established her as a leading director in contemporary world cinema. Given the honors the festival had bestowed upon Denis in the past and her sterling reputation as a filmmaker at the time, one might have anticipated that *Trouble Every Day* would meet with a warm reception at Cannes. This did not turn out to be the case. A gruesome tale of sexual cannibalism in which the main characters suffer from a bloodlust that compels them to attack and feed on their partners during intercourse, Denis's new film departed from her earlier work in ways that many of her former admirers found deeply disturbing. Signaling their uneasiness with *Trouble Every Day*, the festival organizers screened it out of competition and scheduled its premiere late at night. Even so, the audience at the opening, unprepared for the visceral nature of the film, reacted violently. Viewers booed it roundly and walked out of the theater in droves; some even reportedly fainted during its more graphic scenes. Not surprisingly, critics savaged the movie, dismissing it, in the words of one reviewer, as a "risible disaster" (French par. 1), a "mixture of pretentious sexual philosophising and necrophilic romanticism without intellectual rigor or erotic excitement" (par. 4). Denis's eloquent defense of her work at the tense post-screening press conference as "an adventure at the frontier of the poetry of horror" (Peary par. 3) fell largely on deaf ears. *Trouble Every Day* emerged from the festival as a *film maudit*, one whose terrible reputation has to this day prevented it from receiving the attention that it deserves.

In retrospect, it seems clear that Denis's film provoked such a hostile reaction at Cannes precisely *because* it mixes poetry with horror, challenging the critically established boundary between European art and popular cinema. While there are many ways in which *Trouble Every Day* aligns itself with the tradition of the art film – its elliptical approach to storytelling, its sensuous visual style, its minimal use of dialogue, and its thematic interest in transgression and desire, for example – it also manifests a strong kinship with the horror movie. Consider the broad outline of the film. It tells the story of Shane Brown (Vincent Gallo), an American pharmaceutical company representative, who travels to Paris with his new wife, June (Tricia Vessey), to locate Dr. Léo Sémeneau (Alex Descas), a scientific researcher with whom Shane previously worked in Guyana. We discover that Shane has fallen prey to a mysterious disease – linked somehow to Léo's controversial experimentation with the effects of exotic plants on human behavior – that triggers violent thoughts and behavior when he becomes sexually aroused. Shane has come to Paris in the hope that Léo can cure him before he hurts June, who is unaware of his illness. Unbeknownst to Shane, Léo's wife, Coré (Béatrice Dalle), is in the advanced stages of the same disease and Léo has already been searching feverishly for a cure, to no avail. While Léo is working at his laboratory during the day, he is forced to keep the rapacious Coré locked in her bedroom to prevent her from seducing and murdering anonymous men – something we see her do early in the film when she escapes from her home and claims a victim at a nearby truck stop. Cutting back and forth between Shane's desperate hunt for Léo and Coré's frenzied attempts to escape captivity, *Trouble Every Day* builds inexorably toward two climactic acts of violence. Coré ravishes and then ravages a teenage boy, a curious next-door neighbor who breaks into her home with a friend to investigate its enigmatic, oft-glimpsed occupant; soon afterward, she ends her own life by setting fire to the house that has served as her prison. Shane, despairing over the possibility of a cure, at last gives in to his bloodlust and mutilates a maid who works at the hotel where he and June are staying – a young woman with whom he has carried on a wordless flirtation since their arrival. When June subsequently discovers him washing his victim's blood off himself in the shower, they exchange a long, silent look, his gaze tortured, hers wavering between tender concern and dawning horror. "I want to go home," Shane says finally, as a thin rivulet of gore runs down the translucent shower curtain. The film fades to black.

As this synopsis suggests, there are a number of narrative elements that link *Trouble Every Day* with horror cinema. Perhaps the most obvious is Denis's use of stock genre characters like the monster and the mad scientist. Combining the traits of the vampire, the serial killer, the zombie, and the Frankenstein monster, Shane and Coré are terrifying yet strangely sympathetic Others who prey on innocent victims, first seducing and then consuming them. Léo plays the role of the mad scientist, a man of overreaching ambition whose controversial research has led to the creation of these monsters. One might also note that, its open ending notwithstanding, the shape of the plot follows that of many classical horror movies in which we bear witness to the emergence of the monster, its disruptive rampage, and its demise, often in some sort of conflagration. The mood of melancholy and dread Denis establishes in her film and the major themes she explores – the devolution of the human into the animal, the connection between eroticism and death – clearly have roots in the horror genre as well.

In addition to the narrative elements *Trouble Every Day* has in common with the horror movie, there are also shared formal characteristics. Chief among them is Denis's graphic depiction of violence and gore. Like much modern horror cinema, *Trouble Every Day* exhibits a fascination with what Isabel Cristina Pinedo calls the "ruined-body-as-spectacle" (60), utilizing makeup effects and an unblinking camera to show, in fetishistic detail, the destruction of the human form. This fascination is most vividly on display in the film's climactic scenes, when we see Shane and Coré literally tear their victims apart as their cannibalistic urges overtake their carnal desires and lovemaking turns into bloodletting. Other formal debts to the horror movie include the claustrophobic compositions and off-center framing Denis and her long-time cinematographer, Agnès Godard, favor, as well as the use of subjective camerawork to evoke Shane's perspective as he stalks his victim at the end of the film. Finally, the disquieting musical score performed by the British minimalist pop group Tindersticks evokes suspense and a sense of foreboding native to horror. In all these ways and others, *Trouble Every Day* demonstrates a scandalous engagement with popular cinema that flies in the face of what Catherine Fowler describes as the generally "agreed upon notion of European cinema: as *experimental* (thus with practice informing theory, theories constantly changing, and an emphasis on formal experimentation), *serious* (none of the writer/practitioners ... wants to 'satisfy' his audience, instead each wants to challenge them) and *an art form* ([which] follows from the first two notions)" (4).

In its defiant blurring of the border between art and horror, *Trouble Every Day* is anticipated, as we have seen in this book, by the bulk of Euro horror cinema. Intriguingly, the specifics of its approach are even prefigured in a particular Euro horror movie: Jean Rollin's *La morte vivante* (*The Living Dead Girl*, 1982). The title character in *The Living Dead Girl* is Catherine Valmont (Françoise Blanchard), a young woman who has been dead for two years when the story begins, her corpse perfectly preserved in the family mausoleum next to that of her mother, who has also recently passed away. In the opening scenes of the film, two corrupt employees of a local chemical company, who have apparently made a practice of illegally dumping toxic waste on the isolated and now-deserted Valmont estate, arrive at the crypt with a truckload of barrels to deposit. As they begin to haul the waste underground, an earthquake strikes, causing the barrels to tumble over and break open; the chemicals spill out and seep into the ground, eventually dripping onto Catherine's coffin in the catacombs below. The toxic waste revives her, but although she is as beautiful as ever, she is also zombie-like: mute, slow moving, and driven by an insatiable appetite for human flesh. Interestingly, she retains fragmentary impressions of her former life that lead her back to the family chateau, where she sifts through the jumbled remains of the past. Catherine is particularly drawn to a music box given to her as a child by her lifelong friend Hélène (Marina Pierro). The two women are reunited when Hélène calls to speak with Catherine's mother, not realizing that she has died, and instead hears the sound of the music box at the other end of the line. Hurrying to the Valmont estate in the French countryside, Hélène is overjoyed to find Catherine alive, but devastated by her condition. At first, she attempts to cure Catherine, but when she finds that nothing can diminish Catherine's bloodlust, Hélène becomes Catherine's procurer, luring unsuspecting locals back to the chateau for her to consume. Eventually, when the authorities close in on the two women, they make a death pact rather than risk being separated again. In the film's closing moments, Catherine cannibalizes Hélène in a ritual massacre that, as Rollin has said in an interview, is shot as "a kind of love scene" (Black par. 30).

The similarities between *The Living Dead Girl* and *Trouble Every Day* are very suggestive. The plots of the two films are obviously analogous: both deal with sympathetic female characters who, after falling victim to accidents of science, are driven by an irresistible compulsion to feed on human flesh. Moreover, Denis's film strongly resembles Rollin's not only in its use of graphic violence and gore, but also in its distinctive subversion of genre conventions, defamiliarizing formal strategies, cultivation of a sensuous cinema, and thematic interest in the dark undertones of desire. Compare, for example, the scene in *The Living Dead Girl* in which Hélène, posing as a stranded motorist, brings the young woman who gives her a lift back to the castle for Catherine to devour, with the scene in *Trouble Every Day* in which Coré attacks the teenage boy who, driven by curiosity, breaks into her house with his friend. Each scene revolves around the trespass of the victim into the domain of the monster, who is kept as a virtual prisoner in her own home. The deaths of the victims in both scenes are extremely gory, of course, but what it striking is how similarly these deaths are photographed. Rollin and Denis rely on essentially the same set of specific images: fetishistic close-ups of necks being bitten, fingers digging into torsos, flesh hanging in shreds, and mouths dripping with blood. In addition, both scenes conflate death and eroticism in a distinctive way. Catherine and Coré take an equally sensual, even sexual, pleasure in bloodletting, and the terrified cries and anguished moans of their victims are at certain points indistinguishable from sounds made during the act of love. Finally, both scenes feature a comparably lyrical style – one that emphasizes the poetry as well as the horror of the murders they record. The glossy *cinéma du look* approach favored by Rollin, with its dated use of slow motion and distorted sound effects, is different from Denis's hallucinatory realism, to be sure; both, however, aim to produce a dreamy atmosphere of erotic terror.

Above and beyond their distinctive blend of art and horror, though, *Trouble Every Day* and *The Living Dead Girl* share a commitment to fostering performative spectatorship, which they encourage partly through the postmodern way in which they transgress boundaries and violate norms, using graphic sex and violence to suggest the fragility of the body and the instability of the social contract. Both films also offer a trenchant postmodern critique of Western science, rationality, and masculinity, using the figure of the sympathetic female monster, in particular, to expose and attack the destructive male drive to achieve scientific mastery over an irrational, feminized natural order. Furthermore, *Trouble Every Day* and *The Living Dead Girl* invite performative spectatorship because of how they deterritorialize the viewer's gaze. As Beugnet writes of the climactic scene from *Trouble Every Day* discussed above:

> [It] partly draws its forceful impact from an unsettling of the spectator's position, the framing and scale of the images, as well as the light and the heightened sound effects challenging familiar patterns of orientation and the sense of a definite, superior point of view. In turn, the continuous play on scale and the effect of *"visagéification"* creates uncanny echoes across the spatio-temporal spectrum of the film and opens the door to patterns of identification and embodiment that further unsettle the distinction between pleasure and terror. (*Cinema and Sensation* 107)

Throughout this book, I have argued that such spectatorship-as-performance is the defining characteristic of Euro horror cinema. Upending the conventional viewing experience, Euro horror movies, like *Trouble Every Day*, seek to deterritorialize the gaze and reconfigure the act of viewing as a process of becoming Other. This "unsettling of the spectator's position" (Beugnet, *Cinema and Sensation* 107) prompts viewers to "'perform' and 'think' through issues relating to the construction of contemporary identities" (150). Ultimately, I suggest, it is the fact that both *Trouble Every Day* and *The Living Dead Girl* offer the opportunity for this kind of performative spectatorship that provides the most compelling evidence of kinship between the two films.

My aim in detailing these parallels is not to argue that Denis intended *Trouble Every Day* as a remake of or homage to *The Living Dead Girl*, specifically. I do contend, however, that her work in the film was prefigured by Euro horror cinema as a whole – of which Denis herself is absolutely aware. When asked at the post-premiere Cannes press conference if *Trouble Every Day* had any precedent, Denis cited Dario Argento as a filmmaker whose work she admired and used as a model (Peary par. 4). Clearly, then, Denis consciously drew on Euro horror as a source of inspiration for her extreme art film. And she is not alone. Exactly ten years after the debut of *Trouble Every Day* on the Croisette, Almodóvar's latest film, *The Skin I Live In*, had its premiere at the 2011 Cannes Film Festival. Another scandalous blend of art and horror, it tells the story of a brilliant surgeon (Antonio Banderas) who, traumatized by the deaths of his wife and his daughter, creates an impervious transgenetic skin and performs a series of experimental procedures in which he grafts it onto the body of a young woman (Elena Anaya) whom he has kidnapped with the aid of his maternal assistant (Marisa Paredes). While the film was partly inspired by Thierry Jonquet's 2002 novel, *Mygale*, it also obviously represents a reworking of Georges Franju's classic Euro horror movie *Eyes without a Face* – something that Almodóvar readily acknowledged at the press conference following the film's premiere (Zacharek par. 3). The broad outline of its plot is the same (a gifted doctor driven mad by grief and regret subjects a young woman whom he keeps as a virtual prisoner in his home to a series of cosmetic surgeries with the aid of a fanatically loyal female assistant), as is much of its imagery and tone (the disturbing scenes of medical horror, the eerie mask worn by the young woman to hide her disfigured face, the flashes of dark humor that illuminate the film). Even more important, *The Skin I Live In* prompts the same kind of performative spectatorship as its predecessor. As one reviewer puts it, Almodóvar "play[s] with the audiences [*sic*] perception of reality" (Asdourian par. 3), especially in the way he "psychologically twists the sexuality exuded in the film, making you question your own" (ibid.). Yet Almodóvar is merely the latest internationally acclaimed European auteur whose recent work has manifested a debt to Euro horror cinema; he joins an august company whose ranks include not only Denis, but also Michael Haneke, Catherine Breillat, Gaspar Noé, and Lars von Trier.

I recognize that is quite possible – likely, in fact – that not all of these filmmakers are as cognizant as Denis and Almodóvar are of the parallels between their work and that of Euro horror directors like Rollin and Franju. The point is that these parallels exist regardless, revealing a lineage that stretches from the arthouse cinema of today back to the grindhouse cinema of yesterday. My goal here has simply been to demonstrate that ancestry. Perceiving the trajectory that takes us from Euro horror cinema to contemporary extreme art cinema gives us, I believe, a greater appreciation not only of the historical importance of Euro horror, but also of its continued relevance to discussions of European cinema. In short, Euro horror cinema itself may be dead, but its spirit lives on – one final reason to recommend its rediscovery and reconsideration in the field of Film Studies.

WORKS CITED

Adams Media Research. "Small Disk, Heavy Weight." *New York Times*. 10 July 2005. Accessed 11 July 2005. http://www.nytimes.com/imagepages/2005/07/10/business/11dvd.graphic.html.

Ascheid, Antje. "Speaking Tongues: Voice Dubbing in the Cinema as Cultural Ventriloquism." *Velvet Light Trap* 40 (Fall 1997): 32–41.

Asdourian, Raffi. Rev. of *The Skin I Live In*. Film Stage. 19 May 2011. Accessed 6 June 2011. http://thefilmstage.com/2011/05/19/cannes-review-the-skin-i-live-in.

Ashlin, Scott. Rev. of *Cannibal Holocaust*. 1000 Misspent Hours and Counting. 16 Sept. 2009. http://www.1000misspenthours.com/reviews/reviewsa-d/cannibalholocaust.htm.

Austin, Guy. *Contemporary French Cinema*. 2nd ed. Manchester, England: Manchester University Press, 2008.

Barnes, Brooks. "A Film Year Full of Escapism, Flat in Attendance." *New York Times*. 2 Jan. 2008. Accessed 2 Jan. 2008. http://www.nytimes.com/2008/01/02/movies/02year.html.

———. "In a Distressed Year, Hollywood Smiles." *New York Times*. 21 Dec. 2009. Accessed 21 Dec. 2009. http://www.nytimes.com/2009/12/21/business/21hollywood.html.

———. "A Year of Disappointment at the Movie Box Office." *New York Times*. 25 Dec. 2011. Accessed 27 Dec. 2011. http://www.nytimes.com/2011/12/26/business/media/a-year-of-disappointment-for-hollywood.html?pagewanted=all.

Barnett, Rod. Rev. of *Short Night of the Glass Dolls* (2002, Anchor Bay DVD). Eccentric Cinema. 18 Jan. 2003. Accessed 12 July 2011. http://www.eccentric-cinema.com/cult_movies/short_night_glass_dolls.htm.

Bartolovich, Crystal. "Consumerism; or, The Cultural Logic of Late Cannibalism." *Cannibalism and the Colonial World*. Ed. Francis Barker, Peter Hulme, and Margaret Iversen. Cambridge: Cambridge University Press, 1998: 204–237.

Baschiera, Stefano, and Francesco Di Chiara. "A Postcard from the Grindhouse: Exotic Landscapes and Italian Holidays in Lucio Fulci's *Zombie* and Sergio Martino's *Torso*." *Cinema Inferno: Celluloid Explosions from the Cultural Margins*. Ed. Robert G. Weiner and John Cline. Lanham, Md.: Scarecrow, 2010: 101–123.

Bataille, Georges. *Erotism: Death & Sensuality*. Trans. Mary Dalwood. San Francisco: City Lights, 1986.

Baudrillard, Jean. *Simulacra and Simulation*. Trans. Sheila Faria Glaser. Ann Arbor: University of Michigan Press, 1994.

Benshoff, Harry M. *Monsters in the Closet: Homosexuality and the Horror Film*. Manchester, England: Manchester University Press, 1997.

Berenstein, Rhona J. "Spectatorship-as-Drag: The Act of Viewing and Classic Horror Cinema." *Viewing Positions: Ways of Seeing Film*. Ed. Linda Williams. New Brunswick, N.J.: Rutgers University Press, 1994: 231–269.

Beugnet, Martine. *Cinema and Sensation: French Film and the Art of Transgression*. Carbondale: Southern Illinois University Press, 2007.

———. "French Cinema of the Margins." *European Cinema*. Ed. Elizabeth Ezra. New York: Oxford University Press, 2004: 283–298.

Black, Andy. "Clocks, Seagulls, Romeo and Juliet: Surrealism Rollin Style." *Kinoeye* 2:7 (2002). Accessed 28 Feb. 2007. http://www.kinoeye.org/02/07/black07.php.

Bordwell, David. *The Way Hollywood Tells It: Story and Style in Modern Movies*. Berkeley: University of California Press, 2006.

Bordwell, David, Janet Staiger, and Kristin Thompson. *The Classical Hollywood Cinema: Film Style & Mode of Production to 1960*. New York: Columbia University Press, 1985.

Bordwell, David, and Kristin Thompson. *Film Art: An Introduction*. 6th ed. New York: McGraw-Hill, 2001.

"Box Office: *Hannibal* Takes a Record-Sized Bite." *ABC News*. 11 Feb. 2001. Accessed 9 Aug. 2011. http://abcnews.go.com/Entertainment/story?id=109619&page=1.

Bracken, Mike. Rev. of *Nightmare City* (2002, Anchor Bay DVD). *Epinions*. 19 Sept. 2000. Accessed 12 July 2011. http://www0.epinions.com/review/mvie_mu-1004232/mvie-review-834-11D1FF45-39C7ACCE-prod3.

Brophy, Philip. "Horrality – The Textuality of Contemporary Horror Films." *The Horror Reader*. Ed. Ken Gelder. London: Routledge, 2000: 276–284.

Brottman, Mikita. *Offensive Films: Toward an Anthropology of Cinéma Vomitif*. Westport, Conn.: Greenwood, 1997.

Butler, Judith. *Gender Trouble: Feminism and the Subversion of Identity*. New York: Routledge, 1990.

Carter, Angela. *The Sadeian Woman: An Exercise in Cultural History*. London: Virago, 1979.

Case, Sue-Ellen. "Tracking the Vampire." *The Horror Reader*. Ed. Ken Gelder. London: Routledge, 2000: 198–209.

Chaw, Walter. Rev. of *Trauma* (2005, Anchor Bay DVD) and *The Card Player* (2005, Anchor Bay DVD). *Film Freak Central*. 17 Oct. 2005. Accessed 4 June 2009. http://filmfreakcentral.net/dvdreviews/argentotwofer.htm.

Cherry, Brigid. "Screaming for Release: Femininity and Horror Film Fandom in Britain." *British Horror Cinema*. Ed. Steve Chibnall and Julian Petley. London: Routledge, 2002: 42–57.

Clover, Carol J. *Men, Women, and Chain Saws: Gender in the Modern Horror Film*. Princeton, N.J.: Princeton University Press, 1992.

"Consumer Spending Reaches $24.3 Billion for Yearly Home Video Sales: DVD Players in More than 82 Million U.S. Homes." *Digital Entertainment Group*. 5 Jan. 2006. Accessed 6 Jan. 2006. http://www.digitalentertainmentinfo.com/News/press/CES010506.htm.

Cook, David A. *Lost Illusions: American Cinema in the Shadow of Watergate and Vietnam, 1970–1979*. Berkeley: University of California Press, 2000.

Creed, Barbara. "Horror and the Monstrous-Feminine: An Imaginary Abjection." *The Dread of Difference: Gender and the Horror Film. Ed. Barry Keith Grant. Austin: University of Texas Press, 1996: 35–65.

Daniel, Robert. "The Stendhal Syndrome." Art of Darkness: The Cinema of Dario Argento. Ed. Chris Gallant. Guilford in Surrey, England: Flesh and Blood Press, 2000: 231–235.

Davis, Wade. Passage of Darkness: The Ethnobiology of the Haitian Zombie. Chapel Hill: University of North Carolina Press, 1988.

Deleuze, Gilles. "Coldness and Cruelty." Masochism. Trans. Jean McNeil. New York: Zone, 1991: 8–138.

Deleuze, Gilles, and Félix Guattari. Anti-Oedipus: Capitalism and Schizophrenia. Trans. Robert Hurley, Mark Seem, and Helen R. Lane. Minneapolis: University of Minnesota Press, 1983.

———. A Thousand Plateaus: Capitalism and Schizophrenia. Trans. Brian Massumi. Minneapolis: University of Minnesota Press, 1987.

DeVos, Andrew. "The More You Rape Their Senses, the Happier They Are: A History of Cannibal Holocaust." Cinema Inferno: Celluloid Explosions from the Cultural Margins. Ed. Robert G. Weiner and John Cline. Lanham, Md.: Scarecrow, 2010: 76–100.

Dixon, Wheeler Winston. A History of Horror. New Brunswick, N.J.: Rutgers University Press, 2010.

———. It Looks at You: The Returned Gaze of Cinema. Albany: State University of New York Press, 1995.

Doty, Alexander. Flaming Classics: Queering the Film Canon. New York: Routledge, 2000.

Dyer, Richard. White. London: Routledge, 1997.

Dyer, Richard, and Ginette Vincendeau. "Introduction." Popular European Cinema. Ed. Richard Dyer and Ginette Vincendeau. London: Routledge, 1992: 1–14.

Edelstein, David. "Now Playing at Your Local Multiplexes: Torture Porn." New York Magazine. 6 Feb. 2006. Accessed 17 Mar. 2006. http://newyorkmetro.com/movies/features/15622.

Epstein, Edward Jay. "Hollywood's Death Spiral: The Secret Numbers Tell the Story." Slate. 25 July 2005. Accessed 1 Apr. 2008. http://www.slate.com/id/2123286.

Farmer, Brett. Spectacular Passions: Cinema, Fantasy, Gay Male Spectatorships. Durham, N.C.: Duke University Press, 2000.

Fenton, Harvey, Julian Grainger, and Gian Luca Castoldi. Cannibal Holocaust and the Savage Cinema of Ruggero Deodato. Guilford in Surrey, England: Flesh and Blood Press, 1999.

Fentone, Steve. AntiCristo: The Bible of Nasty Nun Sinema and Culture. Guilford in Surrey, England: Flesh and Blood Press, 2000.

Foster, Gwendolyn Audrey. Captive Bodies: Postcolonial Subjectivity in Cinema. Albany: State University of New York Press, 1999.

Foster, Hal. "Postmodernism: A Preface." The Anti-Aesthetic: Essays on Postmodern Culture. Ed. Hal Foster. Seattle: Bay Press, 1983: ix–xvi.

Fowler, Catherine. "Introduction." The European Cinema Reader. Ed. Catherine Fowler. London: Routledge, 2002: 1–10.

Frayling, Christopher. Spaghetti Westerns: Cowboys and Europeans from Karl May to Sergio Leone. Rev. ed. New York: Tauris, 1998.

Freeland, Cynthia A. The Naked and the Undead: Evil and the Appeal of Horror. Boulder, Colo.: Westview, 2000.

French, Philip. Rev. of Trouble Every Day. Guardian Unlimited. 29 Dec. 2002. Accessed 4 Mar. 2007. http://film.guardian.co.uk/News_Story/Critic_Review/Observer_review/0,,866031,00.html.

Friedberg, Anne. "Cinema and the Postmodern Condition." *Viewing Positions: Ways of Seeing Film*. Ed. Linda Williams. New Brunswick, N.J.: Rutgers University Press, 1994: 59–83.

Gabler, Neal. "The Movie Magic Is Gone." *Los Angeles Times*. 25 Feb. 2007. Accessed 18 Mar. 2007. http://www.latimes.com/news/opinion/commentary/la-op-gabler25feb25,0,4482096.story.

Garber, Marjorie. *Vested Interests: Cross-Dressing and Cultural Anxiety*. London: Routledge, 1992.

Gelder, Ken. "Introduction to Part Ten." *The Horror Reader*. Ed. Ken Gelder. London: Routledge, 2000: 311–313.

Guins, Raiford. "Blood and Black Gloves on Shiny Discs: New Media, Old Tastes, and the Remediation of Italian Horror Films in the United States." *Horror International*. Ed. Steven Jay Schneider and Tony Williams. Detroit, Mich.: Wayne State University Press, 2005: 15–32.

Halberstam, Judith. *Skin Shows: Gothic Horror and the Technology of Monsters*. Durham, N.C.: Duke University Press, 1995.

Halberstam, Judith, and Ira Livingston. "Introduction: Posthuman Bodies." *Posthuman Bodies*. Ed. Judith Halberstam and Ira Livingston. Bloomington: Indiana University Press, 1995: 1–19.

Halbfinger, David M. "Pirates, Penguins and Potboilers Rule the Box Office." *New York Times*. 2 Jan. 2007. Accessed 2 Jan. 2007. http://www.nytimes.com/2007/01/02/movies/02boff.html?ref=davidmhalbfinger.

Hall, Stuart. "Encoding/Decoding." *The Cultural Studies Reader*. Ed. Simon During. London: Routledge, 1993: 90–103.

"Hannibal." *Box Office Mojo*. 9 Aug. 2011. http://boxofficemojo.com/movies/?id=hannibal.htm.

Hantke, Steffen. "Academic Film Criticism, the Rhetoric of Crisis, and the Current State of American Horror Cinema: Thoughts on Canonicity and Academic Anxiety." *College Literature* 34:4 (Fall 2007): 191–202.

Hardy, Phil, ed. *The Aurum Film Encyclopedia: Horror*. London: Aurum, 1985.

Harris, Mark H. "About Us." *BlackHorrorMovies.com*. 18 Aug. 2009. http://blackhorrormovies.com/aboutus.htm.

Hart, Lynda. "Doing It Anyway: Lesbian Sado-Masochism and Performance." *Performance and Cultural Politics*. Ed. Elin Diamond. London: Routledge, 1996: 48–61.

Hawkins, Joan. *Cutting Edge: Art-Horror and the Horrific Avant-Garde*. Minneapolis: University of Minnesota Press, 2000.

Heffernan, Kevin. *Ghouls, Gimmicks, and Gold: Horror Films and the American Movie Business, 1953–1968*. Durham, N.C.: Duke University Press, 2004.

Hill, Annette. *Shocking Entertainment: Viewer Response to Violent Movies*. Luton, England: University of Luton Press, 1997.

Hills, Matt. *Fan Cultures*. London: Routledge, 2002.

———. *The Pleasures of Horror*. New York: Continuum, 2005.

Hollows, Joanne. "The Masculinity of Cult." *Defining Cult Movies: The Cultural Politics of Oppositional Taste*. Ed. Mark Jancovich, Antonio Lázaro Reboll, Julian Stringer, and Andy Willis. Manchester, England: Manchester University Press, 2003: 35–53.

Holson, Laura M. "With Popcorn, DVD's and TiVo, Moviegoers Are Staying Home." *New York Times*. 27 May 2005. Accessed 18 Apr. 2008. http://www.nytimes.com/2005/05/27/business/media/27movie.html?_r=1&scp=7&sq=movie&st=nyt&oref=slogin.

"Home Entertainment Enjoys Another Outstanding Year." *Digital Entertainment Group*. 7 Jan. 2008. Accessed 16 Apr. 2008. http://www.digitalenter

tainmentinfo.com/News/press/CES2008yearEnd.htm.

Howarth, Troy. *The Haunted World of Mario Bava*. Guilford in Surrey, England: Flesh and Blood Press, 2002.

Hulme, Peter. "Introduction: The Cannibal Scene." *Cannibalism and the Colonial World*. Ed. Francis Barker, Peter Hulme, and Margaret Iversen. Cambridge: Cambridge University Press, 1998: 1–38.

Hunt, Leon. "Boiling Oil and Baby Oil: *Bloody Pit of Horror*." *Alternative Europe: Eurotrash and Exploitation Cinema since 1945*. Ed. Ernest Mathjis and Xavier Mendik. London: Wallflower, 2004: 173–180.

———. "A (Sadistic) Night at the Opera: Notes on the Italian Horror Film." *The Horror Reader*. Ed. Ken Gelder. London: Routledge, 2000: 324–335.

Hurley, Kelly. "Reading like an Alien: Posthuman Identity in Ridley Scott's *Alien* and David Cronenberg's *Rabid*." *Posthuman Bodies*. Ed. Judith Halberstam and Ira Livingston. Bloomington: Indiana University Press, 1995: 203–224.

Hutchings, Peter. *The Horror Film*. New York: Longman, 2004.

Jäckel, Anne. *European Film Industries*. London: British Film Institute, 2003.

Jameson, Fredric. "Postmodernism and Consumer Society." *Movies and Mass Culture*. Ed. John Belton. New Brunswick, N.J.: Rutgers University Press, 1996: 185–202.

Kehr, Dave. "Hailing the DVD Distributors: The Best Vault Raiders of 2005." *New York Times*. 30 Dec. 2005. Accessed 9 Jan. 2006. http://www.nytimes.com/2005/12/30/movies/30dvd.html?ex=1136955600&en=23ae1dfaab4456da&ei=5070.

Kiernan, Matthew. "The Horror Box Office for 2007." AMC. 2 Jan. 2008. Accessed 28 May 2008. http://blogs.amctv.com/monsterfest/2008/01/the-horror-box-.php.

Kilday, Greg. "$9.63 Bil Boxoffice for '07 Breaks Record." *Hollywood Reporter*. 6 Mar. 2008. Accessed 28 Mar. 2008. http://www.hollywoodreporter.com/news/963-bil-boxoffice-07-breaks-106299.

Kilgour, Maggie. "The Function of Cannibalism at the Present Time." *Cannibalism and the Colonial World*. Ed. Francis Barker, Peter Hulme, and Margaret Iversen. Cambridge: Cambridge University Press, 1998: 238–259.

Kinder, Marsha. *Blood Cinema: The Reconstruction of National Identity in Spain*. Berkeley: University of California Press, 1993.

King, Geoff. *New Hollywood Cinema: An Introduction*. New York: Columbia University Press, 2002.

Kipnis, Laura. *Bound and Gagged: Pornography and the Politics of Fantasy in America*. New York: Grove, 1996.

Klady, Leonard. "Read Their Lips: Americans Don't Like Dubbing." *New York Times*. 29 Aug. 1999: AR21.

Klinger, Barbara. *Beyond the Multiplex: Cinema, New Technologies, and the Home*. Berkeley: University of California Press, 2006.

Knee, Adam. "Gender, Genre, Argento." *The Dread of Difference: Gender and the Horror Film*. Ed. Barry Keith Grant. Austin: University of Texas Press, 1996: 213–230.

Knight, Rich. "*Troll 2* Is Better than *Citizen Kane*." *Cold Rice and a Little Rat Meat*. 7 Aug. 2009. Accessed 9 July 2011. http://lovethymovies.blogspot.com/2009/08/troll-2-is-better-than-citizen-kane.html.

Kornblum, Janet. "'Shining' Moment for Ryang's Remix." *USA Today*. 22 Jan. 2007. Accessed 25 June 2007. http://www.usatoday.com/printedition/life/20070123/d_digita123_side.art.htm.

Koven, Mikel J. *La Dolce Morte: Vernacular Cinema and the Italian Giallo Film*. Lanham, Md.: Scarecrow, 2006.

Landis, Bill, and Michelle Clifford. *Sleazoid Express: A Mind-Twisting Tour through the Grindhouse Cinema of Times Square*. New York: Fireside, 2002.

Lieberman, David. "Horror Genre Rises from the Dead – Again." *USA Today*. 25 Oct. 2005. Accessed 28 Apr. 2008. http://www.usatoday.com/money/media/2006-10-25-horror-usat_x.htm.

MacCannell, Dean. "Cannibal Tours." *Visualizing Theory: Selected Essays from V. A. R., 1990–1994*. Ed. Lucien Taylor. New York: Routledge, 1994: 99–114.

Mathjis, Ernest, and Xavier Mendik. "Editorial Introduction: What Is Cult Film?" *The Cult Film Reader*. Ed. Ernest Mathjis and Xavier Mendik. New York: McGraw-Hill, 2008: 1–11.

———. "Introduction: Making Sense of Extreme Confusion: European Exploitation and Underground Cinema." *Alternative Europe: Eurotrash and Exploitation Cinema since 1945*. Ed. Ernest Mathjis and Xavier Mendik. London: Wallflower, 2004: 1–18.

Mayne, Judith. *Cinema and Spectatorship*. London: Routledge, 1993.

———. *Framed: Lesbians, Feminists, and Media Culture*. Minneapolis: University of Minnesota Press, 2000.

McDonagh, Maitland. *Broken Mirrors/Broken Minds: The Dark Dreams of Dario Argento*. New York: Carol, 1994.

McKelvey, John W. Response to "What Do You Miss Most in Today's Horror Films?, What's Missing?" *Mobius Home Video Forum*. 4 May 2007. Accessed 20 June 2007. http://z8.invisionfree.com/MHVF/index.php?showtopic=7648&st=20&#entry1100821.

McRoy, Jay. "*Cannibal Holocaust*." *100 European Horror Films*. Ed. Steven Jay Schneider. London: British Film Institute, 2007: 39–40.

Media by Numbers. "Hollywood Doldrums." *New York Times*. 1 Jan. 2008. Accessed 2 Jan. 2008. http://www.nytimes.com/imagepages/2008/01/01/arts/02yearready.html.

Mendik, Xavier. "Detection and Transgression: The Investigative Drive of the Giallo." *Necronomicon: Book One*. Ed. Andy Black. London: Creation, 1996: 35–54.

Minh-ha, Trinh T. *Cinema Interval*. New York: Routledge, 1999.

Modleski, Tania. "The Terror of Pleasure: The Contemporary Horror Film and Postmodern Theory." *The Horror Reader*. Ed. Ken Gelder. London: Routledge, 2000: 285–293.

Moerk, Christian. "The Oscar for Best Zombie Goes To . . ." *New York Times*. 30 Apr. 2005. Accessed 30 Apr. 2005. http://www.nytimes.com/2005/04/30/movies/MoviesFeatures/30wax.html.

Motion Picture Association of America. "Theatrical Market Statistics: 2011." MPAA. Accessed 13 Apr. 2012. http://www.mpaa.org/Resources/5bec4ac9-a95e-443b-987b-bff6fb5455a9.pdf.

———. "U.S. Theatrical Market: 2005 Statistics." *Runaway Production Research*. Accessed 12 July 2011. http://www.stoprunaway-production.com/wp-content/uploads/2009/07/2005-MPAA-Market-Stats-26-pages.pdf.

MovieMaven. "Whats [sic] Wrong with Modern Horror?" *Horror-Movies.ca*. 19 Mar. 2008. Accessed 28 May 2008. http://www.horror-movies.ca/horror_11209.html.

Mulvey, Laura. "Visual Pleasure and Narrative Cinema." *Visual and Other Pleasures*. Bloomington: Indiana University Press, 1989: 14–26.

Nakahara, Tamao. "Barred Nuns: Italian Nunsploitation Films." *Alternative Europe: Eurotrash and Exploitation Cinema since 1945*. Ed. Ernest Mathjis and Xavier Mendik. London: Wallflower, 2004: 124–133.

Naugle, Patrick. Rev. of *Hell of the Living Dead* (2002, Anchor Bay DVD). DVD

Verdict. 19 Feb. 2002. Accessed 11 Aug. 2005. http://www.dvdverdict.com/reviews/helllivingdead.php.

Needham, Gary. "The Bird with the Crystal Plumage." *Art of Darkness: The Cinema of Dario Argento.* Ed. Chris Gallant. Guilford in Surrey, England: Flesh and Blood Press, 2000: 87–94.

———. "Playing with Genre: Defining the Italian *Giallo.*" *Fear without Frontiers: Horror Cinema across the Globe.* Ed. Steven Jay Schneider. Guilford in Surrey, England: Flesh and Blood Press, 2003: 135–144.

Newman, Kim. "Blood and Black Lace." *100 European Horror Films.* Ed. Steven Jay Schneider. London: British Film Institute, 2007: 21–23.

———. *Nightmare Movies: A Critical Guide to Contemporary Horror Films.* New York: Harmony, 1988.

"Nightmare Theatre Presents *Troll 2* with Star George Hardy! at the Silver Screen." *Eventful.* 5 Jan. 2008. Accessed 9 July 2011. http://eventful.com/pensacola/events/nightmare-theatre-presents-troll-2-star-george-ha-/E0-001-008192043-8.

O'Brien, Geoffrey. *The Phantom Empire: Movies in the Mind of the 20th Century.* New York: Norton, 1993.

Peary, Gerald. Interview with Claire Denis. *Gerald Peary: Film Reviews, Interviews, Essays & Sundry Miscellany.* May 2002. Accessed 4 Mar. 2007. http://www.geraldpeary.com/interviews/def/denis.html.

Phillips, Michael W., Jr. Rev. of *After Death* (2002, Media Blasters DVD). *Goatdog's Movies.* 21 Jan. 2006. http://goatdog.com/moviePage.php?movieID=572.

Pinedo, Isabel Cristina. *Recreational Terror: Women and the Pleasures of Horror Film Viewing.* Albany: State University of New York Press, 1997.

Place, Janey. "Women in Film Noir." *Women in Film Noir.* New ed. Ed. E. Ann Kaplan. London: British Film Institute, 1998: 47–68.

Poe, Edgar Allan. "The Philosophy of Composition." *Great Short Works of Edgar Allan Poe.* Ed. G. R. Thompson. New York: Harper and Row, 1970: 528–542.

Rhodes, Gary D. *White Zombie: Anatomy of a Horror Film.* Jefferson, N.C.: McFarland, 2006.

Roberts, Caroline. "*Troll 2* Fans Descend upon the Brattle." *Bostonist.* 16 July 2007. Accessed 22 July 2007. http://bostonist.com/2007/07/16/troll_2_fans_de.php.

Rony, Fatimah Tobing. *The Third Eye: Race, Cinema, and Ethnographic Spectacle.* Durham, N.C.: Duke University Press, 1996.

Ross, Becki L. "'It's Merely Designed for Sexual Arousal': Interrogating the Indefensibility of Lesbian Smut." *Feminism and Pornography.* Ed. Drucilla Cornell. Oxford: Oxford University Press, 2000: 264–317.

Ruby, Jay. *Picturing Cultures: Explorations of Film and Anthropology.* Chicago: University of Chicago Press, 2000.

Russell, Catherine. *Experimental Ethnography: The Work of Film in the Age of Video.* Durham, N.C.: Duke University Press, 1999.

Sanjek, David. "Fans' Notes: The Horror Film Fanzine." *The Horror Reader.* Ed. Ken Gelder. London: Routledge, 2000: 314–323.

Schaefer, Eric. *"Bold! Daring! Shocking! True!": A History of Exploitation Films, 1919–1959.* Durham, N.C.: Duke University Press, 1999.

Schatz, Tom. "The Studio System and Conglomerate Hollywood." *The Contemporary Hollywood Film Industry.* Ed. Paul McDonald and Janet Wasko. Malden, Mass.: Blackwell, 2008: 13–42.

Schneider, Steven Jay, and Tony Williams. "Introduction." *Horror International.* Ed. Steven Jay Schneider and Tony

Williams. Detroit, Mich.: Wayne State University Press, 2005: 1–12.

Schoell, William. *Stay Out of the Shower: Twenty-Five Years of Shocker Films Beginning with Psycho.* New York: Dembner, 1985.

Schulte-Sasse, Linda. "*The Stendhal Syndrome.*" *100 European Horror Films.* Ed. Steven Jay Schneider. London: British Film Institute, 2007: 190–192.

Sconce, Jeffrey. "'Trashing' the Academy: Taste, Excess, and an Emerging Politics of Cinematic Style." *Film Theory and Criticism.* 6th ed. Ed. Leo Braudy and Marshall Cohen. New York: Oxford University Press, 2004: 534–553.

Seltzer, Mark. *Serial Killers: Death and Life in America's Wound Culture.* New York: Routledge, 1998.

Sharrett, Christopher. "The Horror Film in Neoconservative Culture." *The Dread of Difference: Gender and the Horror Film.* Ed. Barry Keith Grant. Austin: University of Texas Press, 1996: 253–276.

Shaviro, Steven. *The Cinematic Body.* Minneapolis: University of Minnesota Press, 1993.

Snider, Mike. "Blu-Ray Grows, but DVD Slide Nips Home Video Sales." *USA Today.* 9 Jan. 2012. Accessed 13 Apr. 2012. http://www.usatoday.com/tech/news/story/2012-01-10/blu-ray-sales-2011/52473310/1.

Snyder, Gabriel. "Pic Biz Does the Splits." *Variety.* 9 Mar. 2006. Accessed 14 Mar. 2006. http://variety.com/index.asp?layout=print_story&articleid=VR1117939523&categoryid=13.

Sobchack, Vivian. "Phenomenology and the Film Experience." *Viewing Positions: Ways of Seeing Film.* Ed. Linda Williams. New Brunswick, N.J.: Rutgers University Press, 1994: 36–58.

Sorlin, Pierre. *European Cinemas, European Societies: 1939–1990.* London: Routledge, 1991.

Stam, Robert. *Film Theory: An Introduction.* Malden, Mass.: Blackwell, 2000.

Studlar, Gaylyn. *In the Realm of Pleasure: Von Sternberg, Dietrich, and the Masochist Aesthetic.* Urbana: University of Illinois Press, 1988.

superhero. "I Watch This Movie Every Day . . ." *Internet Movie Database.* 22 Jan. 2000. Accessed 9 July 2011. http://www.imdb.com/title/tt0105643/usercomments?start=11.

swansong. "On Goblins." *Myspace.* 12 July 2006. Accessed 24 June 2007. http://blog.myspace.com/index.cfm?fuseaction=blog.view&friendID=91992407&blogID=143880048.

Syder, Andrew. "*Short Night of the Glass Dolls.*" *100 European Horror Films.* Ed. Steven Jay Schneider. London: British Film Institute, 2007: 186–187.

Tani, Stefano. *The Doomed Detective: The Contribution of the Detective Novel to Postmodern American and Italian Fiction.* Carbondale: Southern Illinois University Press, 1984.

The Film Fiend. Rev. of *Troll 2.* *Fatally Yours.* 10 July 2007. Accessed 9 July 2011. http://www.fatally-yours.com/horror-reviews/troll-2.

thegreatob. "*Troll 2,* the PCC and Me!" *Musings of a Film Fanatic.* 20 Feb. 2011. Accessed 9 July 2011. http://thegreatob.wordpress.com/2011/02/20/troll-2-the-pcc-and-me.

Thompson, Kristin. "The Concept of Cinematic Excess." *Film Theory and Criticism.* 6th ed. Ed. Leo Braudy and Marshall Cohen. New York: Oxford University Press, 2004: 513–524.

Thrower, Stephen. *Beyond Terror: The Films of Lucio Fulci.* Guilford in Surrey, England: Flesh and Blood Press, 1999.

Tohill, Cathal, and Pete Tombs. *Immoral Tales: European Sex and Horror Movies 1956–1984.* New York: St. Martin's Griffin, 1994.

Tyner, Adam. Response to "a TROLL 2 question." *Mobius Home Video Forum.* 13 Sept. 2006. Accessed 9 July 2011. http://z8.invisionfree.com/MHVF/index.

php?showtopic=3598&view=findpost&p=10115476.

Villinger, Craig. Rev. of *Cannibals* (2007, Blue Underground DVD). *Digital Retribution*. 24 Sept. 2008. Accessed 25 Aug. 2009. http://www.digital-retribution.com/reviews/dvd/0950.php.

Wagstaff, Christopher. "A Forkful of Westerns: Industry, Audiences and the Italian Western." *Popular European Cinema*. Ed. Richard Dyer and Ginette Vincendeau. London: Routledge, 1992: 245–261.

Watson, Paul. "There's No Accounting for Taste: Exploitation Cinema and the Limits of Film Theory." *Trash Aesthetics: Popular Culture and Its Audience*. Ed. Deborah Cartmell, I. Q. Hunter, Heidi Kaye, and Imelda Whelehan. Chicago: Pluto, 1997: 66–83.

Waxman, Sharon. "Summer Fading, Hollywood Sees Fizzle." *New York Times*. 24 Aug. 2005. Accessed 24 Aug. 2005. http://www.nytimes.com/2005/08/24/movies/24slum.html?scp=183&sq=&st=nyt.

Wells, Paul. *The Horror Genre: From Beelzebub to Blair Witch*. London: Wallflower, 2000.

White, Patricia. *unInvited: Classical Hollywood Cinema and Lesbian Representability*. Bloomington: Indiana University Press, 1999.

Williams, Alex. "Up to Her Eyes in Gore, and Loving It." *New York Times*. 30 Apr. 2006. Accessed 26 Apr. 2008. http://www.nytimes.com/2006/04/30/fashion/sundaystyles/30horror.html?scp=153&sq=&st=nyt.

Williams, Linda. "Film Bodies: Gender, Genre, and Excess." *Film Theory and Criticism*. 6th ed. Ed. Leo Braudy and Marshall Cohen. New York: Oxford University Press, 2004: 727–741.

———. *Hard Core: Power, Pleasure, and the "Frenzy of the Visible."* Berkeley: University of California Press, 1989.

———. *Screening Sex*. Durham, N.C.: Duke University Press, 2008.

———. "When the Woman Looks." *Re-Vision: Essays in Feminist Film Criticism*. Ed. Mary Ann Doane, Patricia Mellencamp, and Linda Williams. Frederick, Md.: University Publications of America, 1984: 83–99.

Willis, Andrew. "Spanish Horror and the Flight from 'Art' Cinema, 1967–73." *Defining Cult Movies: The Cultural Politics of Oppositional Taste*. Ed. Mark Jancovich, Antonio Lázaro Reboll, Julian Stringer, and Andy Willis. Manchester, England: Manchester University Press, 2003: 71–83.

Wolf-Sothern, Austin. "Why I Love *Troll 2*: For All the Right Reasons." *Placenta Ovaries*. 1 Nov. 2008. Accessed 9 July 2011. http://www.placentaovaries.net/blog/2008/11/why-i-love-troll-2-for-all-the-right-reasons.html.

Wood, Robin. "An Introduction to the American Horror Film." *Planks of Reason: Essays on the Horror Film*. Ed. Barry Keith Grant. Metuchen, N.J.: Scarecrow, 1984: 164–200.

Yapp, Nate. Rev. of *The Whip and the Body*. Classic-Horror.com. 23 Oct. 2007. Accessed 29 June 2009. http://classic-horror.com/reviews/whip_and_the_body_1963.

Zacharek, Stephanie. "Subdued Pedro Almodóvar Returns to Cannes, and Cannes Returns to Normal." *Movieline*. 19 May 2011. Accessed 6 June 2011. http://www.movieline.com/2011/05/subdued-pedro-almodovar-returns-to-cannes-and-cannes-returns-to-normal.php.

Zalcock, Bev. *Renegade Sisters: Girl Gangs on Film*. New ed. London: Creation, 2001.

Zavarzadeh, Mas'ud. *Seeing Films Politically*. Albany: State University of New York Press, 1991.

INDEX

Note: Illustrations are represented by *italicized* page numbers.

The Abandoned (2006), 219
Abbott and Costello Meet Frankenstein (1948), 143
Abby (1974), 184
academic objections: "art cinema" classification limitations, 40–43; audience, 31–32; cheapness of production, 24–25; *cinéma vomitif*, 36–39; commercial motivation, 23; dated quality, 26–29; dubbing, 27–29; eroticism, 30–31; exploitation, 23–26; graphic sex-violence combination, 36–39; homophobia, 36; horror-pornography association, 10, 30–31; ideological issues, 23; racism, 36; reactionary political content, 34–36; sensationalism, 29–30, 33–35; spectacle v. story, 30–31, 33–35; tastelessness, 23–26
Africa addio (1966), 190
After Death (1989). See *Zombie 4: After Death* (1989)
Aja, Alexandre, 220–21
The Alamo (2004), 91
Albanesi, Gabriele, 223
L'aldilà (1981). See *The Beyond* (1981)
Alice in Wonderland (2010), 91
Alien (1979), 10, 143
À l'intérieur (2007). See *Inside* (2007)
All the Colors of the Dark (1972), 119–121, 127, 223

Almodóvar, Pedro, 10, 224, 231–32
Altman, Robert, 120
À ma soeur! (2001). See *Fat Girl* (2001)
Amer (2009), 10, 222, 223
American audience attraction: American horror film renaissance, 91; audience demographic expansion, 91; blockbuster cinema, 218; digital home video technologies, 88–89; European horror films appeal, 98–99; Hollywood corporatization, 83–87, 89–91, 218; Hollywood cultural irrelevance, 90–91; Hollywood home video domination, 220–21; Hollywood horror film quality, 94–97; Hollywood studio horror division formation, 91; horror film revival, 92–94; horror genre in popular culture, 93–94; interactive entertainment technologies, 87–92; internet, 88; nostalgia, 97–98; video games, 88, 93
American cannibal films: antiethnology, 197–98; globalization/contemporary culture relationship, 197–99; influences, 193–94; nonwhite cannibalism as rationale for imperialism/colonialism, 192–93; performative spectatorship, 216; racial Othering, 193–94; relocation of cannibalism to white mainstream culture, 194–97; travelogue influence, 193; white cannibalism, 189, 194–99
An American Werewolf in London (forthcoming film), 95

243

American zombie films, 204–207, 216. *See also specific films*
Among the Cannibal Isles of the South Pacific (1918), 193
Anatomie (2000). *See Anatomy* (2000)
Anatomy (2000), 219
Andrade, Joaquim Pedro de, 203
Angkor (1935), 190
L'année dernière à Marienbad (1961). *See Last Year at Marienbad* (1961)
Antibodies (2005), 219, 220
Antichrist (2009), 10, 224
anti-colonialism. *See* anti-imperialism
anti-imperialism: antiethnology, 197–98; *Cannibal Apocalypse* (1981), 187–88; *Cannibal Holocaust* (1980), 201–202, 203; colonialism deconstruction, 199–204; *The Mountain of the Cannibal God* (1978), 191–92, 199, 200
Antikörper (2005). *See Antibodies* (2005)
Antonioni, Michelangelo, 8, 24, 107
Apocalypse domani (1981). *See Cannibal Apocalypse* (1981)
Apocalypse Now (1979), 186
April Fool's Day (2008), 95
Aranda, Vicente, 47
Argento, Dario: *The Bird with the Crystal Plumage* (1970), 130–135, *133*, 136, 137; *The Card Player* (2004), 222; *The Cat o' Nine Tails* (1971), 7, 10; *Deep Red* (1975), 8, 128, 136; digitization, 15, 17, 19; European art cinema, 7, 8; as horror auteur, 11; *Inferno* (1980), 19; internet popularity, 12; as model for Denis, 231; new work, 222; 1990s films, 218–19; *Opera* (1987), 128; *Sleepless* (2001), 222; *The Stendhal Syndrome* (1996), 135–141; *Suspiria* (1977), 10, 17, 19, 29–30, 222, 223; *Tenebre* (1982), 128; *Trauma* (1993), 128
Around the World in 80 Days (2004), 91
Arthur (2011), 85
El ataque de los muertos sin ojos (1973). *See Return of the Evil Dead* (1973)
Avatar (2009), 89
AVP: *Alien v. Predator* (2004), 184
L'avventura (1960), 24
The Awful Dr. Orlof (1962), 152

The Awful Story of the Nun of Monza (1969), 175

Bava, Mario: *Bay of Blood* (1971), 10; *Black Sabbath* (1963), 20, 222; *Black Sunday* (1960), 9, 20; *Blood and Black Lace* (1964), 107–116, *114*; digitization, 15; European art cinema, 8; and *giallo* film genre, 9–10; *The Girl Who Knew Too Much* (1963), 9, 20; *Kidnapped* (1974), 20; *Kill, Baby . . . Kill* (1966), 8, 20; *Planet of the Vampires* (1965), 10; re-releases, 20; *The Whip and the Body* (1963), 142–152, 154, 180, 220
Bay of Blood (1971), 10
The Beast (1975), 30–31
Beau travail (1999), 225
La bella Antonia, prima Monica e poi Dimonia (1972). *See Naughty Nun* (1972)
Belle de jour (1967), 126
Belphégor – le fantôme du Louvre (2001). *See Belphégor – Phantom of the Louvre* (2001)
Belphégor – Phantom of the Louvre (2001), 219
Benigni, Roberto, 29
Bertolucci, Bernardo, 24, 107
Best Worst Movie (2009), 77
La bête (1975). *See The Beast* (1975)
The Beyond (1981), 18, 19, 20, 208
Bianchi, Andrea, 16, 208
Bido, Antonio, 223
The Birds (forthcoming film), 95
The Bird with the Crystal Plumage (1970), *133*; art as dangerous, 139, 140; art as liberating, 140; gender destabilization, 131–35; as *giallo* film, 220; subversion of traditional gender roles, 133–35, 136, 137; synopsis, 130–31
The Black Belly of the Tarantula (1971), 34–35
Black Christmas (2006), 194
Black Demons (1991), 36, 208
Black Narcissus (1947), 175
Black Sabbath (1963), 20, 222
Black Sunday (1960), 9, 20
Blacula (1972), 184

INDEX

Blade series, 184
The Blair Witch Project (1999), 197
The Blob (forthcoming film), 91
Blonde Savage (1947), 192
Blood and Black Lace (1964), *114*; as anti-detective story, 115; audience points of view, 111–13; ending characteristics, 108–110; as first *giallo* film, 107; generic identity, 115; as *giallo* film, 220; murder set pieces, 111–12, 114–15; narrative closure repudiation, 108; performative spectatorship, 111–16; plot characteristics, 107–108; production devices, 110; synopsis, 103–104; visceral viewer response, 113–14
Blood and Roses (1960), 35
Bloody Pit of Horror (1965), 151
Blow-Up (1966), 8, 107
The Boat (1981), 28
Il boia scarlatto (1965). See *Bloody Pit of Horror* (1965)
Bones (2001), 184
Das Boot (1981). See *The Boat* (1981)
Born on the Fourth of July (1989), 186
Borowczyk, Walerian, 30, 38
The Bourne Legacy (2012), 85
Breillat, Catherine, 224, 232
British Video Recordings Act of 1984, 38–39
The Brood (forthcoming film), 95
Brotherhood of the Wolf (2001), 219, 220
Buñuel, Luis, 126, 160, 214, 225
El buque maldito (1974). See *The Ghost Galleon* (1974)
Burial Ground (1981), 208

La caduta degli dei (1969). See *The Damned* (1969)
Caged (1950), 169
Calvaire (2004), 219, 220
Candyman series, 184
Canevari, Cesare, 42
Cani arrabbiati (1974). See *Kidnapped* (1974)
Cannibal Apocalypse (1981): deconstruction of white hero-nonwhite villain scenario, 188; moral bankruptcy of post-colonial power structure, 187–88; narrative deconstruction of whiteness, 186–88, 200; as postcolonial zombie film, 220; racial issues engagement, 183; synopsis, 182–83; whiteness-death association, 186–87
Cannibal Attack (1954), 194
Cannibal Capers (1930), 194
Cannibal Ferox (1981), 36, 192, 199, 200
Cannibal ferox (1981). See *Cannibal Ferox* (1981)
cannibal films. See American cannibal films; European cannibal films; *specific films*
Cannibal Holocaust (1980): critical and legislative attacks, 215–16; as critique of exotic exploitation cinema, 203; digitization, 17, 19, 20; fantasy-reality reversal, 203; reversal of "savage" label for nonwhites, 201–202; synopsis, 200–201; whiteness-death association, 201–202
Cannibal Island (1956), 194
Cannibal Tours (1989), 198
Cannibals (1980), 192, 199, 200
Cannibals of the South Seas (1912), 193
Canning the Cannibal King (1917), 193
The Canterbury Tales (1972), 175
Captive Wild Woman (1943), 183
Captivity (2007), 94
The Card Player (2004), 222
Carpenter, John, 92, 219
Carrie (forthcoming film), 95
Cars (2006), 89
Il cartaio (2004). See *The Card Player* (2004)
Casa privata per le SS (1977). See *SS Girls* (1977)
The Case of the Scorpion's Tail (1971), 223
Il castello dei morti vivi (1964). See *Castle of the Living Dead* (1964)
Castle of Blood (1964), 7
Castle of the Living Dead (1964), 20
Castle, William, 120
A Cat in the Brain (1990), 223
The Cat o'Nine Tails (1971), 7, 10
Cattet, Hélène, 222
Cavara, Paolo, 34

C'est arrivé près de chez vous (1992). See *Man Bites Dog* (1992)
La chagrin et la pitié (1969). See *The Sorrow and the Pity* (1969)
Un chien andalou (1929), 214
Child's Play (forthcoming film), 95
Chocolat (1988), 225
Christensen, Benjamin, 175
Citizen Kane (1941), 80
City of the Living Dead (1980), 208
Clash of the Titans (2010), 85
closure repudiation. *See* narrative closure repudiation
Clouzot, Henri-Georges, 9
Cobra Woman (1944), 183–84
Cocteau, Jean, 160
La coda dello scorpione (1971). See *The Case of the Scorpion's Tail* (1971)
Coming Home (1978), 185–86
La commare secca (1962), 107
The Conformist (1970), 24
Il conformista (1970). See *The Conformist* (1970)
Cosa avete fatto a Solange? (1972). See *What Have You Done to Solange?* (1972)
La cotta notte delle bamole di verto (1971). See *Short Night of the Glass Dolls* (1971)
Craven, Wes, 34, 219
The Crazies (2010), 95
Crazy as Hell (2002), 184
Creature from the Black Lagoon (forthcoming film), 91
The Crimson Rivers (2000), 219, 220

Dallamano, Massimo, 35, 223
La dama rossa uccide sette volte (1972). See *The Red Queen Kills 7 Times* (1972)
D'Amato, Joe, 37, 71, 73, 176–180
The Damned (1969), 7
Dante, Joe, 92
Danza macabra (1964). See *Castle of Blood* (1964)
Darkness (2002), 219
The Dark Knight (2008), 84
Dark Shadows (2012), 95
Daughters of Darkness (1971), 19
Dawn of the Dead (1978), 18, 206, 209

Dawn of the Dead (2004), 206, 220
Day of the Dead (1985), 206
Day of the Dead (2008), 95
The Day the Earth Stood Still (2008), 91
Dead Snow (2009), 219
De Angelis, Fabrizio, 209
Death in Venice (1971), 24
Il Decameron (1971). See *The Decameron* (1971)
The Decameron (1971), 175
deconstruction of historical imperialism/colonialism. *See* anti-imperialism
Deep in the Woods (2000), 219, 220
Deep Red (1975), 8, 128, 136
The Deer Hunter (1978), 185
Deliverance (1972), 220
Del Toro, Guillermo, 184
Demoni 3 (1991). See *Black Demons* (1991)
Denis, Claire, 10, 224, 225–232
Deodato, Ruggero, 10, 17, 36, 191, 200–204
Detour (1945), 123
The Devil in a Convent (1899), 175
The Devils (1971), 175
The Devil's Daughter (1939), 184
The Devil's Rejects (2005), 91
Le diable au couvent (1899). See *The Devil in a Convent* (1899)
Diabolique (1955), 9
Les diaboliques (1955). See *Diabolique* (1955)
Diary of the Dead (2007), 95
Dickerson, Ernest R., 184
Docteur Jekyll et les femmes (1981). See *Dr. Jekyll and His Women* (1981)
Død snø (2009). See *Dead Snow* (2009)
Dogtooth (2009), 224
La dolce vita (1960), 7, 160
Doom (2005), 206
Don't Be Afraid of the Dark (2010), 95
Double Indemnity (1944), 123
Dr. Jekyll and His Women (1981), 38
Drudi, Rosella, 71
Drums o' Voodoo (1934), 184
Dumont, Bruno, 224

East of Eden (forthcoming film), 91
8½ (1963), 7

Eisenstein, Sergei, 41
Era Gustoso o Meu Francês (1971). See *How Tasty Was My Little Frenchman* (1971)
Erotic Nights of the Living Dead (1980), 37–38
Et mourir de plaisir (1960). See *Blood and Roses* (1960)
ethnographic filmmaking, 197–98
Eugenie (1970). See *Eugenie... the Story of Her Journey into Perversion* (1970)
Eugénie (1974). See *Eugenie de Sade* (1974)
Eugenie de Sade (1974), 153–56
Eugenie... the Story of Her Journey into Perversion (1970), 156–59, 163, 165, 178, 181
European cannibal films: *Cannibal Apocalypse* (1981), 182–83, 186–190; *Cannibal Ferox* (1981), 36,192, 199, 200; *Cannibals* (1980), 199, 200; critical and legislative attacks, 215–16; deconstruction of historical imperialism/colonialism, 189–190, 199–204, 201–202; experimentation with alternative racial roles and identities, 190; influences, 190–91; *The Mountain of the Cannibal God* (1978), 191–92, 193, 199, 200; nonwhite cannibal and white hero, 189–190; nonwhite cannibalism as rationale for imperialism/colonialism, 192–93; notoriety, 191; racial Othering, 191; reversal of "savage" label for nonwhites, 201–202; typical narrative, 190; whiteness-death association, 201–202

European horror films: academic neglect, 21–22; Americanized versions for television, 13; art film connections, 7–8, 223–232; audience demographics, 68–69; censorship relaxation, 151; character, 7–8; common characteristics, 47–48; contemporary relevance, 232; contemporary social message content, 221; cultural sources, 6–7; current commonality with modern American horror, 219–222; dated quality, 26–29; deluxe DVD sets, 17–19; digital home video market, 14–19; distributors, 13; exploitation movies, 47–48; fan-scholars, 11–13; giallo film genre, 9–14; golden age, 6, 8, 47, 217; golden age film connections, 222–23; "gray market" video companies, 14; hard core pornography appearance, 151; heterosexual s&m, 142–168; historical and political experience variations, 46–47; impact on other films, 8–10; independent publishers, 15; internet sites, 12–13; interpretive protocols, 60; legislation against, 38–39; mainstream drift, 14–15; multiplicity, 46–47; narrative closure repudiation, 43, 49, 55, 56, 57; 1990s films, 218–19; nunsploitation films, 35–36, 174–180; paracinematic qualities, 15, 66–67; performative spectatorship overview, 42–45; personalization, 65–66; "playing dead," 42–45; politicization of spectatorship, 66–69; postmodernism, 42, 48–60; psychoanalytical theory, 39–40; queer s&m, 168–180; racism, 36; re-releases in theatres and film festivals, 20; 2000s films, 232; undecidability, 54; unique aspects, 7–8; viewer responses, 69–70; white zombieism, 208; women-in-prison cinema, 168–174. *See also* American audience attraction; performative spectatorship; *specific films*

European zombie films, 204–206, 208–215. *See also specific films*
The Evil Dead (forthcoming film), 95
Exorcist: The Beginning (2004), 184
Eyes without a Face (1960), 8, 11, 231–32

Far from Heaven (2002), 91
Fat Girl (2001), 224
Father Knows Best (forthcoming film), 91
Fellini, Federico, 7, 8, 24, 160
female protagonist deconstruction, 119–121, 136–38. *See also* male protagonist deconstruction; male-female power reversal
feminist point of view, 120–21, 127–28, 139
Fenech, Edwige, 10
Ferrara, Abel, 138
Final Destination 5 (2011), 95
Footloose (2011), 85
Forbidden Planet (forthcoming film), 91

Ford, John, 4
Forzani, Bruno, 222
The Fourth Dimension (2001), 198
Fragasso, Claudio, 19, 70–74, 208, 218
Fragile (2005), 219
Frágiles (2005). See *Fragile* (2005)
Franco, Jésus "Jess": art cinema influence, 42; *The Awful Dr. Orlof* (1962), 152; *Cannibals* (1980), 192, 199, 200; career, 152; digitization, 16; *Eugenie de Sade* (1974), 153–56; *Eugenie . . . the Story of Her Journey into Perversion* (1970), 156–59, 163, 165, 178, 181; internet popularity, 12; *Lilian, la virgen pervertida* (1983), 152; 1990s films, 218–19; *99 Women* (1969), 169; *Sadomania* (1981), 35, 171–74, 178, 179; *Succubus* (1968), 27, 35, 159, 160–64, 163, 165, 181; supporting roles, 154, 173; *Venus in Furs* (1969), 26–27, 164–68, 167, 178
Franju, Georges, 8, 231–32
Freda, Riccardo, 7, 9, 42, 43
Friday the 13th (1980), 10, 220
Friday the 13th (2009), 95
Fright Night (2011), 95
Frontière(s) (2007). See *Frontier(s)* (2007)
Frontier(s) (2007), 219, 220, 221
La frusta et il corpo (1963). See *The Whip and the Body* (1963)
Fulci, Lucio: *The Beyond* (1981), *18*, 19, 20, 208; *A Cat in the Brain* (1990), 223; *City of the Living Dead* (1980), 208; digitization, 19; European horror influence, 10; *The House by the Cemetery* (1981), 50–60; *A Lizard in a Woman's Skin* (1971), 222; *The New York Ripper* (1982), 19, 35, 117–19, 127; *Zombie* (1978), 36, 208–215, 212
Full Metal Jacket (1987), 186
Funny Games (1997 and 2007), 10, 224

Ganja and Hess (1973), 184
Gans, Christophe, 220
Gantillon, Bruno, 16
Gariazzo, Mario, 37
Garrone, Sergio, 42
Il gatto a nove code (1971). *The Cat o' Nine Tails* (1971)
Un gatto nel cervello (1990). See *A Cat in the Brain* (1990)

Il gatto occhi di giada (1977). See *Watch Me When I Kill* (1977)
gender destabilization/deconstruction: *All the Colors of the Dark* (1972), 119–121; *The Bird with the Crystal Plumage* (1970), 131–35; *Eugenie de Sade* (1974), 154–56; *The New York Ripper* (1982), 117–19; nunsploitation films, 177–78; s&m horror film genre, 145–49, 165, 168; *The Stendhal Syndrome* (1996), 136–39; *Venus in Furs* (1969), 165–68; *The Whip and the Body* (1963), 145–49. *See also* male-female power deconstruction; protagonist gender deconstruction
George Washington (2000), 10
The Gestapo's Last Orgy (1976), 42
Get Smart (2008), 84
The Ghost (1963), 7
The Ghost Galleon (1974), 20
Ghoulies (1985), 71
giallo film genre: academic neglect, 10–14; *All the Colors of the Dark* (1972), 119–121; as anti-detective story, 106–108, 115; art as dangerous, 139–40; art as liberating, 140; audience points of view, 111–13; *The Bird with the Crystal Plumage* (1970), 130–35, 139, 140; *Blood and Black Lace* (1964), 103–104, 107–116; cult following, 104; debates, 104; female protagonist characteristics, 123–24; female protagonist deconstruction, 119–121, 136–38; feminist point of view, 120–21, 127–28, 139; film technology development, 104; gender destabilization, 128–130, 131–35; gender destabilization/deconstruction, 116–141; generic identity, 105–106; genre description, 104; *The Girl Who Knew Too Much* (1963), 9, 20; as Hollywood horror tradition-European art cinema tradition bridge, 104; male protagonist deconstruction, 117–19, 125–28, 132–33, 138–39; male victim gender displacement, 124–25; *The New York Ripper* (1982), 117–19, 127; *Opera* (1987), 128; overview, 9–10, 34–35, 141; patriarchal order disruption, 120–21, 122–23; postmodernism, 116–141; production devices, 110; production era,

104; *The Red Queen Kills 7 Times* (1972), 121–23; renaissance, 104; s&m horror film genre commonalities, 181; *Short Night of the Glass Dolls* (1971), 124–28; spectatorship-as-drag, 117–19; *The Stendhal Syndrome* (1996), 135–39, 140; stigmatization of minorities, 35–36; *Trauma* (1993), 128; visceral viewer response, 113–14; weaknesses, 104. *See also specific directors*

The Girl Who Knew Too Much (1963), 9, 20
Girolami, Marino, 208
Giulietta degli spiriti (1965). See *Juliet of the Spirits* (1965)
Godard, Agnès, 228
Godard, Jean-Luc, 160
Godzilla (forthcoming film), 95
Gothika (2003), 184, 220
Gow the Killer (1931), 190
Grau, Jorge, 7, 208
Green, David Gordon, 10
Gremlins (1984), 71
Grindhouse (2007), 10, 94, 206, 209
Gritos en la noche (1962). See *The Awful Dr. Orlof* (1962)
Guerín, Claudio, 16, 47

Hairspray (2007), 84
Halloween (1978), 222
Halloween (2007), 95
Halloween: Resurrection (2002), 184
Halperin, Victor, 207
Hammer Film Productions, 8
Haneke, Michael, 10, 224, 232
The Hangover Part II (2011), 85
Hannibal (2001), 195
Hannibal Rising (2007), 195
Hardy, George, 77
Harold & Kumar Escape from Guantanamo Bay (2008), 84
Harry Potter and the Half-Blood Prince (2009), 89
Harry Potter and the Order of the Phoenix (2007), 84
Harry Potter series, 76
Harvey (forthcoming film), 91
Haute tension (2003). See *High Tension* (2003)

Hawks, Howard, 4
Häxan (1922), 175
Head Hunters of the South Seas (1922), 193
Der heiße Tod (1969). See *99 Women* (1969)
Hell of the Living Dead (1980), 18, 208
Hellraiser (forthcoming film)
Hemmings, David, 8
Henry: Portrait of a Serial Killer (1986), 220
High Tension (2003), 219, 220
The Hills Have Eyes (1977), 34, 220
The Hills Have Eyes (2006), 95, 96, 194, 220
Histoires extraordinaires (1968). See *Spirits of the Dead* (1968)
Hitchcock, Alfred, 4, 104
The Hitcher (2007), 95
Holla (2006), 184
Hollywood: corporatization, 83–87, 89–91, 218; cultural irrelevance, 90–91; home video market dominance, 220–21; horror film quality, 94–97; interactive entertainment technologies, 87–93; studio horror film divisions, 91. *See also* American cannibal films; American zombie films
The Honeymooners (2005), 91
Hood of the Living Dead (2005), 184
Hooper, Tobe, 34, 92, 219
Hopkins, Anthony, 195
horror cinema genre: American cannibal films, 183–86, 189, 190–91, 193–98; American zombie films, 204–207, 216; Anglo American movies focus, 6; black horror direct-to-video films, 184; blaxploitation horror movies, 184; and Cultural Studies, 5–6, 40, 42–43; European cannibal films, 182–83, 186–190, 199–204; European zombie films, 204–206,182–183; "highbrow" v. "lowbrow" classifications, 4; nonwhite film directors, 184; nonwhite lead actors, 184; scholarly interest in, 3–4; and "Screen theory," 4–5; traditional violence treatment, 143–44; traditional violence-separation, 143–44 *See also* European horror films; *specific directors and films*
horror hybrids, 143–44
Hostel (2005), 10, 91, 95, 222
Hostel: Part II (2007), 10, 94

The House by the Cemetery (1981): boundary transgression, 52, 53–55; genre signpost complications, 53; narrative closure repudiation, 55–57; performative spectatorship, 59–60; postmodern characteristics, 51–57; psychoanalytical theory contestation, 54–55; rationality repudiation, 55; synopsis, 50; *Troll 2* (1990) comparison, 82; undecidability, 52–54; violent disruption, 51–52
House of Wax (2005), 91
House of Women (1962), 169
The House That Screamed (1969), 169
How Tasty Was My Little Frenchman (1971), 203
H6: Diario de un asesino (2005). See *H6: Diary of a Serial Killer* (2005)
H6: Diary of a Serial Killer (2005), 219, 220
Hughes, Albert and Allen, 184
The Human Centipede (First Sequence) (2009), 219
L'humanité (1999), 224

I Am Legend (2007), 184
I Can't Sleep (1994), 225
Iglesia, Eloy de la, 47
Ils (2006). See *Them* (2006)
Images (1972), 120
Images in a Convent (1979), 176–180
Immagini di un convento (1979). See *Images in a Convent* (1979)
The Incredible Shrinking Man (forthcoming film), 91
Incubo sulla città contaminata (1980). See *Nightmare City* (1980)
Indiana Jones and the Kingdom of the Crystal Skull (2008), 84
Un indien dans la ville (1994). See *Little Indian, Big City* (1994)
Inferno (1980), 19
Ingagi (1930), 190
Inside (2007), 219, 221
Insomnia (1997), 219
interactive entertainment technologies, 87–92
The Invasion (2007), 91
Iron Man 2 (2010), 85

Irréversible (2002). See *Irreversible* (2002)
Irreversible (2002), 10, 224
I Spit on Your Grave (1978), 138
I Spit on Your Grave (2010), 95
It's Alive (2008), 95
It! The Terror from Beyond Space (1958), 143
I Walked with a Zombie (1943), 207

J'ai pas sommeil (1994). See *I Can't Sleep* (1994)
Jason X (2001), 184
Jaws (1975), 91
Johnson, Martin and Osa, 193
Journey to the Center of the Earth (2008), 91
Julia's Eyes (2010), 219
Juliet of the Spirits (1965), 24
Juliette (1970), 153
Der junge Törless (1966). See *The Young Törless* (1966)
Jungle Holocaust (1977), 36, 191

The Karate Kid (2010), 85
Kassovitz, Mathieu, 220
Kidnapped (1974), 20
Kidnapped (2010), 219
Kill, Baby . . . Kill (1966), 8, 20
King Kong (1933), 183
King of the Cannibal Islands (1908), 193
King of the Zombies (1945), 206
King Solomon's Mines (1950), 190
Kollegiet (2007). See *Room 205* (2007)
Kubrick, Stanley, 53
Kümel, Harry, 19
Kynodontas (2009). See *Dogtooth* (2009)

Ladies of the Big House (1931), 169
Lado, Aldo, 124–28
Lagerfeld, Karl, 163
Lager SSadis Kastrat Kommandantur (1976). See *SS Experiment Love Camp* (1976)
Land of the Dead (2005), 184
Land of the Lost (2009), 85
Lang, Fritz, 4, 160
Lanthimos, Giorgos, 224
Lanzmann, Claude, 42
Larraz, José Ramón, 19, 35

The Last House on the Left (2009), 95
Last Year at Marienbad (1961), 160
Låt den rätte komma in (2008). See Let the Right One In (2008)
Laurenti, Mariano, 175
Lavi, Daliah, 148
Lee, Christopher, 152
Left Bank (2008), 219
Lemmons, Kasi, 184
Lenzi, Umberto: Black Demons (1991), 36, 208; Cannibal Ferox (1981), 192, 199, 200; digitization, 18, 19; Man from Deep River (1972), 191; Nightmare City, 18, 208; racist content, 36; remakes, 10
Let Me In (2010), 221
Let the Right One In (2008), 219, 221
Les lèvres rouges (1971). See Daughters of Darkness (1971)
Life Is Beautiful (1997), 29
Lilian, la virgen pervertida (1983), 152
Linkeroever (2008). See Left Bank (2008)
Little Indian, Big City (1994), 28
Little Miss Sunshine (2006), 75
The Living Dead at Manchester Morgue (1974), 7, 208
The Living Dead Girl (1982), 228–231
A Lizard in a Woman's Skin (1971), 222
The Lost World: Jurassic Park (1997), 195
Lucas, George, 195
Una lucertola con la pelle di donna (1971). See A Lizard in a Woman's Skin (1971)

Macunaíma (1969), 203
male protagonist deconstruction: The Bird with the Crystal Plumage (1970), 132–33; The New York Ripper (1982), 117–19, 127; Short Night of the Glass Dolls (1971), 125–28; The Stendhal Syndrome (1996), 138–39
male-female power deconstruction, 145–49, 154–56. See also gender destabilization/deconstruction
Maléfique (2002), 219
male victim gender displacement, 124–25
Man Bites Dog (1992), 219, 232
Man from Deep River (1972), 191
Manhunter (1986), 195

Margheriti, Antonio, 7, 20, 151, 182–83, 186–89, 222
Marquis de Sade: Justine (1969), 153
Marschall, Andreas, 223
Martino, Sergio: All the Colors of the Dark (1972), 119–121, 127, 223; The Case of the Scorpion's Tail (1971), 223; The Mountain of the Cannibal God (1978), 191–92, 193, 199, 200
Martyrs (2008), 219, 221
La maschera del demonio (1960). See Black Sunday (1960)
The Mask of Fu Manchu (1932), 183
Masks (2011), 10, 223
Mattei, Bruno, 18, 41, 208
Matton, Charles, 37
Méliès, Georges, 175
Men in Black III (2012), 85
Merenda, Luc, 10
Minh-ha, Trinh T., 198
Miraglia, Emilio, 121–23
Mirrors (2008), 221
Mission: Impossible – Ghost Protocol (2011), 85
The Mist (2007), 94
La monaca di Monza (1969). See The Awful Story of the Nun of Monza (1969)
Le monache di Sant'Arcangelo (1973). See The Nuns of St. Archangel (1973)
Mondo cane (1962), 190
Mondo cannibale (1980). See Cannibals (1980)
La montagna del dio cannibale (1978). See The Mountain of the Cannibal God (1978)
Montero, Roberto, 35
Morte a Venezia (1971). See Death in Venice (1971)
La morte negli occhi del gatto (1973). See Seven Deaths in the Cat's Eye (1973)
La morte vivante (1982). See The Living Dead Girl (1982)
The Mountain of the Cannibal God (1978), 191–92, 193, 199, 200
Ms.45 (1981), 138
The Mummy (1999), 184
The Mummy: Tomb of the Dragon Emperor (2008), 84–85

Mutants (2009), 219
My Bloody Valentine (2009), 95

The Naked Prey (1966), 190
narrative closure repudiation, 43, 49, 55, 56
Nattevagten (1994). See *Nightwatch* (1994)
Naughty Nun (1972), 175
Near Dark (forthcoming film), 95
Necronomicon–Geträumte Sünden (1968). See *Succubus* (1968)
"neo giallo," 222
The New York Ripper (1982), 19, 35, 117–19, 127
Night and Fog (1955), 42
Night at the Museum (2006), 89
Nightmare City (1980), 18, 208
A Nightmare on Elm Street (1984), 52
A Nightmare on Elm Street (2010), 95
Nightmare on Elm Street series, 218
Night of the Living Dead (1968), 34, 206
The Night Walker (1964), 120
Nightwatch (1994), 219
Night Watch (2004), 219
99 Women (1969), 169
La noche del terror ciego (1972). See *Tombs of the Blind Dead* (1972)
Nochnoy dozor (2004). See *Night Watch* (2004)
Noé, Gaspar, 10, 224, 232
Nonhosonno (2001). See *Sleepless* (2001)
Non si deve profanare il sonno dei morti (1974). See *The Living Dead at Manchester Morgue* (1974)
La notte del terrore (1981). See *Burial Ground* (1981)
Le notti erotiche dei morti viventi (1980). See *Erotic Nights of the Living Dead* (1980)
Nuit et brouillard (1955). See *Night and Fog* (1955)
The Nuns of St. Archangel (1973), 35, 175
nunsploitation films, 35–36, 174–180

Los ojos de Julia (2010). See *Julia's Eyes* (2010)
On the Cannibal Isle (1916), 193–94
Opera (1987), 128
Operazione paura (1966). See *Kill, Baby . . . Kill* (1966)

Ophüls, Marcel, 42
El orfanato (2007). See *The Orphanage* (2007)
O'Rourke, Dennis, 198–99
The Orphanage (2007), 219, 221
Orphée (1950). See *Orpheus* (1950)
Orpheus (1950), 160, 162
L'ossessa (1974). See *The Sexorcist* (1974)
Ossorio, Amando de, 20
Ouanga (1936), 184

Le pacte des loups (2001). See *Brotherhood of the Wolf* (2001)
Il paese del sesso selvaggio (1972). See *Man from Deep River* (1972)
Palance, Jack, 152
Palud, Hervé, 28
Paolella, Domenico, 35, 175
Paranormal Activity (2007), 201
Paranormal Activity series, 94
Paranormal Activity 3 (2011), 95
Paroxismus (1969). See *Venus in Furs* (1969)
Pasolini, Pier Paolo, 175
patriarchal order disruption: *All the Colors of the Dark* (1972), 120–21; *Eugenie de Sade* (1974), 154–56; *Eugenie . . . the Story of Her Journey into Perversion* (1970), 157–59, 181; *The Red Queen Kills 7 Times* (1972), 121–23; s&m horror film genre, 145–49, 154–56, 161–64; *The Whip and the Body* (1963), 145–49. See also male-female power deconstruction
Paura nella città de morti viventi (1980). See *City of the Living Dead* (1980)
Peeping Tom (1960), 155–56
performative spectatorship: American cannibal films, 216; American zombie films, 216; audience perception, 61; *Blood and Black Lace* (1964), 111–16; *Cannibal Apocalypse* (1981), 188–89; destabilization in s&m genre, 149–151; destabilization of audience point of view, 213–15; digitization technology effect, 63–64; European horror films, 61–63; European v. American, 62–63; experimentation with alternative racial roles and identities, 188–89; fantasy-reality

reversal, 203; *giallo* film genre, 111–16; grindhouse cinema afterlife, 64–65; *The House by the Cemetery*, 59–60; interactive entertainment technologies, 87–92; *The Living Dead Girl* (1982), 230–31; overview, 42–45; "playing dead," 42–45; queering, 171, 173–74, 177–180; spectatorship-as-drag, 117–19; technical production improvement impact, 63–67; *Troll 2* (1990), 78–82; *Trouble Every Day* (2001), 230–31; visceral viewer response, 113–14; *The Whip and the Body* (1963), 149–151; *Zombie* (1979), 213–15
Petersen, Wolfgang, 28
Pet Sematary (forthcoming film), 95
La piel que habito (2011). See *The Skin I Live In* (2011)
Pineapple Express (2008), 10
The Pink Panther 2 (2009), 85
Piranha (2010), 221
Piranha 3DD (2012), 95
Pirates of the Caribbean: At World's End (2007), 84
Pirates of the Caribbean: Dead Man's Chest (2006), 89
Pirates of the Caribbean series, 84
Pirates of the Caribbean: The Curse of the Black Pearl (2003), 85
Planet of the Vampires (1965), 10
"Planet Terror" (segment of *Grindhouse*) (2007), 206
Platoon (1986), 186
Polanski, Roman, 120
La polizia chiede aiuto (1974). See *What Have They Done to Your Daughters?* (1974)
Poltergeist (forthcoming film), 95
The Postman Always Rings Twice (1946), 123
postmodernism: *Blood and Black Lace* (1964), 107–108; capitalism repudiation, 57–58; European horror films, 42, 48–60; explained, 48–50; *giallo* film genre, 116–141; *The House by the Cemetery* (1981), 51–57; *The Living Dead Girl* (1982), 230–31; principles, 49–50; "reaction" v. "resistance," 58–59; spectatorship redefinition, 59–60; *Trouble Every Day* (2001), 230–31. See also anti-imperialism; gender disruption/deconstruction; narrative closure repudiation; patriarchal order disruption

Powell, Michael, 155, 175
Pressburger, Eric, 175
Price, Dennis, 152
Primeval (2007), 184
Profondo rosso (1975). See *Deep Red* (1975)
Promenons-nous dans les bois (2000). See *Deep in the Woods* (2000)
Prometheus (2012), 95
Prom Night (2008), 95
protagonist gender deconstruction: 117–19, 119–21, 125–27, 132–35, 136–39
Psycho (1960), 104
Pupillo, Massimo, 16, 151

Quarantine (2008), 206, 221
Queen of the Damned (2002), 184
Queenie and the Cannibal (1912), 193
Quella villa accanto al cimitero (1981). See *The House by the Cemetery*
The Quiet American (2002), 91

I racconti di Canterbury (1972). See *The Canterbury Tales* (1972)
"race horror" movies, 184
racial role destabilization, 183, 187, 188, 199–200
racism, 35–36
La ragazza che sapeva troppo (1963). See *The Girl Who Knew Too Much* (1963)
Raimi, Sam, 92
The Reaping (2007), 94
Reassemblage (1983), 198
Reazione a catena (1971). See *Bay of Blood* (1971)
[Rec] (2007), 219, 220, 221
Red Dragon (2002), 195
The Red Queen Kills 7 Times (1972), 121–22, 127, 137
Reed, Carol, 183
La religieuse (1966), 175
Renoir, Jean, 4
Repulsion (1965), 120

La residencia (1969). See *The House That Screamed* (1969)
Resident Evil (2002), 206, 220
Resident Evil: Extinction (2007), 95
Resnais, Alain, 42, 160, 225
Return of the Evil Dead (1973), 20
Rise of the Planet of the Apes (2011), 85
Rivelazioni di un maniaco sessuale al capo della squadra mobile (1972). See *So Sweet, So Dead* (1972)
Rivette, Jacques, 175
Les rivières pourpres (2000). See *The Crimson Rivers* (2000)
The Rocky Horror Picture Show (1975), 77, 143–44
Rodriguez, Robert, 10, 209
Rollin, Jean, 11, 15, 218–19, 228–232
Romay, Lina, 152
Romero, George, 18, 34, 206, 209, 219
Room 205 (2007), 219, 221
Rosemary's Baby (1968), 120, 222
Roth, Eli, 92
The Ruins (2008), 184
Russell, Ken, 175
Rustichelli, Carlo, 110, 112, 146, 149

Sabatini, Lorenzo, 20
Sadomania (1981), 35, 171–74, 178, 179, 220
Sadomania–Hölle der Lust (1981). See *Sadomania* (1981)
s&m horror film genre: Bava, Mario, 142–152; censorship relaxation, 151; *Eugenie de Sade* (1974), 153–56; *Eugenie... the Story of Her Journey into Perversion* (1970), 156–59; gender and sex deconstruction, 165–68; gender and sexual role destabilization, 145–49; giallo film genre commonalities, 181; hard core pornography appearance, 151; heterosexual s&m, 142–168; *Images in a Convent* (1979), 176–180; male-female power deconstruction, 145–49, 154–56; marginalization, 151; nunsploitation films, 174–180; patriarchal order disruption, 145–49, 154–56, 161–64; performative spectatorship destabilization, 149–151; queer s&m, 168–174; *Sadomania* (1981), 171–74; *Succubus* (1968), 160–64; theatrical nature, 180–81; traditional horror film violence treatment comparison, 143–44; *Venus in Furs* (1969), 164–68; *The Whip and the Body* (1963), 142–152; women-in-prison cinema, 168–174
Santos, Nelson Pereira dos, 203
Sauna (2008), 219
Saw (2004), 10, 91, 95
Saw V (2008), 95
Saw IV (2007), 184
Scary Movie (2000), 143
Schlöndorff, Volker, 7
La sconosciuta (2006). See *The Unknown Woman* (2006)
Scott, Ridley, 195
Scream 4 (2011), 95
Scream series, 218
Secuestrados (2010). See *Kidnapped* (2010)
Sei donne per l'assassino (1964). See *Blood and Black Lace* (1964)
A Serbian Film (2010), 219
Serrador, Narciso Ibáñez, 169, 170
Se7en (1995), 220
Seven Deaths in the Cat's Eye (1973), 222
The Sexorcist (1974), 37
Shadow (2009), 219
She (1935), 192
Sheitan (2006), 219, 221
Shimizu, Takashi, 184
The Shining (1980), 53, 81
Shoah (1985), 42
Short Night of the Glass Dolls (1971), 124–28, 132
Shrek the Third (2007), 84, 89
Shyamalan, M. Night, 184
The Silence of the Lambs (1991), 195, 220
Silent Hill (2006), 220
Silent House (2012), 95
Sin City (2005), 194
La sindrome di Stendhal (1996). See *The Stendhal Syndrome* (1996)
Singh, Tarsem, 184
The Skeleton Key (2005), 184
The Skin I Live In (2011), 10, 224, 231–32
Sleepaway Camp (1983), 220
Sleepless (2001), 222

Snakes on a Plane (2006), 184
Snipes, Wesley, 184
Son of Ingagi (1940), 184
Sorel, Jean, 126
Sorority Row (2009), 95
The Sorrow and the Pity (1969), 42
So Sweet, So Dead (1972), 35
Spermula (1976), 37
Lo spettro (1963). See *The Ghost* (1963)
Spider-Man 3 (2007), 84, 89
Spielberg, Steven, 195
Spirits of the Dead (1968), 8
Lo squartatore di New York (1982). See *The New York Ripper* (1982)
Srpski film (2010). See *A Serbian Film* (2010)
SS Experiment Love Camp (1976), 42
SS Girls (1977), 42
A Star Is Born (forthcoming film), 91
Star Trek (2009), 85
Star Wars (1977), 91
Star Wars Episode I: The Phantom Menace (1999), 195
Star Wars series, 76
Steele, Barbara, 7, 9, 12
The Stendhal Syndrome (1996), 130, 135–36, 138–40
The Stepfather (2009), 95
Stephenson, Michael, 74–75, 77
The Strangers (2008), 221
Strangers on a Train (forthcoming film), 91
Succubus (1968), 27, 35, 159, 160–64, *163*, 165, 181
Sugar Hill (1974), 184
Suspiria (1977), 10, 17, 19, 29–30, *31*, 136, 222, 223
Sweeney Todd: The Demon Barber of Fleet Street (2007), 144, 194

Tarantino, Quentin, 10, 209
La tarantola dal ventre nero (1971). See *The Black Belly of the Tarantula* (1971)
Tarzan the Ape Man (1932), 190
Tenebre (1982), 128
Terminator Salvation (2009), 85
Terrore nello spazio (1965). See *Planet of the Vampires* (1965)

Tesis (1996). See *Thesis* (1996)
The Texas Chain Saw Massacre (1974), 34, 220, 222
The Texas Chainsaw Massacre: The Beginning (2006), 194
Them (2006), 219, 221
Thesis (1996), 219
The Thing (2011), 95
The Third Man (1949), 183
The Three Stooges (2012), 85
3:10 to Yuma (2007), 91
Toby Dammit (segment of *Spirits of the Dead*) (1968), 8
Todd, Tony, 184
Tombs of the Blind Dead (1972), 20
Tornatore, Giuseppe, 224
"torture porn," 10
Total Recall (2012), 85
Tourneur, Jacques, 207
Trader Horn (1931), 190
Transformers (2007), 89
Transformers: Revenge of the Fallen (2009), 85, 89
Trauma (1993), 128
I tre volti della paura (1963). See *Black Sabbath* (1963)
Trier, Lars von, 10, 41, 224, 232
Troll (1986), 71
TrollHunter (2010), 219, 221
Trolljegeren (2010). See *TrollHunter* (2010)
Troll 2 (1990): acting, 72–73; American audience indifference, 218; clichés, 72; creative fan activity, 75–76; cult status, 73–75; documentary film investigation, 77; fan art, 75–76, 81–82; fan base development, 74; *The House by the Cemetery* comparison, 82; internet impact, 74–75; mash-ups, 81; midnight screenings, 76–77; originality, 80–81; paracinematic qualities, 82; performative spectatorship, 78–82; production design, 73; production limitations, 71–72; script, 72; stereotypes, 72; synopsis, 70
TRON: Legacy (2010), 85
Trouble Every Day (2001): art film connections, 10, 224, 226, 227–29; cinematic techniques, 228; critical reaction, 225–

26; formal horror film characteristics, 228; horror film connections, 227–232; *The Living Dead Girl* (1982) comparison, 229–231; mood, 227; performative spectatorship, 230–31; popular cinema engagement, 228; postmodernism, 230–31; synopsis, 226–27; themes, 227
Turistas (2006), 184
Tutti i colori del buio (1972). See *All the Colors of the Dark* (1972)
21 Jump Street (2012), 85
20,000 Leagues Under the Sea (forthcoming film), 91
The Twilight Saga: Eclipse (2010), 85
Twilight Saga series, 94

Ubaldo Terzani Horror Show (2010), 10, 223
L'uccello dalle piume di cristallo (1970). See *The Bird with the Crystal Plumage* (1970)
L'ultima orgia del III Reich (1976). See *The Gestapo's Last Orgy* (1976)
Ultimo mondo cannibale (1977). See *Jungle Holocaust* (1977)
Underworld: Awakening (2012), 95
The Unknown Woman (2006), 224

Vacancy (2007), 94
Vadim, Roger, 35
I vampiri (1956), 9, 42
Vampyres (1975), 19, 35, 37
Vampz (2004), 184
Venus in Furs (1969), 26–27, 153, 164, 165–68, 167, 178
La vergine di Norimberga (1963). See *The Virgin of Nuremberg* (1963)
Vertov, Dziga, 225
victim gender displacement, 124–25
The Virgin of Nuremberg (1963), 20, 151
Virus (1980). See *Hell of the Living Dead* (1980)
Visconti, Eriprando, 175
Visconti, Luchino, 7, 24
La vita è bella (1997). See *Life Is Beautiful* (1997)
vodoun mythology, 204–205, 207
voodoo. *See* vodoun mythology

War of the Worlds (2005), 91
Watch Me When I Kill (1977), 223
Welles, Orson, 4
What Have They Done to Your Daughters? (1974), 223
What Have You Done to Solange? (1972), 35
When a Stranger Calls (2006), 222
When Worlds Collide (forthcoming film), 91
The Whip and the Body (1963): anomalous nature, 151; as blend of horror and pornography, 144–45; gender and sexual role destabilization, 145–49; as horror-pornography bridge, 143–44; male/female power deconstruction, 145–49, 154; performative spectatorship destabilization, 149–151, 180; production devices, 150; as s&m film, 220; synopsis, 142–43
White Oleander (2002), 19
White Zombie (1932), 207
Wilson, Ajita, 173
The Wolfman (2010), 95
women-in-prison cinema: classic Hollywood, 169–170; lesbian-criminal behavior connection, 169–171; nunsploitation films similarities, 175–76, 179–180; origins, 169; performative spectatorship queering, 173–74; *Sadomania* (1981), 171–74; stereotypical lesbians, 169–170
World War Z (forthcoming film), 206
Wrong Turn (2003), 194, 222

xXx (2002), 19

Les yeux sans visage (1960). See *Eyes without a Face* (1960)
The Young Törless (1966), 7

Zarchi, Meir, 138
Zombie (1979): commercial success, 208–209; *Dawn of the Dead* (1978) comparison, 209; deflation of white imperialist culture, 212–13; destabilization of audience point of view, 213–15; disintegration of colonialist repression and

oppression, 210–13; homophobia, 36; influence, 10; performative spectatorship, 213–15; as postcolonial zombie film, 220; racism, 36, 212; synopsis, 209–210
Zombie Apocalypse (2011), 206
zombie films. *See* American zombie films; European zombie films
Zombie 4: After Death (1989), 19, 208
Zombiegeddon (2003), 206
Zombie Holocaust (1980), 208
Zombie Honeymoon (2004), 206
Zombieland (2009), 206
Zombies of Mora Tau (1957), 206
Zombies on Broadway (1945), 206
Zombie Strippers! (2008), 206
Zombi 2 (1979). See *Zombie* (1979)

IAN OLNEY is Associate Professor of English at York College of Pennsylvania, where he teaches Film Studies. His publications on European cinema and the horror film include articles in *Quarterly Review of Film and Video* and *Literature/Film Quarterly*.

www.ingramcontent.com/pod-product-compliance
Lightning Source LLC
Chambersburg PA
CBHW071425150426
43191CB00008B/1046